New Theatre in Italy

New Theatre in Italy: 1963–2013 makes the case for the centrality of late-millennium Italian avant-garde theatre in the development of the new forms of performance that have emerged in the twenty-first century. Starting in the Sixties, young artists and militants in Italy reacted to the violence in their streets and ruptures in the family unit that are now recognized as having been harbingers of the end of the global postwar system. As traditional rituals of State and Church faltered, a new generation of cultural operators, largely untrained and driven away from political activism, formed collectives to explore new ways of speaking theatrically, new ways to create and experience performance, and new relationships between performer and spectator. Although the vast majority of the works created were transient, like all performance, their aesthetic and social effects continue to surface today across media on a global scale, affecting visual art, cinema, television, and the behavioral aesthetics of social networks.

Valentina Valentini teaches performing arts and new media at the University of Rome La Sapienza. Her research interests focus on performance in the twentieth century, especially the relationship between theatre, art and new technologies. She is a leading authority on performance and multimedia events, and the author of several theoretical and historical studies devoted to twentieth century theatre.

Routledge Advances in Theatre and Performance Studies

www.routledge.com/Routledge-Advances-in-Theatre–Performance-Studies/book-series/RATPS

New Theatre in Italy
1963–2013

Valentina Valentini

Translated by Thomas Haskell Simpson

Routledge
Taylor & Francis Group

LONDON AND NEW YORK

First published 2018
by Routledge
2 Park Square, Milton Park, Abingdon, Oxon OX14 4RN

and by Routledge
711 Third Avenue, New York, NY 10017

Routledge is an imprint of the Taylor & Francis Group, an informa business

© 2018 Valentina Valentini. Translated by Thomas Haskell Simpson.

First published in Italian by Bulzoni Editore, 2015, Roma.

British Library Cataloguing-in-Publication Data
A catalogue record for this book is available from the British Library

Library of Congress Cataloging-in-Publication Data
Names: Valentini, Valentina author. | Simpson, Thomas (Thomas
    Haskell), 1953– translator.
Title: New theatre in Italy, 1963–2013 / Valentina Valentini ;
    translated by Thomas Haskell Simpson.
Other titles: Nuovo teatro made in Italy, 1963–2013. English
Description: Milton Park, Abingdon, Oxon ; New York, NY :
    Routledge, 2018. | Series: Routledge advances in theatre and
    performance studies | Includes bibliographical references and
    index.
Identifiers: LCCN 2017043376 | ISBN 9781138577251 (hardback) |
    ISBN 9781351267281 (ebook)
Subjects: LCSH: Theater—Italy—History—20th century. | Theater—
    Italy—History—21st century.
Classification: LCC PN2684 .V3313 2018 | DDC 792.0945/
    0904—dc23
LC record available at https://lccn.loc.gov/2017043376

ISBN: 978-1-138-57725-1 (hbk)
ISBN: 978-1-351-26728-1 (ebk)

Typeset in Sabon
by Apex CoVantage, LLC
Printed and bound by CPI Group (UK) Ltd, Croydon, CR0 4YY

Contents

Preface

Premise

New Theatre in Italy: 1963–2013, is driven by the conviction that this dynamic and still vital phenomenon has produced aesthetically significant results that have radically transformed thought and practice not only about theater, but throughout contemporary art. Its achievements are lasting and fully equal to achievements in theater elsewhere in the world. In the period under review, Italy has served as the laboratory, audience, and site of many of what are considered the most important developments in new theater internationally. To name only a few, the Living Theater, Jerzy Grotowski, Tadeusz Kantor, and Robert Wilson all have a long history in Italy, having produced there some of their most influential work.

The richness of thought, complex experimentation, radical creation, degree of existential risk, and uncompromising challenge to established forms, together with its impact on practices in visual art, music, dance, literature, and cinema, make Italian New Theater worthy, first, of being known to emerging generations, and second, of being re-evaluated from a perspective that measures its true dimensions and implications. It is not a matter of picking out this or that specific artistic innovation (although these have succeeded continuously one upon the other) but of reconstructing the variegated braid of relations that have made Italian theater, over the last half-century, into an intensely expressive cultural crossroads, and of rereading the second half of the Italian twentieth century in this light. The study reconsiders the entire New Theater phenomenon by lifting it momentarily out of its ongoing currency as a process *in fieri* (with all the militant posturing, taking of sides, clashes, and ideological positioning that characterize it), while also resisting the temptation to categorize and catalogue phenomena into a summary historical judgment.

A convincing argument can be made that New Theater has made a decisive contribution to the cultural construction of contemporary Italy; thus the reciprocal, interwoven relations between theatrical practice and the cultural life of a nation will surface repeatedly in the book's pages.

We have articulated the historical arc of the period under review into five chronological segments: 1963–67, centered on the birth of Gruppo '63, its dissolution, and the watershed Ivrea Conference; 1968–78, during which New Theater consolidated its identifying characteristics; 1978–88, the era of postmodern theater and its eventual burnout; 1989–99, a period marked by a sentiment of being posthumous; and last, the work that has emerged since 2000, which has gone beyond the concept of spectacle to take the spectator as subject of the scenic action.

From our perspective, the formation of Gruppo '63 began a critical, theoretical, aesthetic, and pragmatic process that called into question the foundations of theater and its practice in response to neo-avant-garde trends in cinema, literature, visual arts, and music. Until that moment, theater was rooted in the conviction that it could renew itself simply by producing new plays. Against the traditional prose theater that dominated the national stage, Gruppo '63 advanced a counter-tendency that regarded the literary text as a mere material trace, graphic and acoustic, to be manipulated freely (in the spirit of Roland Barthes), rather than as a monument to be exalted by a more or less brilliant director and recited by a more or less brilliant actor.

The volume is composed of five historical essays, each dedicated to a decade, that enucleate the salient events of the period under review, with the intention to inscribe theater within a horizon contiguous with the other arts, especially music, literature, and visual art.

Three thematic chapters follow, focused respectively on dramaturgies of the spectacle and the literary text; on the dramaturgy of space; and on the (plural) presence of the actor.

- The chapter on dramaturgies of the spectacle and the text presents case studies of three authors: Pier Paolo Pasolini, Giovanni Testori, and Franco Scaldati.
- The second chapter, on space, examines the ways New Theater contested stale concepts of stage and spectacle with experiments centered on new concepts, including those around environment, event, performance, action, and installation. Concomitant with the theoretical contestation underway, technology created new three-dimensional, virtual, immersive and multisensory spaces that exploded the psychic space of scenic representation.
- The chapter on the plural presence of the actor concentrates on the exploratory forms in which the presence of the actor was manifested, the unprecedented types of actions actors were called upon to perform, the dramaturgical functions they fulfilled, and the vision of the world that actors strove to embody.

New Theatre in Italy: 1963–2013 tells a story that designs its own landscape, using key concepts to plot paths through it. It chooses guides in authors and spectacles which return in different contexts, bestowing some-thing of a family air to the enterprise. The fruit of decades of direct obser-vation, this vision of New Theater should have the feel of lived experience.

Our reconstruction of the phenomenology of New Theater makes use of a multimedia apparatus: a website devoted to the actors, companies, spectacles, and contexts covered in this volume, made up of videos, story boards, reviews, interviews and other archival material (**www.newtheatrein-italy.sciami.com**). Throughout this volume, the insertions [CONTEXTS] or [FOCUS] mean that further material on the given topic can be found on the website.

1 The Sixties

Theatre – literature – music: manifestos, *Querelles*, intermedia: 1963–67

1.1 Fact and atmosphere

At the end of the Fifties, there was still a vital element in Italian culture that had succeeded in not being crushed by the reigning ideological populism, nor had it fallen into the abyss of existentialist subjectivism. This element in Italian society faced head-on the advent of a mass culture in which consumerism constituted the prime mover of social unification. Fundamental changes were underway that would explode at the end of the next decade.

The year 1963 witnessed the launch of the first center-left government in Italian history, which would last until 1968.

In October, 1960, the publishing house Mondadori – in its "Medusa" series, directed by Elio Vittorini – released the Italian translation, by Guido de Angelis, of Joyce's *Ulysses*, the fruit of long years of study and labor. Italian translations of the Frankfurt School (Adorno, Marcuse, Horkheimer), the work of Mayakovski, Brecht, and Walter Benjamin's *Angelus Novus* were already in circulation.

The most salient political events between 1963 and 1967 were the assassination of President Kennedy, the war in Vietnam, the military coup in Greece, the Soviet repression of the Prague Spring, and the growing student revolt, bringing with it the utopian dream of revolution achievable in the short term.

In 1963, Gruppo '63 was founded by a group of writers, poets and critics who maintained an unprecedented open-mindedness toward the visual arts, music, and theater, drawing inspiration and ideas from forms of art traditionally disdained by much of the Italian intellectual class. The fact that the group's first formal meeting took place in Palermo as part of the fourth *International New Music Week* is testimony of their unique and characteristic interdisciplinary spirit.

"The Sixties in Italy", Albert Asor Rosa tells us, "were characterized by great economic and social dynamism, marked by substantial and effervescent cultural and literary production".[1] New periodicals came to life, such as *Marcatré*, *Menabò*, *Quindici*, and *Grammatica*. Familiar magazines, such as *Sipario* (under new editor Franco Quadri) and *Teatro* (under Giuseppe

Bartolucci), redefined their editorial line.[2] Marxism and the radical labor movement – to become important in the next decade – found new expression from the mid-Sixties on in journals such as *Quaderni Rossi* and *Quaderni Piacentini*, the last of which was particularly open to cultural issues, featuring writing by Franco Fortini, Giovanni Raboni, Alberto Asor Rosa, and Goffredo Fofi.

The Living Theatre landed in Italy in 1965, performed *The Brig* at the Venice Biennale, and settled in Rome, presenting *Mysteries and Smaller Pieces* and *Frankenstein*. Eugenio Barba, student and collaborator with Jerzy Grotowski, published *In Search of Lost Theater*, including a text by Grotowski entitled "Performance as an Act of Social Psychotherapy", a radical denunciation of consumer society, the obsession with image, and technological media. *The Drama Review*, directed by Richard Schechner, dedicated an issue to "The New Theater", with articles on the concerts of John Cage, Allan Kaprow and Claes Oldenburg's Happenings, and new dance by Anna Halprin and Yvonne Rainer. Marshall McLuhan published *Understanding Media* in 1964. Jean-Jacques Lebel presented happenings at the Festival of Free Expression in Paris. In New York, Nam June Paik used funds from a Rockefeller grant to purchase his first video camera.

In Italy as elsewhere throughout the world, new musical experiments explored electronic technology and absorbed other realms of art production. In 1955 Luciano Berio and Bruno Maderna had founded the Musical Phonology Lab at the RAI headquarters in Milan, where they created electro-acoustic music.[3] In 1961 Berio presented *Visage*, a voice work with singer Cathy Berberian, while at the International Festival of Contemporary Music in Venice, composer Luigi Nono presented *Intolleranza 60*, a collaboration with visual artist Emilio Vedova, Slavic Studies scholar Angelo Maria Ripellino, and the *Lanterna Magika* of legendary Czech set designer Josef Svoboda.[4]

In 1965 the Feltrinelli bookstore in Rome hosted a Happening by Giuseppe Chiari called *La strada*, during which Chiari distorted television signals, a technique also used by Gianni Colombo in his *Segnali Vobbulati*. Two years earlier, working on John Cage's model of the "prepared piano", Nam June Paik had presented *13 Distorted TV Sets* during the Music-Electronic Television Exhibition at the Galleria Parnasse in Wuppertal, Germany.[5]

In September, 1965, in a moment when the avant-garde Gruppo '63 was formulating their concept of the experimental novel, Silvano Bussotti presented *Passion selon Sade* (with Cathy Berberian, the Bruno Canino/Antonio Ballista duo, Max Neuhaus, Salvatore Sciarrino, and the composer herself) at the Teatro Biondo in Palermo, as part of the *Festival della Nuova Musica*. The performance consisted of a series of *tableau vivants* animated by bands of light and slide projections of the spectacle itself, the author, performers, and people who had nothing to do with it.[6]

In September 1966, musician Giuseppe Chiari presented *What is a Happening?* at the Philharmonic Academy in Rome, in which he provided the answer that a happening, "considers a habitual, everyday action as a mean-ingful action".[7] In June 1967 Chiari debuted *The Solitary Crowd* at the Cul-tural Union in Turin, a musical theater work involving a pianist, 16 actors, a painter, and a camera operator. Chiari's activity demonstrates the way music was opening up toward the visual arts, along lines indicated by the Fluxus group. Just as the visual arts were adopting modes of theater, music adopted visual modes, with scores that called on musicians to translate acoustically the graphic signs written on score sheets, or images projected onto screens, or to follow a sequence of instructions.

The brainchild of Antonino Titone, *International New Music Week* in Palermo ran from 1960–68. Titone also created *Collage*, a magazine dedi-cated to new music and the visual arts, which survived from 1963–70. The first issues were "spoken"; that is, communicated orally rather than through print. Titone justified this mode of production by listing the follow-ing factors:

> the vertiginous progression of the insufficiency of writing, in direct pro-portion to the increasing density of interweaving threads in intermedial space; the movement of poets and writers toward new projects based on the contamination of systems; the use of new media (radio, televi-sion) and recording techniques that lead to a re-evaluation of vocal pro-duction, generating a 'new orality" ('sound poetry' and 'Audioriviste'); all of which demonstrate the inadequacy of traditional paper-based magazines.[8]

"At the beginning of the Sixties", Asor Rosa observed, "Writers began to recognize that Italian society was changing – its customs, social atmosphere, and people. Writers organized into groups to toss everything up into the air: language, institutions, social practices, family relations".[9] The so-called "economic boom", with the waves of industrialization that extended into the cultural realm, brought mass media to the forefront, especially televi-sion, but intellectuals were slow to recognize its importance, at least until the student revolts of 1968, when they finally began to accept new modes of cultural production. After the 1964 Venice Biennale, the United States invaded Europe with Pop Art, plunging Italy into a crisis over control of the national cultural tradition. Although La Tartaruga, the legendary, influen-tial gallery he founded in 1954 was among the first to show contemporary American art, and became a furnace of cultural ferment, Plinio De Martiis later remembered the period vividly but with bitterness. He described the Fifties as:

> a frenetic decade, a long, miserable, ragged post-war, but so rich and dense with creativity and genius. Just four names would be enough: Rossellini, De Sica, Fontana and Burri [. . .]. Unfortunately, in the Six-ties (but even more in the Seventies) this originality began to pollute

itself, muddied and corroded by that irreversible process of Americanization, from Pop to Op, Land and Body, Conceptual and Minimal, that colonized and barbarized us, flattening us to the level of a diligent province. More American than the Americans themselves.[10]

The encounter with Marxism, political militancy, and ideological clashes are traits that characterize intellectual and artistic practice in Italy until the Eighties.[11] In this arc of time, intellectuals and artists debated political commitment, linguistic experimentation, and the search for new artistic models. What had become of the novel, poetry, theater? What was the role of the writer and art in politics, society, and ideology?

Answers to these questions can be found in the work of Mario Schifano, whose subjects and compositional methods were mediated and transposed by television. Schifano created films and multimedia spectacles inspired by the multimedia psychedelia of Warhol's Factory, especially the *Exploding Plastic Inevitable* of 1966. At the Piper discotheque [CONTEXTS '60], temple of hip Roman youth, he presented *Grande angolo, sogni e le stelle* [Big Angle, Dreams and Stars, December 28, 1967] with live music performed by the band *Le Stelle*, strobe lights, loudspeakers, and projections of an original film on four panoramic screens.[12] During these years, the music of the Velvet Underground and Pink Floyd, and imagery from television and cinema fertilized the imagination of artists.[13] Italian pop art – according to Tano Festa, who developed it along with Schifano, Mimmo Rotella, Francesco Lo Savio, and Franco Angeli – lifted its icons from the Italian art tradition, such as Michelangelo's *Last Judgment*, rather than from consumer society, as was taking place in the United States. The October 1966 issue of the art journal *Il Verri*, edited by Gillo Dorfles, was dedicated to "Arte Programmata" (a concept and term coined by Umberto Eco), covering work produced by Gruppo T with Miriorama, Gruppo MID, and Gruppo N. Also called "arte cinetica" (Kinetic Art), the principal objective was to stimulate the perceptual activity of spectators.

Poetry too attempted to interact with the social changes wrought by mass media, becoming visual poetry, written and disseminated not through books, but with the same instruments used by advertising, like neon and highway signs.[14]

Within the Architecture Department of the University of Florence, a radical movement contested the contents, methods, and objectives of their profession. The Archizoom group was founded in 1966, followed a year later by UFO, which staged urban and environmental "guerrilla actions". In 1968, Riccardo Dalisi in Naples had architecture students carry out group projects in marginal neighborhoods, creating design objects with recycled and natural materials. This movement sought to overcome the traditional separation of architecture from life, reconceiving it as a creative space for confrontation with social reality.

As for cinema in the Sixties, Gian Piero Brunetta has written:

> For cinema, the Sixties were shot through by a quantity of stimuli, and the work, neglected by critics of the era, vibrates with a shared anxiety and transmits information about deluded hopes, unfulfilled political promises, the breakdown of institutions, and the growing difficulty of interpersonal communication, but also about enthusiasm and the discovery of new horizons, the collapse of many taboos, the need to renovate the basic cultural panorama, the discovery of Brecht and Artaud [. . .] No other country in the world registers – in both quantity and quality – an analogous flowering of talents in such a concentrated period of time.[15]

In fact, between 1965 and 1970 there were as many as 400 production houses in operation in Italy, thanks in part to a 1965 law, n. 1213, that provided incentives for the creation and diffusion of film. Documentary and investigative film became powerful anthropological and sociological instruments in the hands of committed cineastes: Vittorio De Seta made *Banditi a Orgosolo* (Brigands in Orgosolo) in 1961, the same year as *Le italiane e L'amore* (Italian Women and Love), one of the first thematic films featuring episodes by several directors, which became a distinctive genre of the period. Lina Wertmüller, a rare woman director in a role dominated by men, made *I Basilischi* (The Basilisks) in 1963. In 1965, after making several groundbreaking narrative films, Pier Paolo Pasolini released *Comizi d'amore* (Love Meetings) in 1965, a documentary in which the filmmaker toured the peninsula, asking everyday Italians frank questions about their sexual habits and attitudes. In the same year, he made *Uccellacci e Uccellini* (Hawks and Sparrows), in which beloved Variety Theater comic Totò and Ninetto Davoli, a Roman street youth with whom Pasolini had discovered and fallen in love, wandered the urban outskirts of Rome accompanied by a Marxist crow: the film is a funeral oration for neorealist cinema. Francesco Rosi's *La mani sulla città* (Hands On the City, 1963) was a genre-defying narrative (starring method actor Rod Steiger) with documentary elements that investigated corruption in the building trades and real estate speculation in the Naples of the economic boom. The film's epigraph read, "The characters and facts narrated here are imaginary, but the social and environmental reality that produced them are authentic".[16] Luchino Visconti dealt with themes of internal emigration and the myth of the South as "origin" in *Rocco e i suoi fratelli* (Rocco and His Brothers, 1960). Federico Fellini's *La Dolce Vita* (1960) and Michelangelo Antonioni's *Deserto Rosso* (1964) and *Blow-Up* (1965) invented new visual and formal modes of penetrating and portraying the desolation of the rising hegemonic culture of hedonistic consumerism.

Artists and experimental films also came to the fore. Gianfranco Baruchello's 1964 *Verifica incerta* (Doubtful Verification, made with Alberto Grifi) is an early found footage film that recycles and distills a huge quantity of commercial American films of the Fifties.[17] In 1967 Alfredo Leonardi formed the Independent Cinema Cooperative, Filmstudio opened in Rome, the Cappella Underground opened in Trieste, the Brera Cineclub in Milan and Teatro Instabile in Naples. At the Pesaro Film Festival, Alfredo Leonardi presented *Amore amore*, featuring musicians and actors from the Roman musical underground.[18]

Beginning in the early Sixties, Carmelo Bene staged his "against the grain" spectacles in Rome. His *Pinocchio* (restaged in different versions starting in 1962) unmasked the reactionary values behind the nationalist myths of economic progress; in its final scene, actors stomped on the Italian flag [FOCUS]. *Nostra Signora dei Turchi* (Our Lady of the Turks, 1966) exposed religion as mere superstition, with a saint who repeatedly appears to save the protagonist, but then lays in bed, leafing through a lady's magazine. In Bene's work, bourgeois respectability and sexual repression and deviation revealed a complex, conflictual existential dimension, an awareness of a looming void, and the struggle between accepting the individual's condition as one in a mass ("the cretin" character that Bene at times embodied) versus the struggle to overcome oneself. As an actor, Bene rejected any mechanism of identification. He took on the attitudes of the great actor only to ironize and destroy from within the actor's role as mediator between reality and fiction, precipitating a crisis in the concept of the function of theater. In *Pinocchio*, for example, he plunged from the stage down into the house on cords hung like jungle vines; spectators in the front rows were spattered by his spit. Blinding spotlights were aimed at the spectators. *Nostra Signora dei Turchi* made use of a window device to separate the hall from the stage, transforming viewers into voyeurs peering into a room. Objects thrown out the window landed on spectators. Respectable critics and spectators cried scandal, denouncing Bene's baroque mannerisms, woolly reasoning, and vulgarity, but they were enchanted by his character and crowded into the underground spaces where he performed in the Roman *off off* circuit of garages and warehouses that came to form the New Theater scene in Rome, frequented by intellectuals, the young, and the arts community.[19]

1.2 Literature calls for a theater of dissent and experimentation

At the dawn of the Sixties, established theaters – the "Teatri Stabili" (literally, Stable Theaters) run largely on public funds – depended on prominent directors (Giorgio Strehler, Luigi Squarzina, Luchino Visconti, Franco Zeffirelli) to produce grandiose spectacles "cloaked in phony cultural alibis",[20] retreads of classics and familiar themes featuring known stars giving what were considered great performances. Audiences clamored for tickets, for example, to see Marcello Mastroianni play Rudolph Valentino in *Ciao Rudy*, or Anna Magnani as the lead in a stage version of Giovanni Verga's realist short story *La lupa* (The She-wolf) about a sexually voracious peasant woman, which had been considered a breakthrough in 1880.

We have already mentioned the rupture caused by Carmelo Bene, whose phonetic deformations of verbal language made sound into a dramatically expressive element. Rather than slavishly obeying them, Bene manipulated received literary texts, cutting and adding. His *Arden of Faversham*, by an anonymous Elizabethan dramatist, included passages chosen from the writings of Roland Barthes and Gillo Dorfles. In the next decade Gilles Deleuze would define this practice as "making a text minor".[21] The text became a medium that the actor inscribed with his or her own vision of theater. By the late Fifties, experimental work was already underway in the hands of Bene, Carlo Quartucci, Giuliano Scabia, Claudio Remondi, Giancarlo Celli, and Mario Ricci, but it moved to the center of national intellectual debate with the launching of Gruppo '63, the avant-garde writers and critics who began to debate the relationship between literature and theater. A 1965 issue of the theater journal *Sipario* explicitly asked leading literary intellectuals to explain the fracture between the two worlds: "Why don't writers and scholars of literature pay attention to theatre?" In the same period that the Living Theatre was performing *The Brig* and *Mysteries and Smaller Pieces* in Rome, intellectuals such as Italo Calvino, Luigi Arpino, Carlo Cassola, Umberto Eco, Eugenio Montale, Alberto Moravia, Leonardo Sciascia, and Giovanni Testori argued that the problem arose from the lack in Italy of an authentic bourgeoisie and a true national language. Some complained that literary writers refused to allow their texts to be subjected to the mediation of directors and actors, and to the judgment of a live audience.[22]

In late 1966, *Sipario* published a sort of manifesto, *Towards a New Theater Conference* [CONTEXTS '60], which served as a prologue to the watershed Ivrea Conference held the following year. This collective declaration was the mature declaration of a group of artists and intellectuals who called for vigorous theatrical experimentation and denounced the bureaucracy of public theaters, their submission to political demands, and the sterility of an older generation frozen in worn-out roles, closed to international developments, and servile to critics, political power, and stale forms. In place of all that, the declaration proposed to "arouse, collect, value and defend new theatrical forces and trends, in a continuous relation of exchange with every other kind of art, in line with the needs of the new theatrical generations".[23]

It is interesting to read the names of the artists who signed the document:

- Theater artists and critics: Corrado Augias, Giuseppe Bartolucci, Carmelo Bene, Calenda, Gazzolo, Capriolo, Leo de Berardinis, Fadini, Guicciardini, Luzzati, Franco Quadri, Carlo Quartucci, Luca Ronconi, Giuliano Scabia, Trionfo, Roberto Lerici;
- Cineastes: Marco Bellocchio, Liliana Cavani;
- Musicians: Cathy Berberian, Bussotti, Liberovici;
- Semiotician: Umberto Eco.

The visual arts, on the other hand, were absent, despite the interdisciplinary scope of the journal *Marcatré*, to which numerous of the signatories contributed. In fact, fertile relations between theater and the visual arts became established later, in 1967, with the artists of *arte povera*, such as Jannis Kounellis and Carlo Quartucci. Italian Pop artists, instead, moved toward cinema.[24]

Theater began to incarnate a wider cultural demand for change, dissent and experimentation. The first issue of *Quindici*, a review founded in 1967 by ex-writers of Gruppo '63, focused on the deep connection between the Living Theatre and Antonin Artaud. Elio Pagliarani recognized the derivation of the "physical protest" in the work of the Living Theatre from the theories of Artaud, whose "theater of cruelty", he maintained, should surpass the confines of theater to contaminate literature as well. "There is no possible justification today for a notion of literature except for the idea of cruelty, which signifies, still and forever, *rigor, implacable concentration and decision, absolute irreversible determination*".[25] Pagliarani argued that the way to overcome the elitism of the avant-garde was to "get to the head by passing through the senses".[26]

1.3 The "querelle" between literature and theater: Gruppo '63

The year 1963 is the year of director Giorgio Strehler's grandiose version of Brecht's *Life of Galileo* at the Piccolo Teatro in Milan. Lasting five hours, the result of six months of rehearsal at a cost of 230 million *lire*, the overblown event was mocked by militant critic Franco Quadri as "the final docking of Brecht on the aestheticizing shores of a new Arcadia".[27] Against such bloated excess, two standout figures are the Neapolitan actor-author Eduardo De Filippo and the sharp political satirist Dario Fo, regarded as descendants of a rich popular tradition of Italian companies organized around a playwright/lead actor, given new vigor by the essential strength of their performance styles, which spawned a school of actors. To cite Quadri again, "Dario Fo invented a type of spectacle integrating mime with song, deft theatrical mechanisms with one eye on the circus, but above all with a tightrope stretching back to *commedia dell'arte*".[28]

In this context Gruppo '63 formed in Palermo. A first piece, called *Teatro Gruppo '63*, evinces the young writers' predilection for a theater in which the text is used as acoustic material, interweaving literary with theatrical experimentation.[29] Youthful figures such as Nanni Balestrini, Eduardo Sanguineti, and Alfredo Giuliani positioned themselves against the literary establishment, which they identified in Italo Calvino, Giorgio Bassani, Carlo Cassola, Franco Fortini, Elsa Morante, Alberto Moravia, and Pier Paolo Pasolini, accusing them of not recognizing the new languages of mass communication and the social mutation underway due to the economic boom. The neo-avant-garde shifted the endless clash between literary and performance cultures onto a new terrain that engaged both scripted and acted experimentation. From theater, the individuals in Gruppo '63 drew stimulation to transform their writing by making it permeable to the bodies of actors and physical space. They founded the *Compagnia Teatro dei Novissimi* (Theatre of the Newest) in Rome, and in June 1965 staged an evening of four one-acts: *Occhio* (Eyes) by Giordano Falzoni, *Merce esclusa* (Excluded Merchandise) by Elio Pagliarani, *Improvvisazione* (Improvisation) by Balestrini, and *Povera Juliet* (Poor Juliet) by Giuliani. In the last of these, Giuliani utilized a collage technique to assemble discredited, banal texts, transformed by altering the acoustic substance of the words, handling each actor's part as an element in a polyphonic musical score. Conventional critics complained that the linguistic experimentation produced texts that were incomprehensible in a performance setting. The review in *Sipario* avoided judgment on the plays themselves but praised the investment in theater on the part of the neo-avant-garde.[30] Respected scholar and director Vito Pandolfi recognized the event as a positive sign of theatrical ferment in Italy, remarking that the emergence of new playwrights in Italy, long declared an impossible dream, was finally taking place before everyone's eyes.[31] As the writers of Gruppo '63 adopted theater methods into their work, theater companies began to include the new literary generation in their repertoire. Alongside the preferred New Theater pantheon of Beckett, Camus, Ionesco, Mayakovski, Jarry, Genet, and Pinter, one found works by Roberto Lerici (*La storia di Sawney Bean* – The Story of Sawney Bean), Giorgio Manganelli (*Iperipotesi* – Hyperhypothesis), Enrico Filippini (*Gioco con la scimmia* – Play with the Monkey), Germano Lombardi and Gaetano Testa (*Illuminazione* – Illumination), and Balestrini and Giuliani (*Pelle d'Asino* – Donkey Skin).

For the most part, critics – not only the conservative ones – charged Gruppo '63 with returning to the worn-out scandal-mongering experimentalism of the historical avant-gardes. In those years, in fact, the word "avant-garde" carried a negative connotation as something dated and used up. Objecting that their work was self-referential and obsessed with form, Pasolini classed the neo-avant-garde of Gruppo '63 as another sign of the "invasion of the barbarians" into Italy. Critic and theater writer Corrado Augias complained that Gruppo '63 "mostly makes pseudo-theater".[32]

After 1968, literary attention shifted away from New Theater, both because of the dissolution of Gruppo '63 and because a new paradigm in theatrical composition rendered the literature-theater debate superfluous. New Theater had by now consolidated its own systems, with actor-directors who composed original spectacles. The posters for Carmelo Bene's extreme adaptation of Shakespeare's Hamlet read "*Amleto*, by Carmelo Bene", while an added parenthesis specifies "(from Shakespeare to Laforgue)".

Seen in historical perspective, the brief affair between literature and the stage marked by Gruppo '63 appears a result of a fervid period in which theater exercised a powerful attraction for the other arts, literature included.

It offered the writer the chance for a relationship with a living, breathing interlocutor, and gave literature political relevance, a goal particularly dear to Gruppo '63. Surveying the era over 20 years later, Franco Quadri included the work of Gruppo '63 among the most significant achievements of the New Theater movement of the Sixties:

> Here was Mario Ricci returning to myth and fantastic novels, condensing the universe of writers like Joyce and Poe into visually enchanting dream spectacle-games, with actors infinitely repeating gestures in underwater slow-motion prophetic of Bob Wilson [. . .] Here was the figurative and motor dodecaphony imposed by Carlo Quartucci on his actors in his first stagings of Beckett and in texts by the Italian avant-gardists of Gruppo '63, transformed into musical scores for phonemes.[33]

In the Sixties in America, until the advent of Happenings, theater culture was, as in Italy, primarily literary and Eurocentric: the most high-risk work was considered Sartre, Genet, Ionesco, and the new English realists such as John Osborne, Arnold Wesker, John Arden, and Harold Pinter. Artaud became known in the United States and Italy simultaneously beginning in 1963. The Living Theatre made it into *The Drama Review* in 1964, just as the company was evicted from its New York space, and set out for Rome. In 1966, the same journal covered New Theater together with guerrilla and environmental theater, Happenings, psychedelic spectacles, and the off-off Broadway movement.

1.4 *The actor is the poet of oral language:* Pasolini's Manifesto

The years 1967 and 1968 were a time of theater manifestos, declarations of principle and political perspective that gave voice to highly-charged cultural debate. Among them were the *Discussion Topics for a New Theater Conference*, composed collectively by four authors in anticipation of the national conference to be held in Ivrea in June, 1967; Pier Paolo Pasolini's *Manifesto for a New Theater*, which appeared in *Nuovi Argomenti* in the January-March edition of 1968; "In the Belly of Theater", a statement by Giovanni Testori published in *Paragone* in June, 1968; Germano Celant's manifesto, *Notes for a Guerrilla Movement*,[34] which launched *arte povera*; and, translated from English, Richard Schechner's *Six Axioms for an Environmental Theater*. The manifesto became the characteristic literary genre of a historical moment in which not only theater but all the arts sought to change the world [CONTEXTS '60].[35]

In Italy, much of the cultural debate around theater opposed the literary text against the performance text. Intellectuals, critics, and writers took their stand against directors, who they accused of having devalued the word in search of visual and acoustic sensationalism (embodied, as a prime example, in the theater work of Luchino Visconti). While always standing apart from factions, Pasolini shared with the party of literature their diffidence toward spectacle, claiming to prefer the rational over the sensorial. Considerable polemic centered on the controversy about the appropriate language – that is, which type of Italian – to use in theatrical representations. In a sort of preliminary draft of his *Manifesto* that appeared in the March 1965 issue of *Vie Nuove*, entitled "The end of the avant-garde" Pasolini observed,

> A writer knows, for better or worse, the condition of his instrument; that is, language. Actors and directors do not. The impossibility of communicating between the two categories comes from this. Theater people, precisely those who must speak it, do not know that there is no such thing as *common spoken Italian*.[36]

The dilemma, Pasolini concluded, was that "there is no common spoken tongue with which to render written phrases, and dialect theater, although the only theater possible in Italy, is not up to the task of affirming the existence of a national theater".[37] Pasolini argued that the phonemic and acoustical experimentation of the Gruppo '63 approach to language risked destroying the signifying and metaphorical power of the word by presenting it "without shadows, without ambiguity and without drama, like impersonal formulas or academic texts".[38] His real objection to Gruppo '63 was against a literature closed up within itself, while he advocated instead "the will of the author to express a 'meaning' rather than signifieds".[39] Pasolini focused on the responsibility of the intellectual-author (whether writer or director) to reality, and he stigmatized the anesthetizing effect of language with its meaning removed, the disjunction between meaning and the semiotic concept of the signified that he found in the work of the "Novissimi", who were terrified of falling into naturalism.

The theory on theater that Pasolini expressed in his *Manifesto* must be read in the context of his larger body of work on and in theater. After all, Pasolini composed plays before he published his first poems, and returned to theater repeatedly throughout his career even as he decried it as a form. The new generation of critics who advanced the cause of New Theater tagged his *Manifesto* as reactionary and as coming from the establishment, and it was generally ignored, both by the advocates of the new and the institutional theater system.

Today the *Manifesto* is remembered primarily for its most clamorous charge, that "Both the Theater of Chatter (that is, establishment theater) and the "Theater of the Gesture or Scream" (that is, New Theater) are products of the same bourgeois civilization. They have in common their hatred for the Word".[40] This is the accusation that provoked hostile reaction from New Theater, which, for Pasolini, was homogeneous with bourgeois theater, and was incarnated in the Living Theatre, which he made the scapegoat for the international avant-garde with all its trappings: the collective mode of production, the experimental process, the dominance of non-verbal languages, and the dissonant musicality of its verbal performance. These are the characteristics that led Pasolini to invent the negative term "theater of the Gesture or Scream" to identify a form from which he chose to distance himself.

Beyond the narrow partisan sides taken at the time, we can see today that the *Manifesto* enunciated certain concepts by no means opposed to those elaborated by the New Theater. For example, it proposed interest in orality, the centrality of the actor as original creator, and the role of non-verbal languages. For Pasolini in the *Manifesto*, the actor, the vehicle of oral communication, was the "poet of oral language", who should enjoy the same liberty in his own realm as the poet does with written language. This is why the actor must reject the "recited anti-language" of the type of speech found on television. Pasolini insisted that spoken language should be the predominant device of theatrical communication, but, paradoxically, he also granted to the actor and to non-verbal languages an equally decisive role in the overall expressiveness of theatrical representation.

1.5 Theater at the center of society: the Ivrea conference

A watershed moment in New Theater was a national conference held in the town of Ivrea, north of Turin, June 10–12, 1967, which has entered legend as the Ivrea Conference. The three-day event featured talks, workshops, performances, and discussions by leading lights in the national movement, including Carmelo Bene, director Luca Ronconi, Eugenio Barba (whose company, Odin Teatret, was based in Denmark), militant critic and theorist Franco Quadri, voice artist Cathy Berberian, and Dario Fo (although at the time Fo had not yet abandoned the circuit of establishment theater). The most powerful energy, however, came from the presence of young companies, most still very much in formation, from throughout the peninsula, who came in search of critical mass, political and artistic solidarity, inspiration, and conflict. Its initial statement, composed primarily by Giuseppe Bartolucci but bearing 24 signatures, declared, "We believe theater can be used to insinuate doubt, to fracture prospects, to remove masks, to put thought into action. We believe in a theater full of questions, of right or wrong demonstrations, of contemporary gestures".[41]

The road to Ivrea was paved by radical experimentation across genres, by an often willful, deliberate violation of convention. A representative example is *Zip-Lap-Lip*, presented at the Venice Biennale in 1965 by a loose ensemble whose work would prove influential in defining New Theater: Giuliano Scabia, Carlo Quartucci, Claudio Remondi, Rino Sudano, Leo de Berardinis, Anna D'Offizi, and Cosimo Cinieri [FOCUS]. This collective work tested new compositional and performance languages, hand in hand with the search for an anti-bourgeois value system and insistence on abandoning the consumer theater circuit. "*Zip*", wrote the authors in an introduction, "is an essentially visual spectacle, where sound, gesture and projection interact on the same plane".[42] In contrast to and against traditional theater, every element performed an autonomous function, made an equal contribution to the scenic representation, equal to and independent of the actor's recitation. The characters were ten masks that did not correspond to any immediately identifiable type, but developed and transformed in the course of the performance. Language was disarticulated, proceeding by phonetic schemas, almost a musical score. Alternating improvisation with planned segments, the actor exploited all his or her vocal possibilities, choosing keening high notes and extreme timbres, emitting both *forte* and *piano* whispers and hissing, inventing and combining syllabic fragments, breaking multisyllabic words into pieces until they become incomprehensible. In *Zip-Zap-Lip*, each character lived for herself, without concatenation or interaction in dialogue or action. Rather, there were open sections in which the actors dropped their characters to address the spectators "as themselves", in effect leaving behind the theater while unmasking its mechanisms, and enunciating the problematic aspects of performance and spectatorship. They asked, "What is the mission of theater today? What do you expect from theater? A theater of pure entertainment? Political theater? Metaphysical theater? Gastronomic theater? Epic theater? Ritual theater?"[43]

Zip-Zap-Lip was not favorably received by the majority of critics at the Biennale, who masked the inadequacy of their analytical tools with personal disquisitions for or against the avant-garde.[44]

In a memoir, Sandro Lombardi remembers the moment this way:

> It was 1967, and we were breathing an intensely political atmosphere; the love of literature, poetry, or art risked being suspected of lacking political commitment. Implicit orders went around evoking negation, refusal, striving for utopia, dropping out of the bourgeois context; all principles very seductive to the youth of that time. Theater allowed us to reconcile all those diverse needs; it allowed us to follow our own inclinations by grafting them into a collective design.[45]

Before the conference itself, four participant authors (Giuseppe Bartolucci, Ettore Capriolo, Edoardo Fadini, and Franco Quadri) drafted a manifesto, *Discussion Topics for a New Theater Conference*, which sought to identify the guiding principles of the movement, distilled from their observation of the work of artists such as Carmelo Bene, Luca Ronconi, the Living Theatre, Peter Brook, and Giuliano Scabia. The issues they raised mark out the foundations of a new theater, using key terms of the era: laboratory theater, theater collectives, acquisition and experimention with new materials and objects, sound of every imaginable kind, stage space (invoking both the place of performance and the relationship between the performer's space and the spectator's space), and the search for a new audience through new organizational structures. Each element of this new theatrical edifice had its own carefully-reasoned thesis.

"The theatrical location is both the stage and the house, and the elements that compose it constitute the precise formal and conceptual reason underlying the dramatic action". The manifesto thus called for the use of the entire theater, eliminating the distinction between stage and house. It advocated an "alienated and ironic use of objects" whose status was equal to that of the actors, because the actor was "an animated object, a plastic visual and acoustical fact". The performance score might introduce "purely phonetic roles", which, rendered on the page, appeared as visual poetry, graphic traces, drawings, or rhythms.[46] This *Manifesto*, written as guidelines for discussion at the upcoming New Theater conference, took great inspiration from the methods of the Living Theatre, a sort of ideological community with no limiting credo, which recognized no border between daily life and artistic practice. The "Living", as it was nicknamed, transformed uncodified languages – the term "language" here taken in its widest possible sense, including the guttural, the gestural, the non-human – and transported neglected, non-aesthetic materials found outside the theatrical tradition, into performance. The theater described in Bartolucci et al.'s document expanded beyond the performance hall into the street. It proceeded by trial and error, often preferring error. Results were intentionally not anticipated, but discovered along the path. All the expressive languages traditional to theater (including the languages of gesture, movement in defined space and the manipulation of objects) were re-signified, tapping resources coming from dance, the visual arts, and the non-aesthetic. The manifesto also dwelt on the larger organizational apparatus of theater, on the need to locate and develop an entirely new audience. Given the rapid changes in Italian society – a transformation Pasolini identified as nothing less than "anthropological" – it no longer made sense to regard theater as a public service, which was the welfare-state concept that had led to the postwar establishment of public theaters in major cities throughout the nation.

The Ivrea Conference for a New Theater, and analogous initiatives of the era, should be considered as the assertion of a political claim, a claim that theater should penetrate deeply into the social body, and change it. Theater would exist at the center of civil society, in the social present. Political commitment was to be intrinsic to artistic practice, with a tight connection between theater, society, and experimentation.

1.6 Intermedia and musical theater

The Sixties also produced a terrain for experimentation between aesthetic codes frequented by dancers, visual artists, architects, and musicians. There was a powerful interdisciplinary vocation throughout the decade, fueled in part by the activities in the United States and Europe of George Maciunas and Stan VanDerBeek's Intermedia. Exchanges among the arts took the form of musicians engaged in electro-acoustic experimentation, and visual artists who mixed film, video, photography, theater, and television, as in

Rzewski-Pascali's advertising spots.[47] Avant-garde poets made visual poetry. These "interferences" among media and genre altered the nature of each. Artists invaded each other's space. The "Theater of the 101" hosted a spectacle by Sylvano Bussotti presenting music by John Cage. In December 1966, the Piper discotheque in Turin presented an event staged by Carlo Quartucci and Roberto Lerici, two of the creators of *Zip-Lap-Lip*. Visual artist Michelangelo Pistoletto created *The End of Pistoletto*: 25 people standing side by side wearing masks bearing the features of the artist, each holding a sort of reflective steel shield which was made to vibrate to produce sound. Strobe lights moved from the discotheques into the theaters, for example in Balestrini-Ricci's *Illumination*, during which Umberto Bignardi linked moving images to actions carried out by actors, exploring the possibilities of "rhythmic light".

Alfredo Leonardi, the founder of FilmStudio in Rome, created *Organum Multiplum* in 1967, a film that expressed the new culture of the body, intimacy, love and joy, with a soundtrack employing Italy-based experimental musicians, a testimony to the *mènage-à-trois* between composers, independent cinema, and theater. The actors included members of the Living Theatre: the film began and ended with a sequence from the Living's Roman piece, *Mysteries and Smaller Pieces*.[48]

Collage was a characteristic method of composition across media. This technique, derived from Italian futurism and employed first by the historical avant-gardes and then by American Pop Art (which had burst onto the European scene at the 1964 Venice Biennale), turned up for example in Alfredo Giuliani's spectacle, *Poor Juliet*, in dialogues that combined effete social chat with the language of popular gossip sheets. In a 1961 ensemble work entitled *Collage*, poets, painters, and stage technicians collaborated to create a spectacle in which light, color, and movement predominated over dialogue and character. In the script, terms from the visual arts were used to designate musical actions.[49] One of the creators, Aldo Clementi, argued that the term "musical theater" should mean a performance collage in which the musical element regulated the unfolding of the spectacle.[50]

In 1964 Luigi Nono staged *The Illuminated Factory*, a concert for soprano and quadrophonic tape with text by Giuliano Scabia [FOCUS]. The sounds had been recorded during work shifts in the furnace room at the Italsider steel plant in Genoa. The work took the factory itself as an immense resonator and strove to lead concert listeners to a catharsis. The piece's finale closed with a repeated line from Cesare Pavese's poem, "Morning": "The day will come".[51] Inspired in part by photographic montages employed by Brecht for his *War Primer*, the sounds from Italsider, transferred to magnetic tape, denounced the alienation produced by factory labor.[52]

In Nanni Balestrini's *Improvisation*, 1965, actors read word collages made of phrases from evening newspapers, stage directions from Chekhov's *Cherry Orchard*, and instructions from a gymnastics manual.[53] The text of a 1973 piece by the ensemble Gruppo Altro randomly combined selections from the I Ching with physics and biology textbooks and statements by scientists.[54]

In Italy, the ritual aspect of theater, a theater of direct experience that turned spectators into participants according to principles invoked by Artaud and practiced by the Living Theatre, developed in a strongly political direction, imagining a Marxist utopia without classes, in which the authority of the artist over the spectator would be abolished. Domenico Guaccero and Egisto Macchi formed the Musical Theater Company of Rome in 1965, with the goal of setting up "a place for multidisciplinary work where authors, performers (musicians, actors, vocalists) and technicians, working like a team, can make use of the skills of the other to create a strongly participatory theater, polyphonic and relational".[55] In the third section of the piece, *Scenes of Power*, spectators were invited to take part in the musical improvisation by using percussion instruments positioned on the stage among the other instruments. The New Musical Theater abolished musical linearity and the frontal relationship between players and public. A ruling paradigm of the period was that music should be aleatory (based on chance) and improvisational, as in *A(lter) A(ction)*, 1966, by Egisto Macchi, using texts drawn from Artaud's letters selected by Mario Diacono, and sets by visual artist Jannis Kounellis.

What was the relationship in this era between the musical avant-garde and New Theater? Both realms emphasized experimentation and the sharing of projects, productions and aesthetics. The Italian musical avant-garde of the Sixties mixed artistic languages and collective composition in a social laboratory without hierarchies or specialties, in open, natural opposition to the intensely stratified tradition of grand opera.

Notes

1 Asor Rosa, op. cit., 476.
2 During this period, publishing houses concentrated their attentions on theater: not only Einaudi and Feltrinelli, but also Lerici, Officina, De Donato and Editori Riuniti published both texts of spectacles and critical essays.
3 During the Sixties, composers such as Bruno Maderna, Luciano Berio, Luigi Nono, Aldo Clementi and Giacomo Manzoni, along with musicologists such as Luigi Rognoni and Roberto Leydi, created work and conducted research at the Studio di Fonologia in Milan, the third largest European laboratory of its kind, after the Cologne studio and IRCAM in Paris. Cfr. F. Galante and N. Sani, *Musica espansa: Percorsi elettroacustici di fine millennio*, Ricordi Lim, Milan, 2000, 75.
4 Luciano Berio created many works in the genre of New Musical Theater, including: *Mimusique* (1953), two performed actions with text by Roberto Leydi, directed by Giorgio Strehler, with Jacques Lecoq; *Allez-hop* (1959), with text by Italo Calvino, directed by Lecoq; *Esposizione* (1962), with Anna Halprin; *Passaggio* (1962), in collaboration with Edoardo Sanguineti; *Laborinthus* (1963–65), *Opera* (1969–70); *Terminal*, with the Open Theater (1969); and *Un re in ascolto* (1984), again with texts by Calvino.
5 Cfr. J. P. Fargier, ed., *Nam June Paik*, Artpress, Paris, 1989, 70.

6 S. Bussotti, "Marcatré", *La Passion selon Sade*, July-September 1965, pp. 16–18, 350–356.

7 Chiari's "musical compositions" from 1964–67 are collected in a limited edition entitled *Musica senza contrappunto*, with scores of instructions for actions, according to the aesthetics of the Fluxus movement, in which Chiari participated along with Bussotti, inspired by the similar actions by Maciunas and Dick Higgins. In subsequent years, Chiari presented happenings in galleries and museums. Cfr. G. Celant, ed., *Identité italienne, L'art en Italie depuis 1959*, Centre Georges Pompidou, Musée national d'art moderne, Paris, 1981 (Catalogue de l'exposition 29 juin-7 septembre 1981), 164.

8 M. Giordano, "'Collage', un'esperienza di esoeditoria d'avanguardia nella Palermo degli anni Sessanta", in TECLA, *Rivista di temi di critica letteraria e artistica*, n.2, December, 2010, pp. 108–128

9 A. Asor Rosa, "Avanguardia", in *Enciclopedia*, Einaudi, Turin, 1977, vol. II, 202.

10 Plinio De Martiis founded the La Tartaruga gallery in 1953 in Via del Babuino, in Rome. P. De Martiis, "Gli anni originali", *La Tartaruga: Quaderni d'arte e letteratura*, March 1989, nn. 5–6, 3.

11 Franco Fortini criticized Elio Vittorini for his *Letters to Togliatti* which defended a "corporate" independence, but also those who substituted sociological concepts such as "cultural industry" and "social conflict" for the Marxist categories of capital, labor and class struggle.

12 *Le Stelle* was a quartet consisting of a bassist (Giandomenico Crescentini), a drummer (Sandro Cerra), a guitarist (Urbano Orlandi) and a keyboard player (Nello Marini), who Schifano worked with on a multimedia, "psychedelic" project. The first concert, with film projections, was *Anna Carini in Agosto vista dalle farfalle*, in the theater in Via Berlsiana in September, 1967. Such initiatives, combining visual art, cinema and pop music, were inspired by events at Andy Warhol's Factory, such as the *Exploding Plastic Inevitable*, featuring the Velvet Underground. Cfr. A. Moravia and F. Colombo, "Grande angolo sogni & stelle di Mario Schifano", in G. Bartolucci (ed.), *La scrittura scenica*, Lerici, Rome, 1968, 276–278.

13 In popular music, the Sixties were a giant laboratory of new musical forms; Bob Dylan took up the tradition of the American folk singer and became a symbol of youth counterculture, only to be scorned by a fringe of the movement when, in 1965, he abandoned acoustic music for electrified rock. The Beach Boys, with *Pet Sounds*, left behind *surf-pop* to adopt more complex melodies and arrangements. In their album *Sergeant Pepper's Lonely Hearts Club Band*, 1967, the Beatles experimented with long-form compositions and used the recording studio itself as a musical instrument. Frank Zappa and the Mothers of Invention, with *Freak Out!* (1966) deconstructed genres, combining blues, avant-garde music, banal jingles, and rock (thanks to Mauro Petruzziello for his consultation).

14 Cfr. G. Baratta, "Il Portico", *Proposte di poesia tecnologica*, n. 6, December 1965. 22–23.

15 G.P. Brunetta, *Storia del cinema italiano: Dal miracolo economico agli anni Novanta, 1960–1990*, Editori Riuniti, Rome, 1993, 187–190.

16 Ivi, 183.

17 Cfr. G. Baruchello and A. Grifi, "Marcatré", *Una verifica incerta*, nn. 16–18, 1965, 366–369.

18 G.P. Brunetta, op. cit., 184–186.

19 On Lorenzo Mango's role in New Theater, cfr. D. Visone, *La nascita del nuovo teatro in Italia, 1959–1967*, Titivillus, Corazzano (PI), 2010; S. Margiotta, *Il Nuovo Teatro in Italia 1968–1975*, op. cit; M. Valentino, *Il Nuovo Teatro in Italia 1976–1985*, op. cit.

20 F. Quadri, *Il rito perduto: Saggio su Luca Ronconi*, Einaudi, Turin, 1973, 29.

21 Cfr. G. Deleuze, "Un manifesto in meno", in C. Bene and G. Deleuze (eds.), *Sovrapposizioni*, Feltrinelli, Milan, 1978, 69–100.
22 The intransigence of literature toward a genre traditionally considered minor such as theater, and the refusal to submit to the demands of directors, actors and spectators, does not appear so far apart from the attitudes of the writers interviewed by Ugo Ojetti at the end of the nineteenth century (U. Ojetti, *Alla scoperta dei letterati*, Dumolard, Milan, 1895). For both generations of writers, theater was considered mere entertainment, not art, a genre for grade-B writers in service to theater companies and their impresarios.
23 F. Quadri, *L'avanguardia teatrale in Italia (materiali 1960–1976)*, Einaudi, Turin, 1977, 136.
24 Cfr. *Il teatro per cambiare il mondo* (see Chapter 2).
25 Cfr. N. Balestrini, ed., *Quindici, una rivista e il Sessantotto*, Feltrinelli, Milan, 2008. The book consists of a selection of articles published by the journal (from n. 1, June 1967 to n. 15, December 1968). Cfr. also G. Manganelli, "Il Verri", *Cerimonia e artificio*, a monographic issue entitled *Teatro come evento*, n. 25, March 1967, now in Id. L. Scarlini, ed., *Cerimonie e Artifici: Scritti di teatro e di spettacolo*, Oèdipus, Salerno-Milano, 2000.
26 E. Pagliarini, "Quindici", *La constestazione fisica del Living Theatre*, June 1, 1967, 25–29.
27 F. Quadri, "Il vecchio e il nuovo", *Il rito perduto: Saggio su Luca Ronconi*, Einaudi, Turin, 1973, 32.
28 F. Quadri, "Il veccho e il nuovo", cit.
29 For a summary of their initial meeting, cfr. "Marcatré", *Il Gruppo '63 a Palermo*, n. 1, November 1963, 5–13; A. Giuliani, "Il dibattito in occasione del primo incontro del Gruppo '63 a Palermo nel 1963", in R. Barilli and A. Guglielmi (eds.), *Gruppo '63: Critica e teoria*, Testo & Immagine, Turin, 2003, 237–262; which first appeared in N. Balestrini and A. Giuliani (eds.), *Gruppo '63*, Feltrinelli, Milan, 1964. They were a heterogeneous group of novelists, poets and critics characterized by an interest in visual arts, music, and performance.
30 "Sipario", *I Novissimi*, n. 231, July 1965, 40.
31 Cfr. also Alberto Arbasino, "The mere idea that a script might be examined, and be subject to the observations of one of our actors or one of our directors, is enough to fill your spirit with such horror as to drive you to desperate measures: to never leave the world of novels and essays ever again". Cited in M. Rusconi, ed., "Sipario", *Gli scrittori e il teatro*, n. 229, May 1965, 2–14, 35.
32 C. Augias, "Sipario", *Approssimazioni successive a una fisiologia dell'avanguardia*, n. 241, May 1966, 93; cited in D. Visone, *La nascita del Nuovo Teatro in Italia*, cit.
33 F. Quadri, "Avanguardia? Nuovo Teatro", in A. Attisani (ed.) *Le forze in campo*, Mucchi, Modena, 1987, 7–21.
34 G. Celant, "Appunti per una guerriglia", *Flash Art*, n. 5, November-December, Milan 1967. "Elementi di discussione per un convegno su nuovo teatro" was published in *Teatro*, n. 2, 1967–1968, and republished in Giuseppe Bartolucci, *Testi Critici 1964–1987*, Bulzoni, Rome, 2007, 113–123.
35 The essay "Six Axioms for an Environmental Theater", published in *TDR*, n. 39, Spring 1968, and in Italy, the same year, in R. Schechner, *La cavità teatrale*, De Donato, Bari, 1968, is an important theoretical reflection born from the re-elaboration of ideas expressed in Happenings, Intermedia, and Street Theater.
36 P. Paolo Pasolini, *L'italiano 'orale' e gli attori*, in *Dialoghi con Pasolini*, Editori Riuniti, Rome, 1992, p. 178; previously in "Vie Nuove", n. 11, March 18 1965.
37 *Ibidem*.
38 P. Paolo Pasolini, "'La fine dell'avanguardia: Appunti per una frase di Goldman, per due versi di un testo d'avanguardia', and 'Per un'intervista di Barthes'", in Pasolini (ed.), *Empirismo eretico*, Garzanti, Milan, 1972, 130.

39 *Ibidem*, 138.
40 P. Paolo Pasolini, "Manifesto per un Nuovo Teatro", in *Nuovi Argomenti*, January-March 1968 republished in J. Duflot, ed., *Il sogno del centauro*, Editori Riuniti, Rome, 1983, 134–135. In a note, Pasolini explained that by "chatter" he meant playwriting "from Chekhov to the horrible Albee" and by "Gesture or Scream", he meant, "the stupendous Living Theatre".
41 The Ivrea *Manifesto* was first published in *Teatro*, n. 2, 1967–68, 18–25. It can now be found in G. Bartolucci, *Testi critici*, cit., 119.
42 C. Quartucci and G. Scabia, "Per un'avanguardia italiana", in F. Quadri (ed.), *L'avanguardia teatrale: Materiali 1960–1976*, Einaudi, Turin, 1977, 167.
43 Cfr. D. Visone, *La nascita del Nuovo Teatro in Italia, 1959–1967*, cit. (in particular, see pp. 79–92, for the description of *Zip Lap Tip*); see also G. Bartolucci, "Rito laico Beato del Teatro Dionisio", in *Scrittura scenic*, Lerici, Rome, 1968, 68–69.
44 See C. Quartucci and G. Scabia, in F. Quadri, *L'avanguardia teatrale in Italia*, cit., 169–171.
45 S. Lombardi, *Il lavoro dell'attore fra realtà e memoria*, Garzanti, Milan, 2004, 22.
46 "Elementi di discussion per un convegno sul Nuovo Teatro", which here we refer to as the "Ivrea Manifesto", drafted by Giuseppe Bartolucci, Edoardi Fadini, Ettore Capriolo, and Franco Quadri, was offered as a platform of debate at the "Convegno per un Nuovo Teatro", held in Ivrea, June 9–12, 1967. The text was published first in "Teatro", n. 2, 1967–68, 18–25; and republished by Bartolucci in 1972 and Quadri in 1977. Now in G. Bartolucci, *Testi critici 1964–1987*, cit., 119.
47 See the introduction to the catalogue, *Future Cinema: The Cinematic Imaginary After Film* (ZKM, Center for Art and Media, Karlsruhe, 2002–2003). In the exhibition, dedicated to the complex relations between cinema, visual art and new media, theoretician and ZKM director Peter Weibel distinguishes three phases of transformation in cinema, describing "expanded cinema" as a moment of "extension" of cinematic codes and specific cinematic elements.
48 G. Celant, ed., *Identité italienne: L'art en Italie depuis 1959*, cit., 227.
49 Cfr. A. Mastropietro, "Tra improvvisazione e alea: il macro-fenomeno nel teatro musicale delle neo-avanguardie romane", in A. Sbordoni (ed.), *Improvvisazione oggi*, LIM editore, Lucca, 2014, 129–150.
50 Aldo Clementi in D. Visone, *La nascita del nuovo teatro in Italia, 1959–1967*, cit., 29.
51 Cfr. F. Galante and N. Sani, *Musica espansa: Percorsi elettroacustici di fine millennio*, cit., 87.
52 In 1963, Luigi Nono wrote about his idea of musical theater in "Possibilità e necessità di un Nuovo Teatro musicale", in F. Degrada (ed.), *Al Gran sole carico d'amore: Per un Nuovo Teatro musicale*, Ricordi, Milan, 1978, 5–7. Nono's essay was first published in "Il Verri", 1963, 70. He collaborated with Giuliano Scabia on *La fabbrica illuminata*, 1964, in Venice, as well as with Peter Weiss on *Die Ermittlung* [The Investigation], 1965, in Berlin.
53 V. Pandolfi, "Tappe dell'avanguardia teatrale in Italia", *Marcatré*, nn. 16–18, July-September, 1965, 125. Cfr. M. Ricci, "Un altro modello del Nuovo Teatro", in D. Visone (ed.), *La nascita del nuovo teatro in Italian, 1958–1967*, cit., 136.
54 Cfr. G. Altro, *Altro dieci anni di lavoro intercodice*, Edizioni Kappa, Rome, 1981.
55 A. "Tra improvvisazione e alea: il macro-fenomeno nel teatro musicale delle neo-avanguardie romane", in A. Sbordoni (ed.), *Improvvisazione oggi*, cit., 130. This essay features a rich bibliography of new musical theater during the Sixties and Seventies.

2   The Seventies

Setting out: 1968–77

The Seventies in theater trace an arc crossing from the explosion of 1968 to the implosion of 1977. Our memory guides on this journey will be Giuseppe Bartolucci, Marco Belpoliti, Germano Celant, and Franco Quadri.

Throughout Europe and much of the world, deep social and political processes that had been developing since the end of the Second World War came to a head in the late Sixties. In the realm of labor, agriculture definitively ceded its predominance to mass industry, and within industry the service sector came to the fore over manufacture. Cities expanded, seeming to invade and overwhelm the countryside. Great migratory movements within and between nations rapidly altered ways of life, affecting the labor market, creating new habits, needs, desires, and new principles of human rights. Labor unions became stronger, while – with the extension of universal schooling – universities and schools begin to aspire to take a leading role in public life. On the international plane, neo-colonialism entered a crisis phase due to liberation movements in Asia, Africa, and Latin America. The Cold War still held sway among the great powers, but ever-greater diffusion of mass communication became a vehicle for demands for social reform and global peace emerging from below – impulses expressed in art, fashion, and cultural exchange. A widespread movement of protest and revolt spread through the cities. In Italy, this phenomenon was particularly widespread and radical, sometimes uniting students with industrial labor unions, who joined in efforts to overcome the persistent vestiges of fascism, the closed-mindedness of the Church, and the conflicts left unresolved during the process of national unification. To put it simply, Italy entered the contemporary world.

The change was violent. What was soon called the "strategy of tension" began in late 1969, when a bomb exploded in Piazza Fontana in Milan, killing 17 people and wounding 88. To this day the guilty have not been brought to justice. In May, 1974, a bomb placed in a trash can exploded during an anti-fascist demonstration in Brescia, the second-largest city in Lombardy. Eight people were killed and 102 wounded; in this case too, numerous trials have brought no convictions. Later the same year, a bomb on the Italicus train traveling between Florence and Bologna killed 12 people and injured

48. A neo-fascist group claimed responsibility, saying the act was revenge for the killing of a member of their group after the Brescia bombing. In August, 1980, a bomb exploded in the waiting room at the Bologna train station, killing 85 people and leaving more than 200 wounded.

Mass mobilizations by industrial workers and students followed these events and sometimes led to open clashes with the forces of order. The government continued to function but the political scene was reframed, mid-decade, by the alliance forged between the two largest political parties, the Christian Democrats and the Communists – bitter opponents since the establishment of the Republic founded in the wake of the war – led respectively by Aldo Moro and Enrico Berlinguer. National administrative elections of 1976 brought the left-wing to power for the first time, but this achievement was undermined the following year: the alliance of students and the labor movement fractured, triggering the bloody "years of lead", when extra-parliamentary left-wing groups carried out targeted assassinations of judges, politicians, and journalists.

In intellectual life, various strands of French theory coming from Barthes, Foucault, Blanchot, Genette, Deleuze, and others broke down the Positivist-Idealist and historical-materialist paradigms that had held sway in universities since the nineteenth century. In the realm of art, Lea Vergine's pathbreaking study of Body Art, published in 1974, exposed Italy to a boundary-crossing new conception of artistic practice.[1] The following year, art historian Filiberto Menna's *The Analytic Line in Modern Art* affirmed the intimate connection between art practice and critical thought.[2]

Cinema expressed this ferment. "Independent Cinema" emerged, with work by Alfredo Leonardi (*Organum Multiplum*, 1967); Carmelo Bene (*Nostra Signora dei Turchi*, 1968; *Capricci*, 1969; *Don Giovanni*, 1970; *Salomè*, 1072; *Un Amleto di meno* [One Hamlet Less], 1974; and Grifi-Sarchielli (*Anna*, 1972). The 3-hour, 45-minute video *Anna*, by Massimo Sarchielli and Alberto Grifi, can be taken as representative: combining both film and video, the movie presents the daily life of a 16-year-old pregnant Roman heroin addict. Incarnating the cultural climate of the early Seventies, it represents a Rome light years distant from Fellini's *Dolce Vita* (1960), vibrant with revolutionary agitation, the hippy movement, feminism, drugs, and youth protest under the cloud of the Piazza Fontana bombing.

Proponents of "artist's cinema" such as Ugo Nespolo, Bruno Munari, Gianfranco Baruchello, and Mario Schifano (*Satellite*, 1968; *Umano non umano* [Human not Human], 1969; *Trapianto, consunzione e morte di Franco Brocani* [Transplant, Consumption and Death of Franco Brocani], 1969) worked outside the logic of genres and the ordinary channels of production and distribution.[3]

Together with Independent Cinema, the Seventies witnessed the emergence, in Italy as elsewhere, of a new medium: the electronic *nouvelle image*, a field of experimentation where the visual arts met live performance, television and artist's cinema. In New York in 1971, Steina and Woody Vasulka opened the Kitchen Center for Video, Music, Performance and Dance, and Howard Wise founded Electronic Arts Intermix to promote and distribute video art. In the same year in Germany, Gerry Schum and Ursula Wefers opened TV Gallery in Dusseldorf. In Italy, also in 1971, Luciano Giaccari equipped his Studio 970/2 in Varese with videocameras to record spectacles and performances, while Lola Bonora inaugurated the first institutional center for video art at the museum in the Palazzo dei Diamanti in Ferrara, which promoted the U-Tape Festival. In Florence, the production studio Art/Tapes/22 collaborated with the Castelli-Sonnabend Gallery to create video art by a long list of North American and European artists (from the United States: Vito Acconci, Douglas Davis, Simone Forti, Frank Gillette, Allan Kaprow, Joan Jonas, Charlemagne Palestine, Bill Viola; from Europe: Christian Boltanski, Antoni Muntadas, Urs Lüthi) as well as a rising generation of Italians, including Vincenzo Agnetti, Alighiero Boetti, Pier Paolo Calzolari, Giuseppe Chiari, Jannis Kounellis, Giulio Paolini, Gino De Dominicis, and Sandro Chia.[4]

As video art brought disciplines together, it also engaged political issues. In 1976 in Milan, Paolo Rosa and Tullio Brunone founded the Laboratory of Militant Communication, dedicated to using new media in a strategy of counter-information, striving to decodify the semiotics of daily life, to fight the hegemony of mass entertainment and information. The transformation of the once-solitary labor of art into collective practice characterized the multimedia group Studio Azzurro, founded by painter Paolo Rosa, part of the ideological utopia envisioned by artists and intellectuals to make the production and consumption of art socially equal and interchangeable.[5]

A privileged observatory for the promiscuous contamination of arts in the early Seventies was Fabio Sargentini's gallery in Rome, The Attic [FOCUS/CONTEXTS]. Here, Asian, European, and North American artists in various disciplines crossed paths. *The Dance Flight Music Dynamite Festival* in 1971 combined minimalist musician/composers Terry Riley and La Monte Young with dancers/choreographers Steve Paxton, Trisha Brown, and Simone Forti. In another event, Robert Smithson, one of the originators of Land Art, dumped a truckload of boiling asphalt down the side of a stone quarry on Rome's Via Laurentina.

Another highly active center in Rome was Beat 72 [FOCUS/CONTEXTS], organized by Ulisse Benedetti and Simone Carella, which stimulated the research of young theater companies. Poetry and music played key roles in work bridging genres. The contemporary music series New Sonic Forms included leading figures in the musical avant-garde. John Cage's *Theatre Piece*, presented at Beat 72 by a group named Patagruppo, included artist Marco del Re, actress Rosy Di Lucia, and singer Michiko Hirayama.[6]

Rome in those years was an important international center of interdisciplinary experimentation. Achille Bonito Oliva's large-scale exhibition event, *Contemporanea*, held in the underground parking garage of Villa Borghese in 1973 and 1974, brought together visual art, cinema, music, dance, theater, and a section dedicated to counter-information, giving witness to the fertile continuum between social theory, militant cultural criticism, and cultural activism. *Contemporanea* was perhaps the largest of many similar initiatives, including Bonito Oliva's earlier *Vitality of the Negative*, in 1970, and, later, an exhibition devoted to the *Polish Avant-Garde, 1910–1978*, in which Tadeusz Kantor presented an early version of his spectacle *Où sont les neiges d'antan*, which probed the destiny of the avant-garde and the role of the intellectual in the twentieth century.

2.1 Coming out: of theaters, spectacles, roles

It is no understatement to say that during this period, with the nation shaken by killings and contestation from left and right, when the legalization of divorce and abortion seemed to push even the Church into retreat, when teachers and professors were put on trial by student tribunals styled after Mao's Cultural Revolution, theater emerged as never before in Italian history as a national stage of radical aesthetic and cultural experimentation. While there was certainly no shortage of spectacles rendered pretentious and boring by ideological programs of one sort or another, what is perhaps most unprecedented and unrepeatable was the uncompromising openness of the work and its unexpectedly high quality, the more remarkable for the fact that *process* was almost universally stressed as a principle over *results*. With all its contradictions, its dogmas and taboos, this period of virtually unlimited formal experimentation trained a generation truly expert in a craft that, in Roberto Tessari's words, "adhered to the living materiality of representational practice".[7]

In the decade that began in 1968 with the revolt of industrial workers, students, and teachers, and with the challenge to institutional authority and its authorized spokesmen in the press and on television, a core question engaged young practitioners of theater and related arts: Can theater change the world? From this arose the question of means: What instruments, processes, in what spaces, and with what languages can theater reach this goal? Around 1972, a new circuit of ensembles developed an alternative network of spaces and settings in which to produce, perform, and share their work. Following the model of Eugenio Barba's Denmark-based Odin Teatret, which had been inspired in turn by Grotowski's Polish Laboratory Theater, the Third Theater movement created performance spaces, festivals, and performance series that permitted young companies, traveling by van, to carry their spectacles from Palermo to Trieste, from central Naples to the alpine hinterlands. "In the Seventies", remembers theater historian Ferdinando Taviani, "dozens and dozens of groups sprouted up outside the porous walls of the theaters. They resolved the challenges of survival and development by creating new organizational structures, new practices, a new mentality. They exemplified a different kind of daily life in theater. So successful were they that in a second wave, an entire level of theater had formed which had no relationship with – often even no knowledge of – its institutional step-brother".[8]

In the Sixties and Seventies, the clash between the grand ideological-political systems (not only between capitalism and communism, but also between religion and secularism) opened the way for alternatives to the given pathways, even in terms of the problem of how to live daily life. Especially in the Seventies, different types of communities formed, more or less spontaneously, that proposed independent means of educating children, of dress, of feeding themselves. Rather than projecting their militancy toward a future to be realized with political action, they chose to actualize their vision in the now, discarding the normal, normative systems of education, sanitation, labor, and symbolic representation, rebuilding all these structures upon a new basis. Antonio Porta, a poet of Gruppo '63, theorized this cultural alternative as "building the potential of a 'partisan' culture", by which he alluded to the homegrown Italian resistance movement to fascism and Nazi occupation during the Second World War. The poet called for "accepting the revolution and actualizing it within a group", living together "as though" it were truly possible to construct a parallel society.[9] Health care, labor, entertainment, and art were all territories of which to take possession. One of the privileged locations for challenging the system was the public school system, taken to be a structure for reproducing social discrimination and the established relations of power. *Letter to My Teacher*, written in 1967 by a priest, Don Lorenzo Milani, and his students in the alternative school he established in Barbiana, described the teaching methods of traditional Italian schooling as fundamentally repressive. Today the letter remains a persuasive and powerful critique of institutional education.

Class struggle in the workplace accompanied struggles for the environment, health care, the right to higher education, and the struggle at home brought on by the rising feminist movement. Women raised questions about the culture of the body, the claims of love, pleasure, and the vast continent of childhood. In the schools, in neighborhood organizations, in factories, in the prisons, the idea of theater entered a phase of being reduced to zero and then reinvented. Walter Benjamin's reflections on the relationship between the artistic avant-garde and revolution furnished a theoretical foundation for a radical rethinking of the role and function of artistic practice: What is to be done, how, and for whom? In his essay, "The Author as Producer", Benjamin entrusted the task of revolution to the artist: "His work will never be directed solely to the product, but always to the means of production. In other words, his products must possess an organizational function, beyond and before their character as an artwork"[10] For Benjamin, the leading role of the masses, intended here as the culture industry, new media, and socialist revolution, was capable of regenerating and changing the nature of the forms of art. The year 1969 saw the publication in Italy of Benjamin's "Program for a Proletarian Children's Theater", written in 1920 with Asja Lacis, which indicated theater as an instrument of proletarian education.[11]

Both out of ideological commitment inspired by Benjamin/Lacis, and as a source of much-needed income, many New Theater companies applied Peter Brook's games and improvisation exercises for actors to methods they developed for students in schools. Rather than directing their efforts toward a performance product to be consumed, improvisational play was valued as an end in itself, for the new kinds of relationships it made possible, even if only temporarily and in the imagination. But while actors may have believed they were "bringing theater to the classroom", what took place equally was a reciprocal influence, where the world and perspectives of childhood entered the minds and transformed the methods of New Theater companies.

What held together childhood, play, dramatic enactment, and laboratory theater in those years? According to Giuseppe Bartolucci, who was at the center of the movement to bring theater into schools, it was "the materiality of collective research into relations", interdisciplinary teamwork in a laboratory framework, and shared writing and action – all antidotes against "broken didacticism" and "retrograde aestheticism".[12] Bartolucci set up laboratories, libraries, and sites of exchange where theater practitioners and schoolteachers could instruct one another. From this perspective, "children's' theater" offered itself as a territory where radical theory could be put into practice through the reinvention of the techniques, skills, and roles that had heretofore been held to constitute mastery of the craft.[13] The young companies had to imagine an infancy of theater, not as a metaphorical conceit but concretely, in action. To do so they drew lessons from children themselves, from the deaf (as in Robert Wilson), from the insane (as in the work of Basaglia and Scabia at the psychiatric hospital in Trieste), from the disabled, from assembly-line workers (as in the work of Benno Besson in Terni), and from the inhabitants of ignored, marginal, and impoverished neighborhoods (as done by the Giocosfera collective in Rome).

During the period of student and labor revolt, strikes, street actions, distributing flyers, and protest marches were all conceived and carried out as enactments of collection action, following the parameters Erving Goffman proposed in *The Presentation of Self in Everyday Life*, and as a politics of experience, which fed its energies into a theater that reinvented itself outside traditional spaces and beyond its familiar apparatus.[14] The key words were: collective composition versus the subjectivity of the author; process versus product; effectiveness versus formal values; action versus spectacle.

2.2 Theater to change the world

Theater in the Seventies was marked by platoons of explorers, small group or individual expeditions, voyages flowing from east to west, north to south, from the Occident to the Orient, a dislocation in space and sometimes in time. "Out of love for departure", wrote Gaston Bachelard, "we must know how to detach from daily life. The pleasure in travel inheres in the pleasure of imagining".[15] Both figuratively and physically, crossing borders and leaving home meant statelessness. The absence of a place to call one's own motivated the journeying of the Living Theatre, Peter Brook, Jerzy Grotowski, and Eugenio Barba to seek identities elsewhere. Grotowski left behind his fixed company to undertake an evolving series of experiences he named the Theater of Sources. With the Odin Teatret, Barba began his nomadic peregrinations and the practice of "barter theater" in remote places without theater: in the Salento, the southernmost province of the region of Puglia; in Sardegna, in a mountain village; and in indigenous communities in Peru. Carlo Quartucci and Carla Tatò equipped a white-painted truck, *Camion* [FOCUS], as a studio/laboratory/storehouse/stage, and drove it around the country. In Milan, Dario Fo and Franca Rame created the Comune, a place where theatrical practice and performance mixed with social and political action.

About traditional theater spaces, Julian Beck, founder of the Living Theatre, wrote:

> The man in the street would never even enter a building of this sort [. . .] because inside them a code is spoken that has nothing to do with him [. . .] The Living doesn't want to perform for a privileged elite anymore [. . .] Let's get out of the theaters![16]

Beck's cry led the company to stage their performances in the streets, clashing with police, and then to abandon theater entirely in favor of direct political action in remote locations, far from the circuit of production and consumption. In the finale of *Paradise Now* (1968), the actors left the stage and went out into the street, along with any spectators who had accepted their invitation to join their anarcho-pacifist-Reichian tribe. This conclusive action of the ritual of liberation from social and cultural taboo, which the members of the Living Theatre community executed *for* and *with* the spectators, brought real consequences for both, in the sense that it altered their lives, which was the sign that it had been effective. The Living community accepted adepts who joined up to continue their individual process of liberation. The confines between represented and real life were canceled out by erasing the distinction between performers and spectators: they left the theater together, leaving behind its designated spaces and roles. Actors and spectators both abandoned their constraining functions, escaping into the streets of the city.

Responding to international events of the era (the war in Vietnam, the student revolt in Paris, "Prague Spring" followed by its brutal repression, the military coup in Chile against Salvatore Allende's democratically elected government), many radicalized intellectuals and artists turned to direct political action. For others, revolutionary extremism drove them in the other direction, toward a withdrawal from political struggle. Directors, actors, and companies abandoned conventional theater and chose to work in psychiatric hospitals, prisons, schools, and factories, in the conviction that, "a revolution in theater is a contradiction [. . .] the only task of theater is to lead people out of the theaters, into the streets. The duty of theater groups is to make the revolution happen".[17]

The great utopian drive that inspired theater and art during these years of total opposition to the reigning system depended on the faith that theater – by changing its relationship to the surrounding culture – could contribute to altering the social behavior both of actors and spectators. Spectacles that demanded the active contribution of spectators to the event, as in environmental theater, were considered an expression of participatory democracy: taking decisive action on stage meant doing the same in life. The problem was to bring aesthetics and ethics together by forming a like-minded group that functioned as a community, one that proposed to change the world through theater. The model was the Living Theatre, in which lifestyle and dramatic expression coincided totally. To be part of the group and to be an effective performer, you had to share its anarchic ideology. The ideal community of actors and spectators aspired to render theater as essential as ritual in tribal societies.

Among the initiatives that manifested the variegated phenomena of "leaving theater behind" – both as a physical location and as a discipline – are those of collectives who focused their work on children in a variety of social settings, including Giuliano Scabia, Carlo Quartucci's *Camion*, Leo and Perla, and others who invented a different way of making theater.[18] Still others drew inspiration from the vein of political theater growing from Bertolt Brecht and Peter Weiss (author of the avant-garde ensemble sensation *Marat/Sade*, first performed in 1963). Their work focused on social themes and often involved extensive performer/spectator interaction. Performances were staged in closed-down cinemas, project houses, social clubs, in the meeting halls of left-wing political parties. An association named *Nuova Scena* set up an alternative network of theater distribution through the Italian Communist Party's youth association, ARCI (the Italian Recreational and Cultural Association), whose audiences consisted mostly of students, militant intellectuals, and communist labor groups. Through this network, Dario Fo and Franca Rame attracted thousands of spectators to their performances combining agit-prop with farce, and Maoist propaganda with Fo's hilarious improvisation. Examples of these include *Grand Pantomime with Flags and Puppets Small and Medium*; *Mistero buffo* [FOCUS]; *The Worker Knows Three Hundred Words, the Boss Knows a Thousand, That's Why He's the Boss*.

In 1972, after having temporarily stepped away from live performance to create a film, *To Charlie Parker* (1970), Leo De Berardinis and Perla Peragallo decided to move to Marigliano, a lower-class, decaying industrial town ten kilometers from Naples, in order to take on the challenge of living and making theater in an environment seemingly alien to aesthetic expression of any kind. Their work from this period [FOCUS] combined wide-ranging inquiry, sometimes ethical – using theater to raise consciousness against consumer society – and sometimes political: advocating a "theater of ignorance" into which class society could not extend its tools of discrimination; and sometimes more simply existential, with pieces that publicly asked fundamental questions about the meaning of human existence.[19] Gianni Manzella remembers a typical undertaking, when they rented a farmhouse outside town and transformed the barn into a rehearsal hall, bringing in musical instruments bought cheap; a drum set, a saxophone, some woodwinds. Loose rehearsals took place as much in the fields as in the barn. On weekends, they would go into town and perform in the square, initiating dialogue with the local population. The curious would begin to come out to the farm, and some would stay. A sort of very loose company began to take shape, consisting of an auto worker, a carpenter, and an illiterate man who was considered the village idiot.[20]

The spectacles in Marigliano put to the test the ideal of a theater in which the culture of artists and that of the subproletariat might find a means of exchange and reciprocal fertilization. For *Chianto e risate e risate e chianto* (Tears and Laughter and Laughter and Tears, 1974), composed jointly with actors and townspeople, De Berardinis recalled,

> We involved the whole population in the spectacle. Using a film camera to draw them in (sometimes shooting without film) and waving around a tape recorder, we managed to pull a whole bunch of people together into a Multi-Center of painters and sculptors, and together we elaborated a lot of material, but not in a manipulative way. At the end the company had to condense the mass of material down. The result was a comic spectacle that used comedy and plot as vehicles to bring in a lot of local data chosen for its unfiltered, unsifted excessiveness. From a basis in serenity, we exposed the lacerations.[21]

The lesson, according to De Berardinis, was that, "we should measure ourselves in the context of a still-incomplete discourse on class in theater, with the southerners who've migrated north, politicized and not, with the vast outskirts of the cities".[22] The Marigliano theater was a pregnant example of the relationship possible between a group of artists and a "place without theater", an agglomerate neither rural nor urban, a world in which the cultural elements (popular song and theater) had been irreversibly manipulated and adulterated. Giuseppe Bartolucci observed about the Marigliano work that "the mocking of the southern myth aroused a profound cognitive pathos, with a conscious choice in favor of marginalization and deviance that zeroed out populist grand-standing or intellectual presumption".[23]

2.3 *In search of a common base: the manifesto of* arte povera

Starting in the late Sixties, the arts tend to "theatricalize". From the pages of *Artforum*, Michael Fried decried this trend, and like Pasolini in Italy, he thus became a target to strike against, for having expressed a position widely considered conservative; that of the specificity of each form of art.[24] Against this idea, the principle of the event became a common base shared not only in the performance arts, but now in the visual arts as well.

Among the manifestoes produced by artists and critics in this moment, the manifesto of the *arte povera* movement, formulated by Germano Celant, marked out a common liminal terrain between visual art and theater; a terrain soon occupied by Performance Art, Installation Art, and Environmental Art. Adopting the Situationist philosophy of 's *Society of the Spectacle* (1967), Celant maintained that *arte povera* should intervene directly in the social context, to make the tools of painting, music, and theater available to those deprived of such resources. Rather than contemplating and representing, the artist must act, must participate. To achieve this objective, one must prefer the *lived* to the *represented*. This "ecstatic-sympathetic communion with nature" (Celant, 227), this continuum between life and the artwork, was to confer on the artist a ductility and flexibility that prohibited boxing oneself into a stable identity.[25] The artistic product, "merchandise with exchange value", was called radically into question, a perspective which provoked the avant-garde to venture into Performance Art, Body Art, and Land Art, endeavors in which body and landscape were taken up as material and vehicle of artistic action. The key words were participation, collective work, the interchangeability of roles, process versus form, subject and behavior versus object. "If art wants to reach life", observed Achille Bonito Oliva, "it must silence its need for form and act with extreme liberty through the conduct of the artist. Attention must shift from the object to the subject, from the effect to the process". Art must become *povera* by "reducing (art) to the minimum terms, impoverishing signs, reducing them to their archetypes".[26] The duty of *arte povera* was to eliminate the distance that art, with all its apparatus, had created toward the social sphere.

In Italy, the emancipation of the spectator passed through Marxist ideology. The struggle against the capitalist industrial order founded on class divisions coincided with the campaign to liberate the "spectator-slave" from dependence on the artist-intellectual-master. In a 1969 article in *Sipario* entitled, "Activity: A New Form of Spectacle", Michael Kirby (who had succeeded Richard Schechner as editor of *The Drama Review*) discussed the performative dimension of aesthetics in the liminal, intermedial terrain of Performance Art.[27] The idea was to substitute the familiar forms of theater with an action that brought corporality, gesture, and setting to the fore, realizing a truly *live* event in which the author could also be spectator, and the spectator could be integrated into the event as a presence-action, decisive for the realization of the artwork. In this period, the term "representation" began to be used with a negative connotation, in contrast to "event", which existed in the act of its becoming. These traits were shared among Performance Art, Body Art, Land Art, Video Art, by the artists of *arte povera*, and by New Music and New Theater.

In the Seventies, a common denominator among the arts was the search for a common minimal base beneath the specific domain of each form of artistic practice. In an audacious and joyous breaking of boundaries, artist Bruce Nauman played the violin, and musician Alvin Curran taught young actors in the Silvio D'Amico Academy of Dramatic Art in Rome how to orchestrate their voices. There was a fruitful exchange among cinema, visual art, and theater. The cinema screen itself became an object of representation, over and beyond the images projected onto it. Baruchello, Nespolo, Agnetti, and Colombo brought the characteristics of painting to the moving images of cinema by isolating details, decomposing sequences, and freezing frames. The line of continuity and fracture between experimental film, painting, poetry, electronic art, and theater is visible in filmmakers such as Gianni Toti, Alberto Grifi, Silvano Agosti, Guido Lombardo, and Anna Lajolo, who used their cameras as a tool of political struggle, not only in theaters but by filming in prisons, shooting housing protests in the Magliana neighborhood in Rome, and demonstrations for health care outside the Policlinico Hospital. Mario Ricci, Leo De Berardinis and Perla Peragallo, and Carmelo Bene used film projections as dramaturgical instruments in their theater events.[28] Bene in *Our Lady of the Turks*, and De Berardinis and Peragallo in *A Charlie Parker*, made film sequences bleed into live performance and vice versa. Actors' bodies on stage dissolved into image bodies on screen, and projected bodies composed of light materialized as physical bodies bound by gravity.[29]

The New Theater of the Seventies was a laboratory of radical experimentation which led voyages of unknown destination into unmarked territories. Musicians abandoned their inherited repertory and traditional technique: Frederic Rzewski stopped playing the piano, judging it to be a symbol of bourgeois music. Some years before, Fluxus artist Nam June Paik had burned and destroyed a piano, reducing its hammers and keys to ash. In place of concert halls, Alvin Lucier, Vittorio Gelmetti, and Robert Ashley frequented MEV – Musica Elettronica Viva, an alternative space in Rome [FOCUS/CONTEXTS].[30] Their organized improvisations sought to involve the spectator in the production of music.

2.4 The van: travel and rest, load and unload

"Is Theater in the Streets? Weren't we there, in the doorway, face to face with the police? The police, who don't permit theater in the streets, who don't allow life to reach into and overcome the privileged position occupied by art that doesn't want the streets to be free. It was there, in the doorway to the theater, that we understood that we had to go out into the streets".[31]

The militant political commitment that attracted artists and intellectuals during the years of the student and worker movements discovered new expressive possibilities in theater and new ways of involving previously untapped social groups in the struggle. As had happened during the October Revolution in Russia, new forms of theatrical action were born, such as street and guerrilla theater. In the United States, in their processional piece entitled "The Cry of the People for Meat", the Bread and Puppet Theater paraded giant puppet heads in demonstrations against the war in Vietnam. In Italy, Giuliano Scabia staged similar parades with his nomadic theater, and the Comune of Dario Fo and Franca Rame performed political spectacles in factories.

Carlo Quartucci's *Camion* (Truck – [FOCUS]) was an irregular – but for that reason exemplary – work of this sort, an ongoing, traveling spectacle that questioned the roles, locations, and entire apparatus of traditional theater. Rejecting theater, it retained vestiges of theatrical practice as it ventured into other forms of art. *Camion* was a sort of theatrical Land Art, a way of marking a landscape, something between an Allan Kaprow happening and a walk by Richard Long:

> "A van [. . .] like a ship, a vessel, a white page that can also cancel out noises and sounds from the surrounding environment [. . .] I thought of filling the *Camion* with chimpanzees chickens straw aluminum foil birds rabbits colored clothing plants rolls of paper canvases wood theatre flats cords musical instruments paints brushes puppets manikins talking dolls silhouettes of animals fruit crates umbrellas hats grain animal feed old gramophones film stock hanging from steel cables suitcases filled with water gaslights giant tortoises, a glass ant farm".[32]

Carlo Quartucci created his *Camion* after 20 years of spectacles produced in theaters throughout Italy. Prolific, energetic, voracious, unstoppable, he had a genius for aggregating actors, artists (Jannis Kounellis), authors, and playwrights (Gruppo '63, Beckett). In 1970 he inverted the traditional relationship among theater, spectacle, and spectators by leaving the established theater behind to set out on a journey with an actual truck crammed indiscriminately with props, puppets, and actors, so that he could "unload theater" on the road, circus-style.

> *Camion* lives with the people in a village outside Rome or with the people on Portobello Road in London. Tomorrow *Camion* is a puppet master, today it's the person who drives repairs hammers takes care of the truck. . . . And it is also the person who films and photographs it during our short or long trips.[33]

The director functioned like a stagehand; the actress, Carla Tatò, became a narrator, driving the action of *Camion*. The actor, Luigi Mezzanotte, became a quick-change artist, the quintessence of acting, playing games with identity, dispensing with illusion because the stage was no longer there. The team included an author, Luigi Gozzi, who transformed himself into a playwright, picking out performable passages from Ibsen, Melville, and Defoe.

Traveling with *Camion* was an escape from the gray claustrophobia of the theater hall, saving theater's life by restoring it to the light of day and the dark of night, to the highways and byways. It sought out its own audience, surprising people, drawing them in, unloading the tools of its trade in some transitory spot, now saved from the boredom of unremitting repetition. A selection from *A Doll's House* or *Robinson Crusoe* or *Moby Dick* might be performed during a presentation on a chosen social issue; an unstoppable flow in which vision, action, the materials of *arte povera*, the landscapes of Land Art, the gestures of Body Art, and new media promiscuously intermingled.

Camion was the image of a theater without a theater, a theater "struck" (to use the stage jargon for breaking down a show after closing), gone elsewhere, where representation was transformed into action. Carlo Quartucci recalls:

> The itinerant encounter between diverse marginal realities (from the Italian provinces to the scrubby outskirts of Rome) excluded any attitude of "imposition" in favor of experiences of dialogue and exchange. We substituted the term "spectacle" with "ACTION". We didn't have to open the *Camion* up into a stage, *Camion* didn't have to disguise itself as a circus caravan or stage. There is no need to put the man who meets you in the street in the position of being a spectator watching a *Camion* action. Let him believe, and think that *Camion* is there for a real, authentic action.[34]

2.5 A collective book, a body of joy

Taking advantage of an outreach program organized by the city of Turin's public theater, Giuliano Scabia [FOCUS] started organizing projects in marginal neighborhoods focused on issues of social injustice faced by the inhabitants. The state theater soon canceled funding for his work. He then developed a detailed workshop with culminating spectacle in a psychiatric hospital in Trieste, and created a "barn theater" with rural shepherds, utilizing tools of art – puppets, painted images, plays, poetry – to provide a social platform where excluded groups could unite to give voice to their urgently felt concerns. Staged actions focused on themes drawn from the daily life of the inhabitants – their isolation in urban ghettoes, the poor schools – and played a key part in workers' strikes and clashes with the police. Scabia's events took the form of assemblies, political debates in search of a still-uncodified new language. The term *autogestione* (self-management) was used to mean overcoming the alienating division between producers and consumers. The idea was that the people expropriated the means of theater to express their growing awareness of their needs and give definition to their own culture. In 1972 Scabia became professor of dramaturgy at the University of Bologna, a role that provided him with the resources to expand his efforts, to document and record them.

An exemplary project, in 1973, was *Marco Cavallo*, at the Psychiatric Hospital in Trieste, an institution directed at the time by Franco Basaglia, a leading psychiatric reformer who fought to redefine mental illness, and succeeded in restructuring the entire national apparatus for the treatment of the mentally ill. Scabia worked with the mental patients and organized a parade through the streets of the city. His description of the undertaking is worth quoting in full:

> Almost by chance we formed a group of people willing to put their abilities in play, so I decided to use them to try to find a new way of being together. None of us had ever been in a psychiatric hospital or knew anything about psychiatry. We were painters, directors, writers, children's theater people, teachers, philosophers or something else and we had no idea what use our skills and knowledge might prove to have. At first we didn't know what to plan: should we teach drawing? Sculpture? Acting? It wasn't easy. We had no audience to show our work to, no students to instruct in our particular specialties, no children to make laugh, but we faced a human reality that we wanted to help change. On a provisional basis, as though just dropping in, with no duties or clear work relationships, and without being paid, we entered for a period into a hospital that was in a moment of transformation. We were called "the artists" and this definition had been chosen for its ambiguity, and because it permitted us to be recognized by the patients as people extraneous to their treatment and control; extraneous to the asylum. Most of all we wanted to bring about a type of communication, neither codified nor codifiable, that would develop gradually over time. It was a difficult situation, stimulating and absolutely new, but we refused to set up a relationship as experimenters working with guinea pigs. What counted was living the experience, conscious of having to renounce a whole mental structure conditioned by the habits of daily life and our relations with "normal people". Instead we had a relationship with people who were sick, imprisoned and excluded [. . .]. We stayed with the patients for two months (by mutual agreement with the hospital). By composing *Marco Cavallo*, with drawings, songs, dances, and in discussions with the patients, doctors and nurses, we managed to stimulate an atmosphere of tension and communication that included everyone. This atmosphere bestowed on the figure of Marco Cavallo (a blue horse made of wood and papier maché) a sense of collective liberation that was expressed when we led it out into the city, through the streets of Trieste, to San Giusto, into the San Vito quarter. For one day we lived what we would wish forever: we passionately and angrily sang the Marco Cavallo song about the struggle for the marginalized, knowing that we were all very far from liberation".[35]

According to Marco Belpoliti, the distinctive characteristic of Giuliano Scabia's activities was that they combined rigor with improvisation. He had the sensibility to seize upon the unexpected elements that cropped up during group work, grafting into them "traditional archetypes and linguistic metaphors adapted to the occasion", joining avant-garde language play with the peasant roots of Italy's many dialects.[36]

2.6 Between 1968 and 1977: action, post-avant-garde, Third Theater

In his Introduction to an anthology of the magazine *Quindici*, Andrea Cortellessa writes,

> 1968 should not be understood as a point of arrival, that is, as the end of something. It was, rather, the beginning of a cycle that reached its true, ultimate self-immolation in 1977: the cycle of Getting-Out-of-Oneself, of Art together with Politics, and their dissemination into what Blanchot then defined (recalling the Marxist "end of alienation") as *Outside*.[37]

Let us now cross back through the Seventies for an overall view, guided by the two critics most attentive to the Italian and international theatrical scene, Giuseppe Bartolucci (in the magazine *Teatroltre. La Scrittura Scenica*) and Franco Quadri (in the two volumes of his *L'avanguardia teatrale in Italia*).

Bartolucci's periodical, founded in 1971, is an exemplary witness to the interdisciplinary dimension that had been feeding theater since the preceding decade. The first issue, dedicated to the theme of *Action*, scrutinized the new North American avant-garde, from its source, John Cage, to Frederic Rzewski. In dance, he wrote on Merce Cunningham, Anna Halprin, and Simone Forti. He studied the happenings of Allan Kaprow and Robert Whitman and the cinema of Stan Brakhage. The issue concluded with a presentation on the spontaneous theater of Jacob Moreno.[38] The second issue, dedicated to *Sound*, covered Karlheinz Stockhausen, Musica Elettronica Viva, and La Monte Young. The relationship of the new with the historical avant-garde was demonstrated by the inclusion of a text by futurist Luigi Russolo, *The Noises of Nature and Life*, and by a 1933 manifesto on music by futurist founder Filippo Tommaso Marinetti, *La radia*. In an article entitled *The Music of Noise*, Giulio Carlo Argan wrote, in reference both to Mondrian and the noise of automobiles,

> Let it be entirely clear that noise is not a clot, a fragment of real material brutally inserted in a poetic order so as to upset it. It is instead the spiritual element *par excellence*, and the right relationship will not be the reduction of noise to sound, but precisely the opposite.[39]

The theme of sound is constant in *Teatroltre*, with pieces by Giampiero Cane on improvisation in jazz.

The magazine's approach was to read how the historical avant-gardes interacted with the present practices of New Theater; how, for example, Dziga Vertov and Eisenstein had influenced set designer Josef Svoboda (1920–2002) and Leo De Berardinis and Perla Peragallo. The first four issues distinguished diverse languages of sound, image, and body, and promoted a program for the Seventies in the concept of action, which would cross over the ideological, pragmatic, and linguistic boundaries of theatrical tradition. Action was inscribed and actualized in the act of *coming out of the theater*, as described in Bartolucci's article "Notes on Dramatization (Toward Collective Composition)" and in Giuliano Scabia's practice and contributions to the magazine.

Following the principle that action should substitute spectacle, *Teatroltre* focused on the type of theatrical work called *animation*, which began as a form of game-based children's theater but then overcame those narrow confines. The magazine demanded that all recognized languages be zeroed out, so they could be reinvented beyond the narrow realm of art, in society itself. In a very different context, Richard Schechner exhibited an analogous drive when he wrote of extending the boundaries of conventional theater. The American scholar Schechner turned to ritual, while in Italy this same drive for expansion was directed into society, with a strong political connotation. The goal was to penetrate the closed worlds of the schools, factories, urban neighborhoods and the marginalized outskirts of cities. Bartolucci called for digging into social reality, while Schechner advocated the connection between ritual and representation (along with Theodor Shank and Roger Blin). In his spectacle *Musolino the Brigand*, Giuliano Scabia sought to develop methods and a theoretical approach that might map out a new continent that was beginning to emerge in techniques of collective composition, didactic theater, community-based theater, and work with children. Two important texts of this moment of expansion are "Animation, or, On Ambiguity", and "Avant-Garde and/or Animation". In 1976, however, Bartolucci dropped what he termed Image Theater in favor of a new trend, the post avant-garde, which he identified in artists and companies such as Simone Carella, Carrozzone, and Gaia Scienza. By 1977 he had announced the death of animation. In sum, then, between 1968 and 1977 an explosion was followed by an implosion: coming out of the theaters and rejecting art led back into theater and art.

Franco Quadri's *The Theatrical Avant-garde in Italy. Materials 1960–76* uses documentation written mostly by the participants themselves to tell the story of the era's avant-garde theater. In his lengthy "Non-Introduction", written in 1977, the critic analyzed what he regarded as the crisis of New Theater. Among the expansive, explosive gestures of the Seventies, he counted Peter Brook's abandonment of London's Royal Shakespeare Company to found his intercultural company in Paris, and the Living Theatre's self-dividing shift out of theaters and into the streets. For his part, in 1970 Jerzy Grotowski had announced his new path beyond theater:

> It isn't theater that's necessary but something absolutely different. To overcome the barriers between me and you; to encounter you, not to get lost in the crowd, nor in words, nor in declarations, nor among elegantly precise ideas [. . .]. Not to hide myself any longer, to be what I am [. . .]. To find a place where such a being-in-common is possible. And the holy day will become possible [. . .]. Then theater will be eliminated, shame and fear will be eliminated, along with the need to wear a veil, to hide ourselves, and to recite a role that is not ours.[40]

In his "Non-Introduction", Quadri observed that New Theater had grown but the social institutions had remained closed to it, leaving the movement with no outlet, constrained to survive in a narrow circle of festivals and alternative settings, perennially condemned to living a clandestine life, in basements. Quadri saw around him only failed utopias, in ruins. Dario Fo's alternative, independent theater circuit had finally beached itself on an established stage in Milan, the Palazzina Liberty. The animation movement had lost its explosive charge, co-opted by authority (despite the perseverance of Giuliano Scabia, "still the conjuring pilgrim, but even he is ever more tempted by the tranquility of a cozy retirement, where he can savor the pleasure of doing his work on the page".)[41] Disillusionment over the failure of political revolution produced a desire to enclose oneself in a private world. Godard had stopped making films, and Peter Stein and Patrice Chereau, as though to protect themselves, had turned to directing the classics. Speaking of Peter Handke's *A Sadness Beyond Dreams*, a memoir of the suicide of the author's mother, Quadri wrote, "From a literature of attack, some of us have moved on to introspective closure".[42] For Quadri, 1977 represented

> the conclusion of the period of experimentation and search for an alternative: the *heroic period* has been over for some time, and 'theater' becomes once again a unifying word, now that the new language indiscriminately absorbs everything [. . .]. Some claim it's the moment for a new *tabula rasa*, to start over from zero once again.[43]

This *tabula rasa* to wipe out the Seventies would mean turning to the new groups, without seeking any connecting nexus or shared experience with what had come before; a new point of departure. Quadri's position was not dissimilar from that of Bartolucci in the same year.

Surveying the theater of the Seventies, we must touch on the phenomenon of Third Theater, baptized with this name by Eugenio Barba in 1976. Born in the southern region of Puglia, Barba had attended university in Oslo, and in 1961 went to Poland to begin three years of study and collaboration with Jerzy Grotowski, founder of the Polish Laboratory Theater, perhaps the most influential of all the European experimental theater companies. In 1964 Barba returned to Oslo and formed a company, Odin Teatret, from young actors who had been rejected by the state theater training school. Barba was the editor of Grotowski's *Towards a Poor Theater*, published in 1968, which initiated an international network of companies based upon Grotowski's aesthetic principles and the rigorous physical training system outlined in the book – a series of exercises pushed to extremes that at times almost resembled rites of mortification of the flesh. In 1976 Barba described the "base theaters" of the Third Theater movement in these terms:

> There exists a largely ignored theatrical archipelago formed in recent years in many countries in the world, to which little critical attention is given, for which there are few festivals and fewer reviews in the press. It seems to constitute the anonymous extremity of the forms of theater recognized by the world of culture. On one side stands institutional theater, protected and funded for the cultural values it claims to hand down [. . .], and on the other stands avant-garde, experimental, research theater, arduous and iconoclastic, a theater of mutation in search of a new originality, defended in the name of the need to overcome tradition, open to new developments in the arts and society. The Third Theater lives at the margins, often outside or on the periphery of urban centers and the capitals of culture, a theater of people who define themselves as actors, directors, theater people, most of whom never passed through the traditional training schools or apprenticeships, and are thus not accepted as professionals".[44]

For these people, according to Barba, the choice of doing theater was motivated by the need to live a new social model now, in the present, rather than always postponing change in anticipation of a revolution to come: "We cannot only dream of the future, awaiting a total mutation that seems to get farther away with every step we take, leaving in its place all the alibis, the compromises, the impotence of waiting".[45]

A decade later, writing from the perspective of the institutional avant-garde to which Barba sought to create an alternative, Giuseppe Bartolucci dismissed Third Theater with the observation that these companies' training techniques in fact overwhelmed their artistic achievement:

> Physical training enchanted artists and groups, bonding their physical and mental identities, for the severity of the way of life and rigor of the work. Although the companies did not renounce the organization and presentation of spectacles, the training system consumed itself, absorbing a large part of the daily work and limiting the theatrical results; [. . .] the resultant form of communication revealed itself more as a kind of corporal-spiritual liberation than as a means of artistic-theatrical preparation".[46]

2.7 Implosive/expansive

Common to the expansive drive of the arts was a shift of attention from the discrete to the continuous, from the *representational* to the *lived*. Art was not to be sought in the product but in the preparation. Art critic Carla Lonzi published *Self-Portraits* in 1969, a collection of taped conversations with contemporary Italian artists, edited into a collage of overlapping voices accompanied by black and white photographs. Rather than focusing on the aesthetic object, Lonzi centered on process. Fixity was to be avoided through performance, gesture, and self-conduct.[47] In visual arts as in theater, artists adopted the principle of chance, which could liberate the work from limiting meaning and press the spectator to see the sign itself. Discontinuity was privileged, producing non-linear compositions which were not directed toward a defined aesthetic goal. Non-aesthetic materials and behaviors and discarded materials came into use. Dancer-choreographers Simone Forti, Yvonne Rainer, and Trisha Brown all practiced a sort of anti-dance which required no particular training in technique: they stood still, performed simple daily actions, did somersaults, ran, and danced together.

Artists coming from the visual arts, theater, and music made performances and sound installations, cut records, studied anthropology, semiotics, psychology, and broke words into fragments to recuperate the acoustics of written speech. In his manifesto of "epistaltism", visual artist Mimmo Rotella wrote,

> epistaltic language means inventing all the words, unchaining them from their utilitarian function to make tracer rockets aimed against the decrepit edifice of syntax and vocabulary [. . .]; the human voice must not be limited to the monotony of articulated language – it is an inexhaustible source of natural musical instruments.[48]

We have said that the Seventies Line had a double dynamic of dilation and implosion, an outflow from geographical and disciplinary confines in search of a common and universal nucleus – body, gesture, movement. But the voyage finally became centripetal, seeking refuge in theater, as happened in the spectacles produced by an emergent "Image Theater" movement, a term invented by Bartolucci to describe work such as that by Mario Ricci, Memé Perlini, Giancarlo Nanni, and Giuliano Vasilicò.

In his study *The Analytic Line in Modern Art*, Filiberto Menna emphasized the shift that took place in the Seventies from expansion toward subjectivity, a change Menna called "post-conceptual", because, in his view, conceptualism had called out the reasoning behind the subject, in the name of conventional logic. The diachronic and the synchronic, discontinuity and continuity, expansion and concentration, opening toward the world and subjectivity, art's reflection on itself, on the subject and its psychic structures (including the confrontation with the other and the contradictions of the real) are the polarities that marked art in the Seventies. Exemplary of this trend was the painting of Gino De Dominicis, which led viewers into individual mythologies, as did spectacles by Carrozzone and Memé Perlini. At the same time, "the definition 'poor' took concrete form in objects and behaviors that were essentially expansive", vehicles of a practice that claimed the right to *do* rather than merely to *make use of* theater, art, and music.[49]

With its authors and artworks, New Theater nourished the thought and interests of philosophers (such as Gilles Deleuze, who wrote on Carmelo Bene) and scholars and artists in other disciplines. It was a phenomenon articulated in diverse contexts and modes that abandoned traditional theatrical spaces and structures and contributed to the opening-up of closed institutions, such as prisons and psychiatric hospitals. It transformed garages, warehouses, and shuttered factories into art studios and performance halls. Italian theater in the Seventies was a radical, avant-garde phenomenon that spread into and thoroughly permeated the structure of society itself. Its achievements have become so much a part of our conceptual apparatus that what was once revolutionary now seems invisible.

Notes

1 L. Vergine, *Body Art e storie simili: Il corpo come linguaggio*, Feltrinelli, Milan, 1974.
2 F. Menna, *La linea analitica nell'arte moderna*, Einaudi, Turin, 1975.
3 Cfr. G. Piero Brunetta, *Storia del cinema italiano: Dal 1945 agli anni ottanta*, Editori Riuniti, Rome, 1982, 11. According to Brunetta, when state-sponsored cinema entered into a period of economic crisis, it stopped supporting emerging artists, after which point "it becomes impossible, or extremely difficult, to trace a history of national cinema".
4 Cfr. Cigala and V. Valentini, "L'avventura di Art/tapes/22", interview with M. G. Bicocchi, director of Art/tapes/22, in V. Valentini (ed.), *Cominciamenti: Gerry Shum, Art/tapes/22, Lafontaine, Pirri, Eitetsu, Hayashi, Taormina arte 1988: Terza Rassegna internazionale del video d'autore*, De Luca, Rome, 1988, 61–67.
5 Cfr. F. Rosati and M. G. Bruzzone, eds., *Informare contro Informare per (Cinema, televisione, teatro)*, Armando Editore, Rome, 1976.This volume documents the experience of "counter-information".
6 Also important was Michelangelo Pistoletto's experience with Zoo, a group that staged street actions: "We don't work for spectators, we are both actors and spectators, fabricators and consumers [. . .] When you see, hear and smell a spectacle made by Zoo, Michelangelo Pistoletto's theater company, what you think you understand will only be the bark, the envelope, but you will never know what took place until you become actors and spectators on this side of the barriers". M. Pistoletto, "Lo Zoo: Torino fine del XX secolo (Si prepara l'epoca dell'Acquario)", in G. Celant (ed.), *Arte Povera*, Mazzotta, Milano, 1969, 231.
7 R. Tessari, *Teatro italiano del Novecento*, Le lettere, Florence, 2003, 146–147.
8 In A. Attisani (ed.), *Le forze in campo: Per una nuova cartografia del teatro*, Mucchi, Modena, 1987, 192, Ferdinando Taviani distinguishes between the logic of rejection that characterized the attitudes of the artists of the Sixties, and the logic of "distancing" adopted by the Third Theater of the Seventies; the defense of their own identity in the "ghetto", according to Eugenio Barba's

observations in *Il teatro nello spazio degli scontri*, Bulzoni, Rome, 1973. In a list of Third Theater groups, Salvatore Margiotta includes Teatro Evento in Bologna, Teatro della Convenzione in Florence, Teatro Artigiano di Cantù in Milan. *Il Nuovo Teatro in Italia, 1968–1975*, Titivillus, Corazzano (PI), 2013.

9   Antonio Porta, "Tre ipotesi contro la normalizzazione dello scrittore", in *Quindici*, n. 1, June 1967, 25. The concept of "group" was to serve as a structure for production and a political strategy. Porta, of the Gruppo '63, maintained that the only possibility for resisting normalization, was to "increase the potential for a 'partisan' culture, which means accepting the revolution to actualizing it in a group 'as though' it was truly realizable and 'as though' a parallel society could actually be constructed".

10 W. Benjamin, *Avanguardia e rivoluzione*, Einaudi, Turin, 1973, 211.

11 W. Benjamin, 'Il programma per un teatro proletario di bambini", in *Quaderni piacentini*, 1969, 38.

12 G. Bartolucci, "Dall'immagine all'animazione (ipotesi di lavoro per gli anni Settanta)", in *Contemporanea*, CDF Edizioni, Florence, 1973, 28.

13 Ivi, 285. Bartolucci developed this work in the outskirts of Rome through his Teatro Scuola of the Teatro di Roma; Carlo Quartucci and Carla Tatò did similar work at the Centro Culturale Polivalente Decentrato Borgata Romanina.

14 E. Goffman, *The Presentation of Self in Everyday Life* [1959], Italian trans. by M. Ciacci (ed.), *La vita quotidiana come rappresentazione*, Il Mulino, Bologna, 1969. Cfr. G. Scabia, *Teatro nello spazio degli scontri*, Bulzoni, Rome, 1973, a volume containing manifestoes, protocols, and director's notes. In *Lo strillone ha l'ugola stanca*, Ripellino observed, "The principle novelty of this *mare magnum* is the abolition of the borders between the script and the rehearsals, between the preparatory sketch or the roles and the performance, between the stage directions and the actors' lines". (p. 230).

15 G. Bachelard, "Le Avventure di Gordon Pym", in *Il diritto di sognare*, Dedalo, Bari, 1974, 119.

16 J. Beck, *La vita del teatro*, Einaudi, Turin, 1975; cited in F. Quadri, *Lanvanguardia teatrale in Italia*, Einaudi, Turin, 1977.

17 J. Rubin, *Do It: Scenarios of the Revolution*, Simon and Schuster, New York, 1970.

18 Cfr. G. Bartolucci, ed., *Il teatro dei ragazzi*, Guaraldi editore, Florence, 1972.

19 O. Ponte di Pino, "Per un teatro Jazz: Intervista a Leo de Berardinis", in J. Gelber (ed.), *La Connection, con l'intervento di Leo de Berardinis*, Ubulibri, Milan, 1983, 35–50.

20 G. Manzella, *La bellezza amara*, Pratiche editrice, Parma, 1973, 47. Cfr. S. Margiotta, "Il teatro dell'ignoranza di Leo e Perla", in *Il Nuovo Teatro in Italia, 1968–1975*, Titivillus Edizioni, Corazzano (PI), 2013, 242–250.

21 L. de Berardinis, in Franco Quadri, *La'avanguardia teatrale in Italia*, vit., p. 45.

22 *Ibidem.*

23 G. Bartolucci, "Dalla postavanguardia alla nuova spettacolarità", in *Testi critici, 1964–987*, Bulzoni, Rome, 2007, 272.

24 M. Fried, "Art and Objecthood", *Artforum*, June 1967.

25 Celant's text, a sort of manifesto of *arte povera*, is untitled and published at the end of a book of photographic documentation of the works of the selected artists, including De Maria, Pistoletto, Kaltenbach, Long, Merz, Huebler, Beuys, Hesse, Helzer, Van Helk, Kounellis, Weiner, Favro, Nauman, Kosuth, Dibbets (p. 227).

26 A. Bonito Oliva, ed., *Vitalità del negative nell'arte italiana, 1960–1970*, Centro Di Firenze, Florence, 1970.

27 M. Kirby, "Attività: nuova forma di spettacolo", *Sipario*, n. 281, September, 1969, 15.

28 Alberto Grifi collaborated on creating the images for an early spectacle by Leo and Perla, *La faticosa messa in scena dell'Amleto di William Shakespeare*, 1967. Cfr. G. Manzella, *La bellezza amara*, cit., 41.

29 *A Charlie Parker*, by and starring Leo de Berardinis and Perla Peragallo (Film, 35 mm and 16 mm, 1970), was presented at Teatro Abaco, Rome, on December 7, 1970. Another film by the same due is *Compromesso storico a Marigliano* (1971), with photography by Alberti Grifi and edited by Perla Peragallo.

30 A. Curran, *Live in Roma*, D. Margoni Tortora (ed.), die Schachtel, Rome, 2010, 17.

31 J. Beck, *La vita del Teatro*, Einaudi, Turin, 1975; cited in F. Quadri, *L'avanguardia teatrale in Italia*, Einaudi, Turin, 1977, 12.

32 Carlo Quartucci, in F. Quadri, *L'avanguardia teatrale in Italia*, cit., 180.

33 Ivi, 182.

34 Ivi, 185.

35 G. Scabia, *Marco Cavallo: Un'esperienza di animazione in un ospedale psichiatrico*, Einaudi, Turin, 1976, 12.

36 M. Belpoliti, *Settanta*, Einaudi, Turin, 2001 and 2010, 304.

37 A. Cortellessa, "Volevamo la luna", Introduction to N. Balestrini (ed.), *Quindici, Una Rivista e Il Sessantotto*, Feltrinelli, Milan, 2008, 8.

38 The tables of contents of the journal are published in V. Valentini, G. Mancini and G Bartolucci, eds., *Testi critici, 1964–1987*, Bulzoni, Rome, 2007, 385–397. The journal *Teatroltre* consisted of twenty seven issues, from 1971 to 1983.

39 G. Carlo Argan, "La musica dei rumori", *Teatroltre/La Scrittura scenica*, n. 2, anno I, 1971, 13.

40 Jerzy Grotowski in F. Quadri, *L'avanguardia teatrale in Italia*, cit., 15–16.

41 Ivi, 11.

42 Ivi, 10.

43 Ivi, 9.

44 E. Barba, "Terzo Teatro", in *Teatro, solitudine, mestiere, rivolta*, Ubulibri, Milan, 1996, 165.

45 Ivi, 166.

46 Giuseppe Bartolucci, in O. Ponte di Pino, *Il nuovo teatro italiano (1975–1988)*, La casa Usher, Florence, 1998, 28.

47 C. Lonzi, *Autoritratti*, De Donato, Bari, 1969.

48 Cfr. Manifesto, http://fondazionemimmorotella.net/poemi_fonetici.html. Cfr. G. Celant, "Record as Artwork, Disco come lavoro d'arte", in *OFFMEDIA: Nuove techniche artistiche: video, disco, libro*, Dedalo libri, Bari 1977, 76–106.

49 F. Menna, *La linea analitica dell'arte*, Einaudi, Turin, 1975, XXI.

3   The Eighties
Between death and rebirth: 1978–88

3.1 The unhappy conscience of the late seventies

We trace here a series of interconnected events, selected by "affective memory", which took place in an arc of time – the late Seventies and most of the Eighties – that witnessed the phenomenon of terrorism, the actions of *Autonomia Operaia* (the revolutionary radical labor groups), the arrival of postmodern culture, and the late-decade reaction against it, which took the form of a demand for the reintegration of the subject and of history.

Alberto Asor Rosa has observed that a cultural phase came to a close at the end of the Seventies, when disillusioned writers turned hermetic. In his discussion of Italian literature during this period, Marco Belpoliti confirms Asor Rosa's vision:

> *The Name of the Rose* (1980) by Umberto Eco is the novel that closes the Seventies and assays a first, certainly not positive, account of it. The defeat of Guglielmo (the novel's protagonist) and his method of inquiry [. . .] is a reflection of the defeat of intellectuals such as Eco in the face of the tragedy of terrorism.[1]

In the same book, Belpoliti dedicates a chapter to the writers who examined the assassination of Aldo Moro, the Christian Democratic president who was kidnapped by the left-wing terrorist organization the Red Brigades in March 1978, and murdered after being held hostage for 55 days. In her 1982 novel *Aracoeli*, Elsa Morante – who had once exalted the generation of '68, sure they would save the world – described the end of political utopias. In their place, in her *Drawing Notebook, Letters to the Red Brigades*, she described a world transformed by "violence, massacres, political assassinations". Morante declared, "The world is now dominated by the Unhappy Multitude; not different people, but the same, transformed".[2]

The 1980s exhausted the idea of a genre of militant literature which had been practiced in Italy since the 1920s, and which culminated in the figure of Pier Paolo Pasolini, who was murdered in 1975. This form of literature had ultimately propagated, in the words of Italo Calvino, "a vision of Italian society as the failure of all political projects".[3] In *Seven Years of Desire*, his collection of articles and essays written between 1977 and 1983, Umberto Eco described his times as marked by a crisis of reason: "The final balance is negative – the system has not been modified, the left has been defeated, terrorism has dissipated precious energies, the rebellion of the youth movements has ended its journey in irrationalism and vitalist aestheticism".[4]

Between the mid-Seventies and the first years of the Eighties, semiotics came to the fore in Italy as a discipline that promised to bring an analytic dimension to art, an approach of decomposition, of subdividing the whole into parts. Italo Calvino described the semiotic approach in these terms: "The world in its various aspects is ever more seen as discreet rather than continuous. I employ the word "discreet" in its mathematical sense: a discreet quantity is one composed of separate parts".[5] In 1979 Calvino released *If On a Winter's Night a Traveler*, while Eco published *Lector in fabula*, with the subtitle *Interpretive Cooperation in Narrative Texts*. Eco's text configured a model reader whose cultural horizon (an encyclopedia) included the intertextual competency necessary to fruitfully access a given text. Calvino's novel, on the other hand, plunged the reader into a world made of literature, offering the reader a plurality of means of narration, each layered into the other – an effective example of postmodern meta-novel.

The same year of 1979 saw the birth of *Alfabeta*, a monthly journal of international scope, bringing together writers including Nanni Balestrini, Paolo Volponi, Francesco Leonetti, Antonio Porta, Maria Corti, Umberto Eco, Pier Aldo Rovatti, Gianni Sassi, Mario Spinella, and Gino di Maggio. In June of that year, the *Poets' Festival* took place in Castelporziano, near Rome, organized by writer and critic Franco Cordelli and Simone Carella (Beat '72), financed by Rome's new left-wing administration (especially by Renato Nicolini, who as Cultural Assessor promoted the cultural renovation of the capital city, with a particular devotion to ephemeral events). Together with the *City of Theater Festival* that had taken place the previous year, the *Poets' Festival* rejected the idea of theater as a laboratory open only to specialists, and aimed instead to "call together an entire generation of poets – fathers and sons together – to settle their debts once and for all".[6] The project of making spectacle out of poetry removed its aura of being for initiates only, catapulting it instead into the unpredictable domain of the mass event: 10,000–15,000 visitors attended over the course of three days. While in theatrical spectacles such as Carrozone's *Point of Rupture* (1979), and Falso Movimento's *Tango Glaciale* (1982 [FOCUS]), the metropolitan imaginary was reconstituted on stage (with flashing neon lights and sonic vibrations projected onto the audience), the *Poets' Festival* directly evoked the unpredictable "urban marvelous", accepting the risk of attrition between the fragility of poetry and the vital, destructive energy of huge assemblies of people.

The new postmodern spectacle was directed at a mass public, rather than the limited one of so-called underground theater. It privileged technologies capable of involving an audience more vast than that of a live event. Post-modern theater strove to overcome the ephemeral nature of the theatrical spectacle by using reproducible formats (film, sound recording, video) while at the same time trying to appeal to a popular audience.

For Italian television, Carmelo Bene created a technologically and formally innovative program, one of Italy's first broadcasts in color, about Russian poetry. Giving it the title *Bene! Four Different Ways of Dying in Verse* (1979), he explored the possibilities of electronic media by weaving together selections from four renowned poets of the Twenties (Block, Mayakovski, Yesenin, Pasternak).

MTV began broadcasting in the United States on August 1, 1981. Music video – a device for the promotion of product – became a successful formula that pioneered a new video aesthetic, disseminated in Italy through the first private television channels. Another significant phenomenon in this cultural shift was video-theater programming, in which important stage directors were able to produce great works of theater for video, without having to reduce or adapt the original texts.

At the threshold of the Eighties, conservative governments came to power both in Europe and the United States. Margaret Thatcher became prime minister of the United Kingdom in 1979, while in 1981 a former Hollywood and television actor named Ronald Reagan became president of the United States. In Germany, the Christian Democrat Helmut Kohl became Chancellor in 1982.

In the preface to his 1981 book, *Odin's Brecht*, Eugenio Barba declared that the Third Theater (whose ethic joined the profession of theater to the practice of daily life) had by now disappeared, "decimated by penury of means, by the absence of a strategy, by rivalry, by war among the poorest, by disunity".[7] Isolated from the circuit of commercial theater, separate even from the New Theater scene, walled up in a diversity that admitted no exchange with other realities, the Third Theater in Italy by now survived only thanks to a network sustained by Odin Teatret and Barba himself. Some years later, Franco Quadri described the situation in these terms:

> After a period of study, the postmodern line would grow out of the post-avant garde, positioned counter to the Third Theater, which had a brief period of explosive growth centered on the immediacy of ensemble culture, privileging festivals and street performances in the orbit of the Piccolo Theater, in Pontedera, and the annual Santarcangelo Festival.[8]

Once its phase of expansion had exhausted itself, this mode of organization and performance came to be integrated into the activities of public libraries and social service agencies, transformed into the genre of social-service theater, an auxiliary of welfare-state services for the aged, children, the handicapped, immigrants, and marginalized communities such as the Rom people.

In the realm of cinema, Gian Piero Brunetta characterized the Italian situation as,

> pre-apocalyptic, anemic, aphasic, paralyzed, [. . .] void of ideals, absent
> of values, [. . .] The tone of the new artists is uncertain, their physiog-
> nomy fugitive, [. . .] their work cannot be measured by any method,
> system of reference or traditional standards of judgment.[9]

Critics lamented not only the lack of masterpieces but of any critical-intel-
lectual-social terrain capable even of recognizing one: "In a framework of
progressive structural decomposition of the system, irregular phenomena
proliferate, polycentric and diffused throughout the national territory".[10]
Italian cinema was without ideas or language, smugly autobiographical, isolated from society, with auteur ambitions nourished by television models,
devoid of recognized masters, and it tended to privilege – in terms of practical training – television, the Home Video market, and the cinema festivals.
In this context, it was easier to create a first film than to develop an evolving
career. Among 300 or so young directors who emerged in this period, some
of the most notable (listed with their first works) are Nanni Moretti (*Io
sono un Autarchico*, 1976), Silvio Soldini (*L'aria serena dell'Ovest*, 1990),
Roberto Benigni (*Tu mi turbi*, 1983), Massimo Troisi (*Ricomincio da tre*,
1981), Gabriele Salvatores (*Sogno di una notte d'estate*, 1983), Mario Martone (*Morte di un matematico napoletano*, 1992), Giuseppe Tornatore (*Il
Camorrista*, 1986), Antonio Capuano and Antonietta De Lillo (*Una casa
in bilico*, 1985), Francesco Calogero (*La gentilezza del tocco*, 1987), and
Gianni Amelio (*Colpire al cuore*, 1983).

New dance came to the fore in Italy in the early Eighties. In 1981 and
1982, the Teatro Circo Spazio Zero in Rome organized two dance series:
the first, dedicated to German *Tanztheater*, presented Pina Bausch to
Roman audiences for the first time. The second, on American postmodern
dance, brought Steve Paxton, Simone Forti, Lisa Nelson, and Pooh Kaye.[11]
The same years saw the debut of the Carolyn Carlson Company, with
Eleven Waves and *Underwood* (featuring dancers Giorgio Rossi, Raffaella
Giordano, Roberto Castello, Michele Abbondanza, and others). Carlson
had been hired by the prestigious La Fenice Theater in Venice to set up a
laboratory for dance research and training which would lead to the creation of a permanent company. Also in the early Eighties, performances by
Parco Butterfly (with Julia Anzilotti, Virgilio Sieni and Roberta Gelpi), by
Sosta Palmizi (with Roberto Castello, Giorgio Rossi, Raffaella Giordano,
and Michele Abbondanza) and by Enzo Cosimi demonstrated the existence
of a new dance movement, which found expression in festivals and dance
series featuring both established companies and new choreographers.[12]

During these years, dance and theater companies frequented the same
locales, their experiences jointly fueled by a wave of new American dance
pioneers such as Simone Forti, Deborah Hayes, and Steve Paxton, who had

been invited to Rome for residencies at Fabio Sargentini's Attico center [CONTEXTS '80].[13] New Theater and New Dance shared analogous production modes (such as workshopping and improvisation) and favored the contamination of artistic languages, the demythologizing of technique, the idiosyncratic characteristics of each dancer or performer, and the expressivity of the body and movement. New Theater furnished to dance an analogous universe of theory, artistic practice, and performance opportunities (in the form of performance spaces, circuits, series, festivals, and settings for critical debate). An example of this was the creative and formal relationship between a dance company, Parco Butterfly, and performers grouped under the umbrella of Magazzini Criminali. The models for these dancers were Merce Cunningham and Pina Bausch, with de-personalization and anti-athleticism on one side, and deep introspection and the expressivity of the dancers on the other. But these artists also took deep interest in the more theatrically-oriented work of Robert Wilson, Tadeusz Kantor, Meredith Monk, Peter Brook, and Jerzy Grotowski.

The spectacle *The Courtyard* (Sosta Palmizi, 1982, FOCUS) brought new Italian dance to the attention of critics and audiences, indicating a precise aesthetic and choreographic direction. In an almost empty space (a cement floor with soil spread on it, white sheets hung on lines, an old-fashioned traveling chest), six bizarre creatures moved like animals – a man-turkey, man-rooster, woman-worm, man-rabbit – in a series of tragic, grotesque, and at times comic situations.[14]

3.2 Neo-avant garde/post-avant garde/postmodern/ trans-avant garde

We can distinguish two periods within the chronological arc covered in this chapter, 1978–86. The first began with the 1978 assassination of Aldo Moro and ended with the *Metropolitan Landscapes* conference in Rome in 1981, a period marked by disorientation and grief – the core of the so-called "years of lead". In 1979, in the journal *Teatroltre*, Giuseppe Bartolucci identified a new trend for which he invented a neologism, *la nuova spettacolarità* (The New Spectacularity), and in 1981 he curated a conference on the theme entitled *Metropolitan Landscapes*, featuring the two most important western theorists of postmodernity, Jean-François Lyotard and Jean Baudrillard, along with theater companies, critics and scholars in various disciplines.

During the second period, from 1981–86, Italian postmodern theater came to full flower with a number of exemplary spectacles, such as *Crollo Nervoso* (Nervous Breakdown) by Magazzini Criminali (1980, FOCUS), *Tango Glaciale* by Falso Movimento (1982), and *Eneide* (Aeneid) by Krypton (1983). In the wake of these breakthrough spectacles, a sense of crisis soon began to arise. In 1986 a conference in Modena, *Le Forze in campo* (The Forces at Play), curated by critic Antonio Attisani, brought together artists, actors, directors, critics, and scholars of several generations to launch a new movement that would surpass postmodern theater by pacifying the conflict between New Theater and Third Theater, and by reintegrating the literary tradition and texts that had been deconstructed by New Theater, which had shaken the entire aged edifice of dramatic tradition.

These diverse pathways that overlapped and wove together across the arc of the Eighties rapidly transformed the landscape of New Theater. For example, the poetic theater that Federico Tiezzi elaborated in his trilogy, *Perdita di memoria* (Memory Loss) radically remodeled the aesthetic of the "saboteur of signs" which he had proposed only several years earlier.

In order to avoid a unidirectional gaze in recounting the complex history of New Theater, from the avant-garde crisis to the hegemony of postmodern theory, we need to combine diverse viewpoints. "The history of New Theater", Lorenzo Mango observed, "is the story of many changes, many diversities that constitute an identity, both historical and aesthetic, as singular and specific as it was multifarious and plural".[15]

Between 1975 and 1977, in the pages of *Teatroltre*, Giuseppe Bartolucci signaled two births and two funerals: the emergence of the "post-avant garde" upon the ashes of the "neo-avant garde" (and the death of the Theater of Images), and the rise of the New Spectacularity, which in a single gulp had devoured the post-avant garde. In 1975 Bartolucci answered the question he posed to himself: "Where is the avant garde headed? In a certain sense, toward its own demise, its sunset. In another sense it proceeds toward its own redefinition, its refoundation".[16] What signs of decline had the critic discerned? They were numerous: for some, the temptation to create a product, and for others, the opposite temptation, toward an essentially romantic existential desperation (Leo and Perla, *Rusp spers*, 1976). At the same time a self-destructive instinct manifested itself (*The Garden of the Forked Paths*, 1972, Carrozzone) along with "the end of the use of the body as had been developed by Grotowski-Barba". Bartolucci listed further signs of end times as "the end of the proliferation of interdisciplinary elements"; "the end of an ideological utopia" (as in the Living Theatre); the "rejection of the product in favor of experience"; "the use of the negative path for an extremist re-foundation of theater practice"; and a growing turning-away from political and popular theater.[17] The post-avant garde substituted for the superabundance of the Theater of Images with analytic-scientific rigor, linear movement, and actions that rejected interpretation. These were the years of *Autonomia Operaia* (the extra-parliamentary, radical, workers' autonomy movement), the '77 Movement, and the assassination of Aldo Moro.

The path leading from the post-avant garde to the New Spectacularity was pioneered by Simone Carella, who dematerialized the spectacle, emptying theaters of actors and spectators. *Esempi di Lucidità* (Examples of Lucidity, 1978), exploited technologies of reproducibility to escape from the enclosed theater, built *La città del teatro* (The City of Theater), and transformed poetry into mass spectacle. Postmodern theater took shape in the early Eighties within the framework of the New Spectacularity, with iconic spectacles such as *Crollo Nervoso, Tango glaciale*, and *Eneide*, which together constructed a recognizable aesthetic, featuring a *mixage* of hetero-geneous music, environmental soundscapes, actor-dancers, and spaces that exalted two-dimensional surfaces upon which to project images taken from mass media and cinema.[18]

In 1980, art critic Achille Bonito Oliva invented the concept of "Trans-avant garde" by identifying a common trait among artists such as Enzo Cucchi, Sandro Chia, Francesco Clemente, and Mimmo Paladino. Typical of their art was a self-distancing from the practices of the historical avant-gardes and neo-avant gardes, and especially from conceptual abstraction (including technological experimentation and interculturalism) in favor of the local and anthropological spaces of lived experience, figuration, and the manual artisanry of artistic labor.

The vast exhibition realized by Germano Celant in Paris at the Centre Pompidou in 1981, entitled *Identité italienne*, represented a sharp reaction against the new trend, in the sense that it affirmed, against the new post-modern direction of the trans-avant garde (which Celant characterized as "pompiérisme e . . . fauvisme populiste" seeking to astonish with bizarre images), the power of the conceptual and militant attitude of the traditional Italian avant-garde.[19] Celant opposed the internationalism of the Sixties to the rejection of idealism and hostility toward political militancy that he saw in postmodern culture. He considered the trans-avant garde a form of reac-tionary "return to order", which evoked even the specter of national social-ism; an anti-intellectual, cynical form of painting, born against the backdrop of the economic and political crisis of the late Sixties. While presenting itself as emerging from the antipodes, the trans-avant garde, in Celant's view, in truth represented the regressive aspects of postmodernism.[20]

3.3 Postmodernism: the metropolitan landscape

The architectural exhibition *The Presence of the Past* at the Corderie dell'Arsenale in Venice (with Franco Purini, Robert Venturi, and Hans Hol-lein) reflected on the impact of postmodernism. In the same year, the *Metro-politan Landscapes* conference in Rome focused on postmodern thought in art, evoking terms such as nomadism, low practices, surfaces, and decenter-ing, all of which were destined to become crucial to the conceptual repertory of the period.[21] The conference identified a new aesthetic that emphasized inertia, implosion, the end of history and of progress, the setting-aside of rationalism, of alterity, and the erasure of the distinction between subject and object. The concept of the "simulacrum" theorized by Jean Baudrillard transferred its properties to the spectacle. According to the new paradigm, at the base of simulation there is no longer any principle of representa-tion. Therefore, there is no longer any dialectic between actors and specta-tors, between stage and life.[22] Art historian Filiberto Menna observed that postmodern eclecticism had broken down ideologies and theories, especially the opposition between history and the present, nourishing a "culture of narcissism" that nullified critical analysis, preferring to fold itself into a hermetic private universe.[23]

Thus took place a progressive detachment from the neo-avant gardes. Concepts such as dialectics, conflict, antagonism, utopia, revolution, and subversion were archived and substituted by terms such as catastrophe, strategy of appearances, seduction, and reversibility. The theoretical-philosophical tools of modernism, now useless, were scrapped. The sensation of the end of things, experienced as uncompensated mourning provoked by the defeat of the revolutionary illusion, found in postmodern though a sort of resignification and inversion of its meaning. Rather than being lived as loss, catastrophe was magnified into a horizon of meaning and translated into an epistemology of a world in ruins, which was not to be mourned, but to be lived hedonistically, a world of sensorial excitation, of low frequencies that dulled logical thought in favor of immersion and flow.

Critics and scholars who participated in the *Forces at Play* conference in Rome described a theatrical scene that had rapidly allowed itself to be seduced by mass media. Theatrical practice had integrated itself into the system of information, into the cultural imaginary and rituals of mass entertainment and leisure. *Aeneid*, an emblematic spectacle of postmodern theater, transformed the verses of Virgil's epic poem into a pop song, the "Story of Aeneas", sung live by Pietro Pelù of the group Litfiba, before a pink and violet backdrop with projections of seagulls and horses. Immersed in the blazing light of the burning of Troy, spectators were blasted by sonic booms and lightning bolts, perceptually plunged into audio-luminous excitation.

With the "object aesthetics" of Haim Steinbach, Jeff Koons, Guillaume Bijl, and John Armleder, art reconstructed the world at its natural scale. The human being (transformed into a "shopping subject") was no more important than the object. The distinction between art and entertainment collapsed, while the history of art became an iconographic archive to be drawn from as *bricolage.*

In *Tango Glaciale*, a cult spectacle of postmodern theater, the image bank was metropolitan, that of the mass media (its slogan was "Naples like New York!"): cinema, comic books, advertising, rock music, the dark glasses and trench coats of Hollywood gangsters. The sound score mixed diverse repertoires: Debussy and Astor Piazzolla, Peter Gordon, and Penguin Café. Projections reproduced comic book graphics in a way new to the Italian stage.

> Once again we're being given the myth of America, the metropolitan America of our imaginations, re-lived through the shiny icons of advertising and romantic comedy, a place outside time, stereotyped and intangible, like a comic book, evoked by wallpaper images of wild animals and exotic flowering oases projected on the scenic backdrop.[24]

In *Crollo Nervoso* (Nervous Breakdown) by Magazzini Criminali, 1980, we see neither Los Angeles, nor Saigon, nor Mogadishu (although all are named in the spectacle), nor any other real historical-geographical reference point, but a homogenized idea of the urban metropolis, a mish-mosh that makes it impossible to distinguish either place or identity. There are no longer separate cities, but a single metropolis without borders. The metropolis of the future would abolish the dualism between center and periphery in favor of the steppe, a homogenous space devoid of center or any fixed points of reference; a desert without past or history.[25] If in its "analytic" phase Magazzini Criminali "built spaces with no roots" onto which they inscribed depersonalized action and abstract gesture, in its postmodern phase they preferred mass locations, sports stadiums like the Olympic Track and Field Stadium in Munich, where they performed *Ins Null* (*Verso lo zero*) (1980). In *Crollo Nervoso* (where sequences from *Star Wars* and Kubrick's *Space Odyssey* were projected), science fiction inspired de-contextualized atmospheres and images. As theorized and practiced in the field of design by Alessandro Mendini, appropriation – adopted as a compositional technique – legitimated incongruity as a positive value. Mendini was the founder and director of the design magazines "Modo" (1977–79) and "Ollo" (1988-) and director of the most important Italian architectural reviews, "Casabella" (1970–76) and "Domus" (1979–85).[26] The musical aesthetic of Magazzini Criminali took inspiration from ambient music, whose icon was Brian Eno, as well as from the mythology of rock, according to which music itself was less important than the transgressive figure of the musician, embodied in figures like Jimi Hendrix and Janis Joplin, Lou Reed, and David Bowie.[27] The group's technique of appropriating pre-existing music (which was nothing less than thievery, as Sandro Lombardi has stressed) overturned the traditional relationship between production and consumption, privileging the listener, who was transformed into the producer of an infinite musical repertory (analogous to the phenomenon of the DJ in the era's discotheques).

In this period, a miscellany of media and genres (cinema, television, advertising, sport, comics, music, science fiction) fueled the formats utilized by Magazzini Criminali as they transformed from a theater company into a producing organization. They organized live concerts (*Last Concert Polaroid*, Rome, 1976) and released records (under the name Magazzini Criminali Music) such as *Crollo nervoso* (1980), *Notte senza fine* (Endless Night, 1983, with a cover by Mario Schifano), and *Honolulu, 25 dicembre* (produced in Brussels). They also put out a magazine, first named *Il Carrozzone* and then *Magazzini Criminali*, which served as yet another instrument of the group's communication strategy, involving friends, critics, and intellectuals who supported their work, and included image maps of texts of their work combined into a graphic staging of their aesthetic imaginary, with film stills, pornography, body culture imagery, sex, and fashion [CONTEXTS '80].[28]

The extreme heterogeneity of forms and the deconstruction of any regulating criteria bestowed great expressive and experimental freedom upon theater in this era. Paradoxically, postmodern theory – imported into Italy in the early Eighties through Baudrillard, Lyotard, and Jameson – furnished perhaps the last unifying context within which artistic and aesthetic production could interact and proceed within a theoretical-philosophical framework. The Nineties, on the other hand, would suffer for the absence of such a center, and bear instead the burden of being *posthumous*, survivors of the end of ideology.

3.4 Theoretical reflection: anthropology and postmodern = intercultural

The question of the avant-garde cannot simply be set aside by declaring its historical exhaustion, because the avant-garde has a transhistorical function; it does not simply coincide with whatever phenomenon appears to be new in a given era. As Rosalind Krauss has observed, the avant-garde always contains within itself its own failure. To be avant-garde, Krauss maintains, an artist must be able to reinvent the medium that she or he uses.[29] To better understand the changes that took place in the Eighties in theater, both in Italy and internationally, we shift our perspective to the analyses of Richard Schechner and Bonnie Marranca on the crisis of the neo-avant gardes and the arrival of a postmodern aesthetic. In his 1981 essay, *The Decline and Fall of the (American) Avant Garde*, Schechner listed the following causes as contributing to the decline of the New York avant-garde:

- The split between the dramatic text and the performance text, in the sense that the author of the spectacle came to substitute the writer. In contrast to writers of dramatic texts such as, for example, Edward Albee or Henrik Ibsen, Robert Wilson and Richard Foreman are authors of performance texts that no one else could ever stage.
- The weakening of the methods of transmission of the techniques of New Theater from one generation to another. Instead, an artist's formation is now an autodidactic process, therapeutic, stamped with the technologies of self-help, a *pastiche* in which Asian practices such as yoga and T'ai Chi are absorbed and applied outside their traditional context.
- The crisis of ensemble theater, brought on by the difficulty of holding divergent positions within a single collective, as well as by the emergence of the solo performer, whose creations cannot be reproduced by another artist.
- The absence of a sustainable economy, and ignorance of means by which this condition might be modified.
- The obtuseness of a trend in journalism that reacted against experimentation, together with the inability of more rigorous critics to affect public opinion.

- The end of political activism and the inclination of artists to engage the marketplace, mass media, and the entertainment industry.[30]

These changes lead us to the problem of postmodern theater as approached by Bonnie Marranca, a scholar highly attentive to the New Theater scene. In *Performance, a Personal History*, (1998), Marranca noted the disappearance of the barricade that had previously separated the avant-garde from mass culture:

> Previously, the downtown arts community functioned as a subculture, opposed to the exigencies of the marketplace and populist demands, and reveling in its own intellectual rigor, advanced forms and vocabularies. Now, many of the terms of contention have become irrelevant for younger generations".[31]

In the same year in which he analyzed the causes of the New Theater crisis, Richard Schechner, with his characteristic intellectual impartiality, identified a series of key concepts of postmodernism: polycentrism and relativism (the cosmos has lost its center and the center is everywhere); orality; environment; flow; reflexivity (being inside and outside at the same time, detached and immersed, without clear separations); interculturalism (in place of internationalism); and the integration of the verbal with the non-verbal. In synthesis, he observed, the postmodern is indeterminate, ahistorical, holistic, and ritualized.[32]

To return to Italy, it is important to remember that between the end of the Seventies and the early Eighties, along with semiotics, both anthropology and postmodernist theory were spreading. The enthusiasm for semiotics soon waned (in Italy, in fact, it had manifested rather weakly), taking with it the hope that semiotics might be able to say something about the contemporary scene, about the body, about the senses. Semiotic theory began to waver between not wanting to give in to the deconstructionist drift (that is, the thesis that it is impossible to fix any meaning at all) and, on the other hand, not wanting to submit to any hierarchically established ordering criteria.

As semiotics faded, anthropological and postmodern theory came to the fore and converged toward a zeroing-out of time and history in favor of space, of the horizontal, of cultural syncretism. Schechner's essay, *Restoration of Behavior*, first published between 1981 and 1983, was a theoretical synthesis of the effort to cross anthropology with postmodern theory, which established the basis for Performance Studies.[33]

Ideologically, however, anthropology and the postmodern remained separate. Theatrical anthropology, which may have originated in Italy with Ferruccio Marotti's research in Bali in the 1970s, was fueled by annual sessions of the International School of Theater Anthropology (ISTA), organized by Eugenio Barba and held for the first time in 1979. ISTA was a laboratory of research combining theater practitioners, critics, and students from Europe,

Africa, Asia, and the Americas, which produced a network of exchange on technical aspects of the art of the performer, including both empirical methods and fundamental speculation into what constitutes the core difference between the actor's body and the everyday body. Each annual session focused on selected aspects of the theme, investigated through workshops, conferences, demonstrations, and performances.[34]

What philosopher Gianni Vattimo wrote in his book *La fine della modernità* (The End of Modernity) about the debate between anthropology and hermeneutics may help us to inscribe this tendency in a more ample epistemological framework. If anthropology is thought of as a discourse on cultures of the "other", wrote Vattimo,

> this alterity comes to be somehow 'regulated' or, if you like, exorcised, with a metaphysically inspired appeal to a common humanity, a super-historical essence, inside the confines of which lay all human phenomena, no matter how different they may appear.[35]

In the context of theater, the performative constants described by Schechner, the biological universals stressed by director Peter Brook, and the pre-expressive laws identified by Eugenio Barba, all pursue this intercultural comparative method of an "ideal common unity".

Interculturalism has offered a kind of compensation for the loss of all the singular national identities. But this transference from the international to the intercultural has produced a paradoxical synonymy between multiculturalism and the global monoculture brought on by new technologies. What was once divergent (the plurality of cultures and the reduction of the world to a global village through mass media), by millenium's end found itself assimilated into the concept of "trans-territoriality", this too connected telematically. The anthropological perspective has furthermore given theoretical legitimacy to the way artistic practice has left behind the orbit of the text in preference to context, even beyond the spectacle. This tendency was flanked by the postmodern exaltation of the aesthetics of social behavior, of the diffuse artwork, and the irrelevance of the author. Arriving by different pathways, anthropology and postmodernism rendered obsolete the idea of art as a specific practice traditionally interrogated only from an aesthetic viewpoint. Now, art must be subject also to sociological, psychological, and gender studies interpretation.

Just the same, Performance Studies, as a field, has not fallen on particularly fertile ground in Italy. Rather than broadening and deepening research, Performance Studies has mostly led to a thinning of historiographical and theoretical substance (certainly in terms of semiotics, psychoanalysis, and the Marxist tradition), with an attraction toward "low" practices, which are the melting pot of the contemporary.

Looking back over this period, Schechner has justly criticized both Performance Studies and Cultural Theory, settings where postmodern, post-structuralist, and post-colonial theory (dwelling especially on the failure of the diverse currents of Marxism) enjoyed free play. In his essay on the "Conservative Avant-garde" (2010), he attributes to these theories the fault of having sustained the world-view of what he calls the university-trained "conservative avant garde" of today, as opposed to the era when budding artists learned freely from one another:

> Theory's role in leading to a conservative avant-garde is demonstrable. The poststructuralists and postmodernists so current from the 1970s to the turn of the twenty-first century (and far from passé today), and the "restored behavior" or "surrogation" advocates, emphasized repetition, citation, deferral of meaning, the circulation of ideas, and the impossibility of defining, over even of individuating, "originals". . . . Increasingly, artists respond to the global situation and their own attenuation by redoing avant-garde classics. MoMA's Abramović retrospective drew record crowds – to what? To a famous artist sitting in state? To see signature performances that were edgy when first done but are now safely museumified/mummified?[36]

In "Can We Be the (New) Third World?", Schechner carried still further his critique of Performance Studies and Performance Theory – the latter of which was, in fact, largely Schechner's own invention – which posited relations between theater, ritual, and anthropology. His theories had led, in the words of Mabel Giraldo, "to a theatricality outside the field of art and aesthetics, positioned midway between the human and social sciences, becoming an inferior, marginal art, devoid of epistemological and aesthetic identity".[37]

This observation accords with those of Bonnie Marranca, who has charged that the methods of Performance Studies have ultimately contributed to the marginalization of theater as a phenomenon of western culture, the devaluing of the artwork as an object of interpretation, as a result of formal discipline, now replaced by the idea of artistic work as a type of merchandise without quality. The distance and mutual autonomy of author and spectator have been lost, in favor of a hypothetical communion with no distinction among roles.[38]

3.5 Dawning: the artwork reborn

Within this framework, we might locate a spectacle such as *Cuori strappati* (Torn Hearts, 1983), by Gaia Scienza, either *beyond* the vise-like grip of the neo-avant garde and the postmodern, or even in a caesura *between* the two, as a rejection of the spectacularity of works such as *Crollo nervoso* and *Tango Glaciale* – a shift in discourse toward the horizon of the work of art. By the mid-Eighties, many in Italy felt the need to question the postmodern vision of the relation between theater and world. In his posthumously-published

Lezioni americane (American Lessons), Italo Calvino made a sort of prophetic testament of essential principles to be safeguarded in art: Lightness, Rapidity, Exactness, Visibility, and Multiplicity. There do exist right paths and wrong paths, Calvino insisted, but they must be redefined on every single occasion. The decade had been particularly turbulent for many of the leaders of the various neo-avant gardes, who lived with the daily anguish of disappearing suddenly from the scene or of coming to be seen as survivors in a world that had completely exhausted the meaning of their actions.

In a talk entitled "Crossing the Desert" given during the *Forces at Play* conference in 1986, Giuseppe Bartolucci expressed the thought of many present when he insisted on the need to overcome the postmodern aesthetic of spectacularity and mass-media entertainment. A new strategy was needed, one focused on artwork that would aspire to integrity without forgetting the shattering of certainties that had taken place. He called for a search for new narrative forms capable of reintegrating tradition.[39] Many interventions during the conference (including those by Franco Quadri, Claudio Meldolesi, Ferdinando Taviani, Lorenzo Mango, Franco Ruffini, Oliviero Ponte di Pino, Gianni Manzella, Mario Martone, Giorgio Barberio Corsetti, Federico Tiezzi, Claudia Castellucci, and Cesare Ronconi) agreed that a moment of transition was underway, one that demanded new aesthetic and practical approaches and a new lexicon. The terms used since the Sixties to define "New Theater" – avant-garde, neo-avant garde, theater research, experimental theater, minor theater, Third Theater, base theater, ensemble theater – no longer fit. Some demanded that the ideology of opposition between official theater and alternative theater be dismantled, so as to open the door to integration. Others feared that New Theater, its pluralist diversity lost, would crystalize into a museum display.

What were the risks entailed in re-introducing the literary text into the practice of composition for the stage? Federico Tiezzi, who had passed from the Theater of Images to analytic theater and then on to the postmodern, launched a new challenge at the *Forces at Play* conference:

> The grand spectacle has dried my eyes, which need a new way of seeing, purer, simpler and at the same time more vigilant, more active and (a strange word, from '68, which I was too young to experience) more committed and more severe.[40]

Poetry, emotion, humanity, universality, the abandonment of formulas were the concepts that Tiezzi inscribed in his thinking about a theatre of poetry, "outside the hypertrophy of the visual and the complication of the gaze".[41] In his spectacle, *Portrait of the Artist as a Young Man* (1984), the Caspar David Friedrich painting *The Wreck of Hope* entered the stage, saved from the flood.

The crisis of postmodern aesthetics, which in Italian theater had meant the crisis of the companies centered around the new spectacularity, had led to a new code word, which Giuseppe Bartolucci expressed as conceiving spectacle as a work of art.[42] He called for a return to literature, to writing for the stage, which is to say planning and composing a work of art (the term in Italian, *opera*, reveals an approach to spectacle as an artistic labor, neither minimalist performance nor mass-media mimesis) by integrating the horizontal (space, perception, sensibility) with the vertical (time, and the discrete logical thought inherent to writing), so as to hold at bay both narcissist intemperance and the protagonism of the spectator.

From this perspective, the new coincided no longer with Debord's white screen, nor with John Cage's gesture of shutting the piano, nor with Naim June Paik's act of destroying it. On the contrary, the idea was to regenerate theater by exploiting its specific and special instruments. For Franco Quadri, this necessarily involved the literary text, with an actor who would incarnate it, becoming its vehicle. Virtually everyone who took part in the debate agreed that the analytic dimension of New Theater, the practice of decomposition and reduction of theatrical codes to an absolute minimum, had been exhausted. The same was true of metropolitan spectacularity. It was therefore necessary to delve into the complexity of stage composition, including both the literary text and the actor, and make use of institutional spaces, which meant stepping beyond the ideology of political opposition.[43] For some, the proposed change in direction invoked a return to order after the Dionysian excess of the Seventies and Eighties. For others, it meant facing the challenge of rejecting the protective, safe schemas of dramatic convention. Gerardo Guccini characterized the demand to return to story, character, and text as "re-theatricalization", a recuperation of the very concept of theater that the preceding years had attempted to zero out.[44]

Spectacles such as *Notturni Diamanti* (Diamond Nocturnes, 1984) and *Il Cavaliere Azzurro* (The Azure Knight, 1985) by Solari-Vanzi; *Genet in Tangiers* (1984), *Ritratto dell'attore da giovane* (Portrait of the Artist as a Young Man, 1985), and *Vita immaginaria di Paolo Uccello* (Imaginary Life of Paolo Uccello, 1985) by Magazzini Produzione; *Il Ladro d'anime* (The Thief of Souls, 1985) by Giorgio Barberio Corsetti; *Lo spazio della quiete* (The Space of Quiet, 1984), *Le radici dell'amore* (The Roots of Love, 1985), and *Atlante dei misteri dolorosi* (Atlas of Painful Mysteries, 1986) by Teatro Valdoca, all re-integrated the element of time that postmodernism had expelled and reified as an entity external to events. Verbal communication and literary mythology also made their return.

The new dramaturgy sought to return to the infancy of language, using onomatopoeia and animal sounds (as in the mute characters in Tiezzi's *Portrait of the Artist*), and deploying the whole sonic-textual-phonic repertory of infantile imitation of the world. The capacity to communicate, to put oneself into contact with the world through language, to overcome stuttering, was developed through the mediation of models and figures drawn from the patrimony of art and the personal cultural repertory of individual artists. The *Memory Loss* trilogy, by Magazzini Criminali, built on the poetic memory of ancient Greek tragedy mediated through contemporary authors such as Genet, Artaud, and Pasolini, and through myths and heroes taken from literature and cinema. Fassbinder became a character in the piece, as did the legendary comedian Totò, played by actor Sandro Lombardi. In the same company's *Genet in Tangiers*, Marion d'Amburgo embodied the voice and movement of Anna Magnani.[45]

But after its period of silencing, aphasia, and errancy, the reborn artwork must not regress back to the traditional theater of roles. Bartolucci admonished the companies present at *Forces at Play* not to lose track of the discipline of writing for the stage, not to drift toward modernity's notion of interpretive dramaturgy.[46] In Teatro Valdoca's *Atlas of Painful Mysteries* (1986), the word returned to the stage, forged anew through its encounter with "the school of poetry" in the verse of poets Mario Luzi (1914–2005), Franco Fortini (1917–94), and Milo De Angelis (1951-). Verses by Aeschylus and Paul Celan were written and unscrolled on cartouches, and whispered, like words on tiptoe, through terracotta megaphones. In the text of the same company's *Ruvido umano* (Rough Human, 1986), lines taken from Rilke and Allen Ginsberg were vocally modulated from a scream to a whisper to evoke a dimension of the virgin dawn of time, reshaped through verbal language, through language's capacity to transform the real.

In Giorgio Barberio Corsetti's *Descrizione di una battaglia* (Description of a Battle (1988, FOCUS), word and action engaged as equals in a duel of their ability to specify, creating a harmonious counterpoint. In this spectacle, mental space and stage space coincide in a story, *La Tana* (The Den), which constituted the narrative and thematic framework of a montage of texts. The Den was the stage, a blank page upon which the author constructs a world, populating it with the phantoms of his/her mind. Theater and writing find their objectification in a white wall, a page where signs appear through the physical effort of actors who dig into and cleave its surface. A thematic and structural equivalence develops between the means of the stage and those of literature, potentiating both. The polyphonic montage in *Description of a Battle* creates a multiplicity of meanings and layers that render the spectacle complex and stratified, a place of intersection and interaction among the work of the actors, the space, and texts from Kafka. Mirroring among the literary texts that provided the fuel and material for the actors' improvisations, for their gestural and choreographic exploration, led to a close intersection between written word and plastic, dynamic space. One guided the other, testing its resistance, and layering in an organic process of assimilation of the highly visual text of Kafka into the living, reactive body of the actor. The process in this work did not create the sort of "elsewhere" produced when a text is mechanically transported onto the stage. The equality between the verbal and gestural scores configured itself like a cell with two nuclei formed from material evolved through a process of organic assimilation of the text; the "Kafka-ization" of the physical space. A repertoire of movements, poses, actions, sounds, and verbal emissions formed the material with which the spectacle was composed. The montage of the two scores in the course of ordering the scenes (the layering of three stories each into the other) was comparable to the polyphonic montage described by Eisenstein: A central theme developed through a counterpoint of diverse voices, each repeating a motif with variations.[47] The duel between the verbal score and the plastic, gestural score of the actor, the full equivalence and coexistence of both, became possible not only when the actors assumed Kafka's immaterial, textual body into their own tangible bodies, but also thanks to the gestural character of Kafka's writing, which is particularly assimilable to the stage, a place where gesture becomes ideogram, in the way dreamed of by Meyerhold and Kafka.

Notes

1 M. Belpoliti, *Settanta*, Einaudi, Turin, 2010, 56.
2 Ivi, 44.
3 Ivi, 102, 59.
4 Ivi, 58.
5 Italo Calvino, cited in A. Asor Rosa, *Storia europea della letteratura*, Einaudi, Turin, 2009, 559.
6 F. Cordelli, "Dalla battaglia di Castelporziano", *Teatroltre*, n. 19, 122; Cfr. G. Bartolucci, "Osservazioni su Castelporziano", *Teatroltre*, n. 19, 127–132.
7 E. Barba, *Brecht dell'Odin*, Ubulibri, Milan, 1981, 7–8. For a summary of the debate on Terzo Teatro, cfr. M. Valentino, *Nuovo Teatro*, Titivillus, Corazzano (PI), 2014.
8 F. Quadri, in AA.VV., *Le forze in campo: Per una nuova cartografia del teatro: Atti del convegno di Modena, 24–25 maggio, 1986*, Mucchi, Modena, 1987, 17. The first failed encounter between Eugenio Barba, the lead figure in Terzo Teatro, and Nuovo Teatro took place at the Ivrea Conference in 1967, when Barbe and his company presented their training methods, which were criticized harshly by representatives of Nuovo Teatro, such as Carmelo Bene and Mario Ricci.
9 F. Piero Brunetta, *Storia del cinema italiano*, vol. IV, Editori Riuniti, Rome, 1993, 519.
10 Ivi, 520.
11 L. Bentivoglio, *Tanztheater, dalla danza espressionista a Pina Bausch*, Di Giacomo, Rome, 1982; D. Bertozzi and S. Barbarini, eds., *New York: Nuova danza-new dance*, Di Giacomo, Rome, 1982.
12 Cfr. *Collage*, an international journal of new music and contemporary visual art (1963–1970), founded by Antonio Titone, who had organized week-long new music festivals in Palermo from 1960–68. www.unipa.it/tecla/rivista/2_rivista_giordano.php
13 F. Sargentini, R. Lambarelli and L. Masina, eds., *L'Attico, 1957–1987*, A. Mondadori-De Luca, Milan-Rome, 1987.
14 Cfr. M. Palladini, *I teatronauti del chaos: La scena sperimentale postmoderna in Italia (1976–2008)*, Fermenti, Rome, 2009, 43–44.
15 L. Mango, "La decostruzione del nuovo", in M. Valentino (ed.), *Il Nuovo Teatro in Italia, 1976–1985*, cit., 17.
16 All citations from G. Bartolucci, "Dalla postavanguardia alla nuova spettacolarità", in *Testi critici*, Bulzoni, Rome, 2007, 244–297; also in G. Bartolucci, L. Mango and A. Mango, *Per un teatro analitico esistenziale*, Studio Forma, Turin, 1980; and in *Teatroltre*, n. 14.

17 G. Bartolucci, *Testi critici, 1964–1987*, cit., 249.
18 M. Valentino, *Il Nuovo Teatro in Italia, 1976–1985*, cit.; F. Pitrolo, *What Was Before Isn't Anymore: Image, Theatre, and the Italian New Spectacularity, 1978–1984*, University of Roehampton, London, 2014.
19 G. Celant, *Identité italienne: L'art en Italie depuis 1959*, Centre Georges Pompidou, Musée National d'Art Moderne, Paris, 1981 (Catalogue de l'exposition 25 juin–7 septembre, 1981), 20.
20 H. Foster, *The Return of the Real*, MIT Press, Cambridge, MA, 1996.
21 Cfr. G. Bartolucci, M. Fabbri, M. Pisani and G. Spinucci, eds., *Paesaggio metropolitano*, Feltrinelli, Milan, 1982; G. Bartolucci, "La traversata del deserto", in A. Attisani. (ed.), *Le forze in campo*, cit., 23–31.
22 G. Bartolucci, "Domande a Jean Baudrillard", in *Paesaggio metropolitano*, cit., 63.
23 F. Menna, "Identità e legitimazione dell'arte", in *Paesaggio metropolitano*, cit., 105–110; Cfr. also *Alfabeta*, n. 22, 1981.
24 S. Sinisi, *Dalla parte dell'occhio, esperienze teatrali in Italia, 1972–1982*, Kappa, Rome, 1983, 193.
25 Ivi, 103, nn. 37, 38.
26 A. Mendini, *Paesaggio casalingo*, Domus, Milan, 1979; *Architetettura addio*, Shakespeare, Milan, 1981; *Existenz maximum*, Tipolito Press, Florence, 1990; *The International Design Yearbook*, Laurence King, London, 1996.
27 S. Lombardi, "La noche repetida", in R. Bonfiglioli (ed.), *Frequenze barbare*, La Casa Usher, Florence, 1981, 212–213.
28 A list of theater companies who record discs in this period would include: Litfiba's *Eneide*, with their music for the spectacle of the same name by Krypton; G. Scienza, *Il Ladro di Anime*, 1985; D. Bacalov, *Diario segreto contraffatto*, produced by DoppioZero, Rome, 1985; O.A.S.I., *Il Cavaliere azzurro*, with music for the spectacle by Marco Solaro and Alessandra Vanzi; and P. Milesi, *The Nuclear Observatory of Mr. Nanof*, with music for the video by Studio Azzurro, directed by Paolo Rosa.
29 R. E. Krauss, *L'originalità dell'avanguardia e altri miti modernisti*, Elio Grazioli (ed.), Fazi Editore, Rome, 2007. Cfr. V. Valentini, "Détournement dell'avanguardia", in AA.VV and Biblioteca Teatrale (eds.), *Memorie delle cantine Teatro di ricerca a Roma negli anni 60 e 70*, Bulzoni, Rome, 2006, 47–65.
30 R. Schechner, "The Decline and Fall of the (American) Avant-Garde", in *The End of Humanism. Writing on Performance*, Performing Arts Journal Publications, New York, 1982, 11–77
31 B. Marranca, "La politica della performance", in Id., *American Performance, 1975–2005*, V. Valentini (ed.), Bulzoni, Rome, 2006, 47–65. Originally appeared in *Performing Arts Journal*, vol. VI, n. 1, 1981.
32 R. Schechner, "The Crash of Performative Circumstance: A Modernist Discourse on Postmodernism", *Triquarterly*, 1981, 52. Cfr. "Conservative Avant-garde", *New Literary History*, n. 41, 2010.
33 Cfr. V. Valentini, "Professione cartografo", in R. Schechner (ed.), *La teoria della performance*, Bulzoni, Rome, 1984, 11–38.
34 E. Barba and N. Savarese, *The Secret Art of the Performer: A Dictionary of Theatre Anthropology*, Routledge, London, 2005.
35 G. Vattimo, *La fine della modernità*, Garzanti, Milan, 1985, 153.
36 R. Schechner, "The Conservative Avant-Garde", cit., 29–52.
37 M. Giraldo, "Richard Schechner: da Restoration ai Performance Studies. Un'indagine preliminare", in *Comunicazioni Sociali. Journal of Media, Performing Arts and Cultural Studies*, n. 1, April 2016, pp. 138–149.
38 B. Marranca, "Pensando all'interculturalismo", in *Biblioteca teatrale*, n. 54m aprile-giugno 2000, 25–44.
39 Cfr. G. Bartolucci, "La traversata del deserto", cit., 23–33.

40 F. Tiezzi, "Il quarto testo è lo spazio-pensiero", in *Le forze in campo*, cit., 87.
41 Ivi, 85.
42 G. Bartolucci, "L'opera contro il deserto", in G. Mancini and V. Valentini (eds.), *Scritti critici, 1964–1987*, cit.
43 V. Valentini, "Il teatro è il luogo dove trova scampo il reale", *Le forze in campo*, cit.
44 G. Guccini, "Teatri verso il terzo millennio: il problema della rimozione storiografica", *Culture Teatrali*, nn. 2-3, primavera-autunno, 2000, 11–26.
45 V. Valentini, "La drammaturgia del disgelo", *Frigidaire*, Maggio 1986.
46 G. Bartolucci in O. Ponte di Pino, *Il Nuovo Teatro italiano, 1975–1988*, cit., 28.
47 V. Valentini, "I principi costruttivi del montaggio nel teatro contemporaneo", in P. Montani (ed.), *Sergei Eisenstein: oltre il cinema*, Edizioni Biblioteca dell'immagine, La Biennale di Venezia, 1991, 80–103.

4 The Nineties
Ideology, a vice to flee: 1989–99

4.1 Revisionism and conciliation

The fall of the Berlin Wall in 1989, marking the end of Moscow's hegemony and the extinction of the Soviet Socialist Republic, stands as the most important political event of the last decade of the twentieth century. One of its effects was the war in Yugoslavia, while the Gulf War unleashed a succession of uncontrollable violence and destruction in the Middle East. Conservative governments in the United States and Europe (Reagan, Thatcher, Putin, Berlusconi), and, soon thereafter, the global financial collapse, provoked a reaction that knocked the achievements of the Sixties and Seventies (civil rights and social programs) off their hinges and ushered in the privatization of the public sphere, while the AIDS epidemic in the United States re-awoke a new activism that entered the terrain of art, with ACT-UP and innumerable other manifestations. In this period, the Western Empire entered a crisis; the axis of the world shifted toward the east, triggering a virtual financial bubble that sparked massive human migration, as the value of labor (including intellectual labor) declined in the face of the pressure exerted by a global workforce numbering in the billions.

Decisive events took place in Italy: the Italian Communist Party (the PCI) became the Democratic Party of the Left (PDS); in 1992, mafia bombs in Palermo, Sicily, killed magistrates Giovanni Falcone and Paolo Borsellino; the *Mani Pulite* (Clean Hands) investigation uncovered *Tangentopoli* (Bribesville), a system of corruption that permeated the political structure to the core, which resulted in the collapse of the First Italian Republic, and which in turn led to the rise of magnate Silvio Berlusconi and the frenzy of corruption he injected into Italian civil society.

The Nineties witnessed the triumph of Neo-liberalism and the weakening of the ideological divergence that had set east against west, left against right, and socialism against capitalism. Certain ideas began to fade away, such as dialectics, the struggle for a better society, the utopia of possible revolutions, and art as means for envisioning a reality different from the dominant one, with the individual as a creative force. The intellectual middle class declined, as did the working class, together with a growing difficulty, brought on largely by technological change, of distinguishing the real from the imaginary.[1] The notion of trans-territoriality favored the homogenization of cultural identities. With the fall of the socialist regimes in Eastern Europe, people and entities such as the Soros Center, Microsoft, Bill Gates, and Rupert Murdoch propagated on a global scale a certain standard model of art which was held to be typical of global industrial society.

The impulse to reabsorb, amoeba-like, phenomena which in past decades had been ideologically antagonistic to one another produced revisionism and cultural syncretism, an attitude expressed by a Mexican guerrilla leader who enjoyed a brief vogue, Subcommandant Marcos, as "considering the current state of things to be ineluctable, ostracizing any critical reflection, representing as irrational anyone who refuses to accept the natural state of society and the marketplace".[2] Anything that directly opposed the dominant apparatus could longer stand. In Theater, success came to artists who practiced a weak form of flat, sentimental social protest that pacified spirits, using models derived from television, such as in the spectacles of Pippo Delbono and Emma Dante.

"Globalization" was the term that came into use to indicate the new worldwide arrangement of political-economic relations. In Rome, the *Molteplici culture* (Multiple Cultures) exhibition in 1992, curated by Carolyn Christov-Bakargiev, brought into view art from what had been formerly called the Third World, its aesthetic supported by the idea that integration and the assimilation of cultural difference is a positive value for its own sake. In Paris, the *Magiciens de la terre* (Magicians of the Earth) exhibition, curated by Jean-Hubert Martin, in 1989, spread the post-colonial, multicultural discourse that contributed to breaking down the oppositions between the First and Third Worlds, between center and periphery, and between east and west, by magnifying the hybridity of identity. In the visual arts, the "project" came into fashion, along with the figure of the curator – a new sort of *deus ex machina* – who grafted pragmatic managerial skills onto those of the critic.

A new phenomenon emerged of self-managed social centers, developed by groups of theater artists who occupied abandoned urban buildings and used them for the production and presentation of spectacles. This was the case with Link in Bologna, Interzona in Verona, and both Rialto Sant'Ambrogio and Angelo Mai in Rome. In these spaces, collectives conceived, workshopped, mounted, and performed their own work while also organizing events and series that hosted experimental theater, music, and dance.

The Nineties also saw the advent of digital technology, the expansion of computer networks and the personal computer – in a larger sense, the coming to light of "virtual worlds". These technologies altered the means of both production and delivery of cinema and initiated the transfer to digital formats of both still and moving images, thereby levelling and homogenizing what had once been a range of support media. The broad accessibility and moderate cost of digital technology transformed video art from a marginal sector of artistic experimentation into a central one.

Technological development advanced step by step with the growing attraction exercised by now-obsolete technologies and industrial archeology. The delivery system of the movie industry – that is, the traditional movie theater – now seemed out of date, as did the medium of film itself. Fewer and fewer movies were shot on celluloid film, as digital cinematography became standard. And yet numerous visual artists returned to celluloid and its associated mythography precisely for its evocative power in the popular imagination. Both photography and music underwent analogous crises.

As the Nineties progressed, many on-line theater journals appeared in Italy, taking the place of printed ones and making up for the reduction in space accorded to theater in the daily newspapers, which preferred to cover entertainment, especially television. The role of the critic, crucial through the mid-Eighties, became ever less important in the Nineties; the militant critic was replaced by the curator. By the end of the decade, the internet began to transform the means of communicating, archiving, and researching theater both new and old. Archives and libraries invested resources in digitization while theater companies increased their visibility, publishing their work through video sharing platforms, Youtube, Vimeo, and similar means.

In the Nineties, as Marco Belpoliti has said, postmodern design that depended on citation was replaced by Transitive Design, which "connected past to future with neither nostalgia nor projective ambition, but simply by the principle of continuous mutation".[3] New architecture by Jean Nouvel, Robert Venturi, and Renzo Piano resulted from computer design software, according to which, Belpoliti observes, "there is no longer a model to imitate, but, rather, the possibility to imagine and simulate, via the computer, infinite forms of the object".[4] If, he continued,

> lack of depth is the sign of the postmodern, which works on the fragment, on a cracked and incomplete totality, the Nineties instead aimed at a homogeneous treatment of form and space. Deleuze's *Fold* had a great deal of influence on architects; surfaces expand, fold, invaginate, and form pockets, so that the distinction between interior and exterior, depth and surface is emptied of meaning.[5]

Façades were re-imagined as giant screens, in competition with cinema and television. In contrast to Le Corbusier's idea of the city as an ordered, rational system, "space today is not made to be inhabited, but to be traversed; the nomad's tent is the prototype, the city a dynamic labyrinth". Seeking refuge from one type of labyrinth, people sought out another, the shopping center, "without windows, with totally unexpressive external walls of smooth cement, uninhabitable architectures where the flow of time seems imperceptible, without the perils that the metropolis holds for the *flaneur* of the past".[6]

In *Peripezie del dopoguerra dell'arte italiana* (Postwar Vicissitudes of Italian Art), art historian Ada Chiara Zevi wrote, "The analogies with the

Seventies are evident but, seen clearly, more apparent than real. In common between the two decades: rejection of pictorial essentialism, projection beyond the frame, diaspora of designated locations".[7] The great difference was that in the Nineties there was no longer any opposition to the system. In a review of the *Transavanguardia* exhibition at Castello di Rivoli in 2002, which he fiercely opposed, Germano Celant demonstrated the similarity of the new movement to *arte povera*, which *Transavanguardia* had claimed to subvert: both manifested the visible signs of the collapse of difference.[8] The central paradigm of the Seventies had been the "environment", which in the Nineties took the form of site specific work (with social impact) and multimedia installations (often interactive), both of which showed a marked interest in the role of the spectator. The common characteristic among much environmental art was the arousal of the perceptual sphere. Video dominated, as in Studio Azzurro's *videoambienti* (videoenvironments), which wove time, space, and spectators into a relational fabric. This group's first interactive installations (*Coro* and *Tavoli*, 1995) were forcefully motivated by the intention to re-enliven a spectator drugged by the mediatic system. The "mediatization" of individual and collective experience was re-routed toward sharing and doing. Nicholas Bourriad proposed relational aesthetics as a paradigm and compositional principle for artistic production in the Nineties: rather than emphasizing an artistic result, through feedback and human interaction the spectator's intervention completed a process.[9]

In its first years, the decade's reaction against postmodern aesthetics led to a rediscovery of the human emotions that had been banished by the conceptualism of the Seventies. Bill Viola, the North American artist known for his single-channel videos and installations, began a cycle of work in 1995 that went under the title of *The Passions*. The artist explained,

> The general idea I started from was to go to the root, the source of my emotions and emotional expressions. During my artistic training in the Seventies, these were prohibited zones, but I find myself to be completely at the mercy of these potent emotional forces, much deeper than the sentimentalism I had been taught to avoid.[10]

In 1992, Jeffrey Deitch curated the *Posthuman* exhibition at Castello di Rivoli. In 1999, Francesca Alfano Miglietti presented *Rosso*, a revival of Body Art updated with post-punk narcissism, at Milan's PAC. In Mike Kelley's environments of these years (as in contemporaneous novels by the Italian pulp and cannibal movements), abjection, regression, and disgust became aspects of aesthetic reflection and art practice, alongside the fear of a dehumanized cyborg universe.[11] The *Gioventù cannibale* (Cannibal Youth) anthology of 1996 presented new writers united by a pulp vision of reality that overwhelmed the distinction between popular and experimental fiction.[12] Departing from Lacan's definition of the temporal fragment suspended "between two deaths" (physical death and the fading of memory), the *Between Two Deaths* exhibition at the Karlsruhe ZKM in 2007 attempted to analyze the spirit of the time: gothic fashion, horror films, and latent vampirism expressed the insecurity and fear that rendered conservative society incapable of movement. The need to take up the modernist past once again made the archive into a diffuse metaphor and object of activity. Jerzy Grotowski died in Pontedera in 1999, in the same year as Sarah Kane's suicide in London.

Italian new dance, a phenomenon of New Theater since the mid-Eighties, published *Manifesto 1992. Dance As Contemporary Art* [CONTEXTS], motivated by the need to declare its identity and role. Italian dancers faced the challenge of leaving behind the dominant models that had functioned as their training schools, to discover and affirm a Mediterranean individuality. The *Manifesto* summoned dancers to seek a corporal, material, and relational *genius loci* based on "the gravity of weight and contact between bodies and with the earth". In comparison to French *nouvelle danse*, which was postmodern and parodic, Italian new dance centered on the figure of the choreographer-author-dancer, with her complex labor of conception, creation, and composition. The manifesto claimed a Mediterranean cultural identity, a free mental nomadism to be cultivated in solitude: "The artistic diversity that has always characterized us is our source of power, a pointedly Italian (more precisely, Mediterranean) poetics, which has long been reductively interpreted as creative weakness, because it did not reproduce the reigning fashionable traits". The contemporaneity of new Italian dance consisted in its dialogue with other artistic languages; not a heterogeneous assemblage, but a contamination that expressed integration and unity.[13]

Perhaps the single work that most characterizes the Nineties is Matthew Barney's cycle of films, the *Cremaster Cycle* (1994–2002), in which the artist combined his function as auteur with his own performance, drawing, sculpture, and installations. Five feature-length films constituted an "aesthetic system" including pre-modern regression, solid postmodern roots, and the mythmaking typical of the neo-avant gardes. Barney's cycle had both a monumental and a spilling-over quality reminiscent of the nine-play cycle of the same era by Socìetas Raffaello Sanzio, entitled *Tragedia Endogonidia*. The *Cremaster Cycle* turns on a vast gamma of diverse myths of seemingly irreconcilable types, from Masonic legend to Richard Serra, Joseph Beuys, and the legendary escape-artist Houdini. Drawing from the most disparate sources, the five videos that constitute the Cremaster Cycle syncretize such motifs as sports, biotechnology, the classical tradition, American popular entertainment (rodeo and football), puritanism, the Irish saga, and the personality cult of the artist. The revisionist ambiguity of the Cremaster Cycle derives from a pre-modern dimension which, subjected to the processes of postmodern hybridism, takes up the mythologies of the neo-avant garde and turns them inside out. The result is a formidable system of self-mythification based on profoundly regressive moral and aesthetic values.[14] Art actualized globalization in this decade by absorbing and promiscuously mixing all forms of artistic practice, including those which had always positioned themselves as irregular.

4.2 Inhabiting transition. The balance of "Pregress"

Drawing up a balance sheet of New Theater in the era from the Sixties to the Eighties, Giuseppe Bartolucci analyzed the fracture between political and artistic practice, which he ascribed to the inability of the instruments of art to produce social change. Although it had shared with the political movement of 1968,

> the vitality of provocation and the insurrection of the new and the different, the avant garde ceased to be a utopia of social renewal. The avant garde crossed a threshold into the myth of existence as disorder, of living as drowning, and made artistic practice into an activity of consolidation followed by flight, proceeding by error and in mad disorder.[15]

At the 1986 conference in Modena – which we will here take as marking the shift from the Eighties to the new decade – Antonio Attisani reflected on the changes happening in society and theater and how they might be managed. He stressed the need to eliminate ideological schemas and factionalism and spoke against the use of poetics as totalizing systems, noting the negative effect of such tendencies not only in the work but also in the lives of theater practitioners. He thus advocated the decommissioning of the great theatrical models (The Living Theatre, Jerzy Grotowski, Eugenio Barba, Peter Brook, Tadeusz Kantor), and proposed in their place a revisionist critical approach:

> We know we are inhabiting a transition at the end of an unstable century [. . .]. Theater finds itself in a minority status (after the postmodern emphasis on mass spectacle) [. . .] which does not signify its death, but a change of state, and not isolation, but a different kind of interaction with other media. Theater must work on this new status of difference without ideological haste, leaving behind the confusion of poetics with theology, and must direct its interest anew to the 'traditions' (perhaps more those of our grandparents than those of our parents).[16]

Also at the Modena conference, theater historian Ferdinando Taviani reiterated his objection that New Theater posited the avant-garde against tradition, when in fact, he charged, the principal of novelty that governed New Theater was entirely congenial to assimilation by the contemporary marketplace. The collection of essays *Il Nuovo Teatro italiano, 1975–1988*, edited by Oliviero Ponte di Pino, argued for an inclusive reconciliation of contrasting positions, insisting that New Theater should be capable of including diverse and multifarious spirits under the rubric of the new, in line with the continuity between the historical avant-gardes and contemporary theatrical phenomena.[17]

At the end of an historical and aesthetic cycle, the priority was to stabilize what had been consolidated during the previous phase, and thus recognize the legitimacy of theatrical production that had achieved a distinct level of quality in a new generation of theaters, which the state officially classed as *teatri stabili di innovazione* (Permanent Theaters of Innovation).[18] Among these, Ravenna's Teatro delle Albe had found a way to establish permanent roots while also maintaining a position outside the mainstream. Since its beginnings in the mid-Eighties, this company had configured itself as a sort of alternative pole outside the conflict raging between Third Theater, which identified with Eastern traditions, poverty, and ritual, and the urban post-avant-gardists, who favored high technology and Warholian transgression. The Albe company remained free of this clash of "sandals versus Nike" by conceiving theater as a language of the present, by restoring drive and urgency to a medium capable of telling stories about its own time.[19] In an interview, one of the company's founders, Marco Martinelli, asked, "Is it really true that theater is condemned to the museum and tired formal repetition, unable to hear the clamor of life?"[20] The Albe pursued an interrogative: What is happening *today* in social communication, in our ethos, in the arts, in politics, in affective relations? What characterizes contemporaneity, what distinguishes ours from other historical periods? The questions echo those of Paolo Virno: "What makes our present into an *era*, that is, an absolutely singular constellation of forces/actions/ideas/conflicts?"[21] This is the problem of the "ontology of the present" that Foucault spoke of in *Moi, Pierre Rivière, ayant égorgé ma mére, ma soeur et mon frère: un cas de parricide au XIX siècle*,[22] and even earlier, in *The Archeology of Knowledge*. What does it mean to ask oneself about the place and time in which we speak and act, to elaborate a now that excavates the present, undermines it and puts it at risk? The Teatro delle Albe founded its theatre on the actor, but also on texts, making historical authors such as Aristophanes and Molière into contemporaries of living authors such as Marco Belpoliti, Martinelli himself, and the other actor/playwrights in the company, such as Ermanna Montanari and Luigi Dadina. The Albe combined Senegalese fables with Carlo Goldoni, Euripides with Nevio Spadoni, Alfred Jarry with Karl Valentin. Theirs was (and is) a theater of feeling, both comic and tragic, that worked with linguistic pastiche (including but not limited to Senegalese Wolof and Italian dialects such as romagnol and pugliese) and that exploited transgressive gestures in paradoxical spectacles that pushed sentiments and passions to their extremes [FOCUS]. In the situations and stories they represent, their spectacles attempted to comprehend how the present we live in manifests itself in its precise historical confluence: What are the essential problems that this present time is working out? The striving to reach "outside" and "beyond" the limits of the art form, which had so deeply informed theater in the Seventies, now fertilized the production of Teatro delle Albe. By sharing experiences with other companies, transplanting their practice into other geographies (rural Senegal, public schools in Chicago, the infamous Scampia housing project in Naples), by involving children and adolescents, Teatro delle Albe put its own present at risk in order to better recognize and comprehend the present shared by all.

4.3 Being posthumous

After the conference in Modena in 1986, Giuseppe Bartolucci withdrew from the scene, thereby removing from center stage a figure who since the Sixties had combined, in an unprecedented way, the functions of avant-garde creator and militant critic. Times had changed. This was the era of the rise of Silvio Berlusconi, another combined figure, who simultaneously functioned as political chief, entrepreneur, media mogul, industrialist, and master of the revels. New Theater lost any sense of having a center, of having any propulsive momentum; those who reached out to grasp it came up with empty hands. The internal conflicts that had so raged between opposing visions of art and contrasting systems of thought ran out of steam, now pacified into a tendency toward accommodation, not only toward artistic rivals but toward the cultural institutions of the state. The anthropological principal of interculturalism became a rationalizing instrument of globalization. The vexed question of the relationship between theater and literature continued, but at a lower boil. Some spoke of a return to the theater of poetry; others went so far as to advocate the creation of a National Theater. Franco Quadri, a theater and cultural critic a half-generation younger than Bartolucci, took particular interest in a constellation of new companies from the region of Emilia Romagna, including Fanny & Alexander, Masque Teatro, Motus, and Teatrino Clandestino.[23] This region had distinguished itself for the capacity of its cultural institutions to develop and sustain theatrical initiatives of diverse types. There were permanent centers, such as Ravenna's Teatro delle Albe and Leo de Berardinis's site in Bologna; emerging and consolidated ensembles, such as Teatro Valdoca and Socìetas Raffaello Sanzio; and festivals, including the Santarcangelo Festival, Crisalide, and Bertinoro, where companies shared work and came into contact with international developments.

Two of the founders of Motus [FOCUS], Daniela Niccolò and Enrico Casagrande, asked themselves what remained for theater practitioners in the new era.[24] In the absence of a unifying and identifiable characteristic, theater in the Nineties struggled for recognition, standing outside the familiar classifications in terms of movements, aesthetics, and ideology. In one direction there was a pull toward isolation, according to which doing theater was regarded as thoroughly solitary subjectivity, but an impulse toward aggregation pulled in the opposite direction at the same time, toward a search for shared strategies of resistance. A performance series entitled *Teatri '90*, organized by critic Antonio Calbi in Milan in 1997, strove to feature the continuity between the past era of New Theater, now dead, and the young companies of Emilia Romagna. The surviving traits of the old in the new were unmistakable: the same self-reflection; the same refusal to follow mentors; the exaltation and exploitation of banality, kitsch, trash tv, and horror; and the rejection of the author in preference for anonymity, which now incarnated in the form of rave parties and the Luther Blissett hoax (a loose collection of artists who shared a single name). Niccolò and Casagrande described the scene as "impregnated with a strange, ironic lack of differentiation between the learned and the unlearned, between high philosophy and pop conformism".[25] It was only to be expected that Motus identified the internet as a model for a new aesthetic language and space, a new realm to explore as theater.

Scholar Gerardo Guccini reacted to the *Teatri '90* series by arguing that it was impossible to conceptualize the younger companies as belonging to a movement, because each was an isolated case, each an "independent microcosm".[26] But another critic, Massimo Marino, argued that the companies included in the series were all, "contaminated by the visual arts, based on extremes of the body and poetry, close to performance art, and inspired by the digital universe and that of the cyborg".[27] For his part, Franco Quadri agreed that they were "devoid of a shared discourse", but he observed that "they share a self-definition as orphans, the rejection of the fathers, who may – however unconsciously – have existed".[28] From our perspective today, if we except those whose work fell outside the theatrical circuit (for example, those who performed in social centers), we can say that the younger companies in fact tended to be born in the ripples around the slightly older companies, such as Teatro delle Albe, Teatro della Valdoca, and Socìetas Raffaello Sanzio. However various, they generally tended to oppose neo-avant-garde formalism and exalt the "liberating" promise of technology, while devaluing the aesthetic object per sè and centering their attention on the spectator.

In a text with the tone of a manifesto published in 1996 in the periodical *Patalogo*, the Motus company asked what remained to be done by groups like themselves who arrived after the sunset of the post-avant garde, who agreed neither with the demand for the total erasure of the heredity of the recent past, nor with the postmodernists who claimed that all creation is mere rehashing, citation, and recycling.

> We're immersed in a condition of continuous, unwitting, undirected transitions that carve out our perceptual and creative processes. We are the first generation that grew up under state-sponsored television filled with commercial advertising. We were stamped by Japanese cartoons and Disney documentaries, adolescents in the magnificent Eighties, who re-lived the years of protest as mere fashion revival, [. . .] with everything present but reabsorbed, sedimented, narcotic.[29]
>
> [CONTEXTS]

In such a condition, what principles could work as levers for a reaction against economic globalization and homogenization? The answer was not to be sought in the metropolis that fueled the imagination of the Eighties (syncretic, horizontal, sophisticated, and centrifugal), but in the periphery, the abandoned spaces, in distance as internal space. In reaction against the loss of centrality of the actor/character dyad, the body was to be exalted, its chains of identity unlocked. A magazine named *Virus* spread the message that,

> ever more often, artists use their bodies for images, actions, performance [. . .], so that the skin, the eyes, the hands, the legs, [. . .] become territories of meaning, terminals of de-territorialization, horizons of transit [. . .], new maps of non-identity.[30]

This vision popularized Guattari and evoked the misunderstood cyborg, with an implicit shout-out to Artaud's body without organs. The Nineties actor was to offer herself up as a robotic cyberpunk object-machine, a body reified and deformed. "It is the animal actor, the thing actor, the machine actor who exhibits the body object within a stage language that has expelled the divine, abolished the domination of the word, of logos, and thus of God".[31]

The Theaters of the Nineties, therefore, were "those who came after", seeking an aesthetic framework in which to locate themselves in literature (following Pessoa, Alda Merini, Ben Jelloun, Ballard, Samuel Beckett), in the visual arts (Marcel Duchamp, Francis Bacon, Andres Serrano, Cindy Sherman, Pipilotti Rist), and in philosophy (Foucault, Deleuze-Guattari, Baudrillard, and Virilio).

In its spectacle *Nur Mut, la passeggiata dello schizo* (Nur Mat, Schizoid on a Stroll, 1996) Masque Teatro referenced Deleuze and Guattari's *Anti-Oedipus* and cyborg culture: the actor-presences were artificial even when presented live, because technology deformed their voices and bodies, in a performance space codified more as an art installation than a traditional stage, or an enclosed setting designed to circumscribe the viewing experience and constrict the gaze of spectators. Physical obstacles (scrims, plexiglass cases, walls) separated audience from the stage, forcing viewers to resort to other senses, such as touch and hearing. In the 1999 spectacle *Eva futura*, the exchange between organism and machine created a device that constructed and animated the stage space without distinction between the mobile and the immobile, between architecture and body.[32] These were the years when the French artist Orlan subjected herself to extreme plastic surgery, documented on video, to transform her face, and Donna Haraway wrote the *Cyborg Manifesto*.[33] Cinema was present in these spectacles as a sort of collective imagination bank and as a code, using film montage to organize the live spectacle. Sound scores elaborated by a new artistic figure, the sound designer, dominated the scene in full artistic autonomy, using taped live sounds from diverse sources, such as the body, the environment, or mere noises (like the sudden gunshots in Socìetas Raffaello Sanzio's version of *Hamlet*). Sound scores were manipulated by new software and techniques such as dub, techno, and electronic sampling.

Teatrino Clandestino's *Variations on Hedda Gabler* (2000, FOCUS), established an ambiguous slippage between the actor's corporal body and its presence in digital images. Video determined the relationship between the actions of live actors, positioned far upstage, and large-scale close-ups of their faces projected onto a downstage scrim; the real was small and far away, the virtual large and close. The veil effect of the scrim separated spectators from the action, but allowed them to see through, to peer in, reaching toward the actors' real bodies. Broadcast through headphones, sound and vocalizations created a tangible, plastic acoustic space. In these *Variations*, there was no relation between literary text, gesture, action, character, and verbal emission. The splitting of the body-mind unity and the mutual exchange between live and reproduced reality sparked the recognition that the properties that constitute being alive no longer pertain exclusively to the human organism.

In Teatrino Clandestino's *Madre e Assassina* (Mother and assassin, 2004, FOCUS), the here and now of the theatrical event was entrusted to off-stage voices emitted live by the actors. Invisible, they embodied characters, noises, and words. The treatment of the voices was modeled on television, with children's voices produced by adult actors parodying cartoons. Dialogues in slang and common speech that carried the plot forward came from the world of trash TV: a journalist character blithely commented on the case of a mother who had murdered her children. In another moment, a lead character arrived in the television studio to read a letter in which he confessed to the murder while speaking directly into the "camera eye", that is, to the spectators in the theater. The spectator could not tell whether what was seen was physically present on stage (an enclosed space hung with transparent scrims onto which images were projected) or whether the images were merely pre-recorded, despite their three-dimensional appearance.[34] In these representative spectacles of the Nineties, setting, sound, technology, and spectator combined to construct the dramaturgy.

4.4 A televisual pre-theater telling true stories

A particular feature of the complex landscape of theater in this period was the marked success of television broadcasts of narrations of historical events by solo performers, a genre termed "*teatro civile*" (Civil Theater) or "*teatro di narrazione*" (Theater of Narration). The widespread reaction against ironic postmodern spectacle converged with remaining vestiges of politically militant Third Theater to spark the phenomenon of actor-author-narrators, alone on stage, who presented a sort of anti-spectacular spectacle aimed at rediscovering the frank integrity of simply telling stories, which here focused especially on true accounts of events from Italy's postwar history: the anti-fascist resistance, tales of workers' struggles, and ecological and political catastrophes. Marco Paolini, Ascanio Celestini, Marco Baliani, Laura Curino, and numerous others developed performances combining historical research with personal experience into monologues presented in theaters large and small, in piazzas, on the radio, and finally on television, with extraordinary success.[35]

The Story of Vajont, by Marco Paolini, created a sensation when broadcast on national television in 1992, recounting the national hubris that led to the building of a spectacular dam high in the Italian Alps, which triggered a landslide in 1963 that killed more than 2000 villagers in less than three minutes. In *Olivetti. The Roots of a Dream*, first presented in 1996, Laura Curino alternated between speaking in first person and embodying the voices of the mother and wife of Camillo Olivetti, who the monologue evoked as a humane industrialist who practiced a compassionate, ethical capitalism. In 1998, Marco Baliani re-lived on stage, and then in a live television broadcast set in the Roman Forum, the anguish of his unresolved feeling of complicity in the kidnapping and murder of Aldo Moro, from his perspective as a political militant living in Rome in the late Seventies. Ascanio Celestini's *Radio Clandestina* went farther back in time to reconstruct a tragic episode of the anti-fascist resistance in Rome, when a bloody partisan bombing of Nazi occupiers led to the retaliatory execution of over 300 Italian prisoners in the Fosse Ardeatine.[36]

These pieces all used direct, straightforward communication to arouse deep empathy in spectators, combining facts of great emotional impact and personal memory with a denunciation of the arrogance of power. The stories brought repressed national traumas into the light by drawing on primary sources that guaranteed authenticity and veracity: the testimony of simple bystanders, men-in-the-street, relatives, and survivors recorded in police reports, trial records, or by independent investigators. The goal of these spectacles was to reconstruct a truth buried under the manipulated versions of history distorted by media and politics. The narrators tended to speak in the name of a tenacious struggle of common people, against the efforts of those responsible for the traumas to conceal their actions.

Along with the interest of their subject matter, these solo performances appealed to audiences thanks to the style of direct address and the colloquial language of the speakers, far from the inflated rhetoric typical of much aesthetic and public discourse in Italy. The linear narration, including diverse voices, joined a sort of "just me and you" relationship set up by the performer with listeners, a reaction against the self-referential narcissism associated with much New Theater. The oral style of the narrators emphasized the spoken word, offered up not so much to counter the written word or the text, but against the dominance of the visual aspect and the use of speech for its rhythmic and musical properties, which had characterized New Theater. These performers emphasized simple familiar language and spoke as though in an informal conversational flow – although in fact many were later published in book form. The essential nature of these performances, in which acting and theatricality were reduced to a minimum, was more similar to television programming than to theatrical spectacle, in particular for the alternation they tended to feature between factual testimony and imaginative reconstruction. The narration in Ascanio Celestini's *Radio Clandestina* is punctuated by the tape-recorded voices of assembly-line workers at a Piaggio motor scooter plant in Pontedera, Tuscany, while in *Scemo di Guerra* (Shell-Shocked), the recorded voice of the author's father intervenes to recount his memories of war. The stories themselves, featuring elements of crime news and investigative reporting or counter-information, also increased the apparent synthesis of theater with television. Audiences were drawn in by the very absence of spectacular elements, the freedom from artifice and fiction; there was something about these performances that evoked memories of listening to stories as a child. The speakers shifted smoothly between character and persona, between artifice and conversation, while addressing the spectator directly. In effect, a particular mode of performance developed into a genre that borrowed certain qualities from television variety show entertainers or talk show hosts, who played on interaction with their audience.

The phenomenon of live narration flowered, in the context of contemporary aesthetics, in a moment when the confines between artistic disciplines were becoming more opaque. "Narrative theater" took shape as a reaction against a wider loss of specificity, favoring a "return to the beginnings" toward a "pre-theater", in a way similar to what was happening in cinema, where the advent of digital technology drove some filmmakers back toward the primitive technologies of pre-cinema. Fleeing from the predominance of space, authors sought to recuperate the element of time as narrative, striving to start over from the beginning. But rather than realizing the essential *opera* envisioned by Giuseppe Bartolucci, this genre tended to adopt the codes of orality practiced by mass media, with the result that this "pre-theater" had a decidedly televisual feel. In other words, theater renewed itself by "re-mediatizing" itself, mirroring itself in television, a more current medium.

4.5 Almost an epilogue

The period of great political change we have examined in this chapter began with the end of the postwar world order and was assailed by a multitude of tensions. It would be misleading to reduce the complex phenomenology of theater in this era, its creators, and the spectacles they created, into a few essential characteristics, key words, and concepts. Nevertheless, it is fair to say that artists in the Nineties were often haunted by a widespread sensation of being "posthumous", of feeling like a survivor of a catastrophe that had left the past in ruins. There was a sense of absolute singularity which, subjected to the pressures of the new world market and its media, accentuated individualism and an anxious desire to ride rapidly succeeding waves of fashion by seizing on new technologies, creating environments, mounting installations.

With the recognition that an era of theater had come to an end, the time came to clear the space of mimetic and anti-mimetic theories and start all over again from the poem, the song, the ceremonial word, and gesture. In this sense, the Nineties began and ended with the expression of a need for regeneration, a need to establish new roots. It was a "minor" expression, in that it was always overwhelmed by the louder, more imposing, more reassuring clamor of the new information technologies, the so-called "net", which heralded a cold future while evoking a warmer past – thus the interest in pre-cinema and pre-theater. The period of transition was animated by opposed drives – integration *versus* disintegration, recomposing *versus* dematerialization – which led artists to imagine new bodies composed of new, post-human materials, whether cyborg or composed of light, or sound, or elastic matter that stretched even beyond technology. The final decade of the twentieth century mobilized to overcome the prescriptions of postmodern aesthetics and to mark out a territory free of ideology, free of formal norms, from which to look out in multiple directions. Behind stood traditions to be restored, sentiments and emotions to be re-integrated, into a new way of being that all recognized as transitory, syncretistic, and revisionist.

The trilogy *A passo d'uomo* (At a Walking Pace) created by the duo Rem & Cap between 1990 and 1992 is exemplary in this respect.[37] The performing couple that had always held center stage in the company's work up to now, submitting masochistically to their invented machinations, disappeared from the scene. In their place came a group of young actors who had been trained in the company's workshops. Through the trilogy, the new actors developed a ritual aimed at re-capturing and re-founding the lost realm of theater. The first step was the building of a sacred place, a "paradisus", where drama, in the form of a fragment of Euripedes' *Alcestis*, could finally take place. The collective entity of the Chorus was to be re-established, a community that must take on the responsibility of healing the rupture between individual and society, father and son, between choral voice and solo. The first spectacle of the trilogy reconstituted the history of theater, from the Greeks to Pirandello's *Six Characters in Search of an Author*, from its origin to its final crisis. The second piece (*Leggenda*, 1990) involved the re-conquest of the territory of the story, the telling of ancient myths buried under layers of consciousness. The final piece of the trilogy (*Personaggi*, 1992) re-integrated the dispersed figure of the character in a celebratory ritual of the exit from the scene of Rem & Cap themselves. The *A passo d'uomo* trilogy posited the need for rebirth and the re-appropriation of certain fundamental essences of theater through a ceremony of initiation, in which the young actors overcame challenging perils under the guidance of the two old masters.

Notes

1 V. Valentini, "Sull'(im)possiblità di esistenza della critica", in *Bibliote Teatrale*, n. 54, aprile-giugno, Bulzoni, Rome, 2000, 11–24.

2 Cfr. Marcos, *Il nostro programma: ossimoro! La destra intellettuale e il fascismo liberale*, Sandro Ossola (trans.), *Il manifesto*, 7 agosto 2000, 5.

3 M. Belpoliti, "Design transitorio", in Id. *DoppioZero: Una mappa portatile della contemporaneità*, Einaudi, Turin, 2003, 109–113.

4 Ivi, 171.

5 Ivi, 170.

6 Ivi, 168.

7 A. Chiara Zevi, *Peripezie del dopoguerra dell'arte italiana*, Einaudi, Turin, 2005, 521.

8 Ivi, 467.

9 N. Bourriad, *Estetica relazionale*, Postmedia, Milan, 2010 (*Relational Aesthetics*, Presses du reel, Paris, 1998).

10 Interview with Bill Viola, in J. Walsh (ed.), *Bill Viola: The Passions*, Getty Publications, Los Angeles, 2003, 119.

11 Cfr. H. Foster, *The Return of the Real: The Avant-garde at the End of the Century*, MIT Press, Cambridge, MA, 1996; trans., *Il ritorno del reale: L'avanguardia alla fine del Novecento*, Postmedia Books, Milan, 2007, 128. Cfr. M. Perniola, *L'arte e la sua ombra*, Einaudi, Turin, 2000. Cfr. D. Haraway, *A Cyborg Manifesto: Science, Technology and Socialist-Feminism in the Late Twentieth Century. Simians, Cyborgs, and Women*, Routledge, New York, 1991.

12 Cfr. The anthology edited by D. Brolli, *Gioventù cannibale*, Einaudi, Turin, 1996. Cfr. Also E. Mondello, *La narrative italiana degli anni Novanta*, Meltemi Editore, Rome, 2004.

13 A. Senatore, *La danza d'amore: vent'anni di danza contemporanea in Italia*, UTET, Novara, 2007.

14 V. Valentini, "Cremaster, un monumento alla forma-merce", in A. Fasolo (ed.), *Matthew Brney, Cremaster Cycle*, Bulzoni, Rome, 2009, 11–26. Cfr. also N. Dusi and C. Saba, eds., *Matthew Barney o dell'Opera interdisciplinare: Polimorfismo, multimodalità, traduzioni*, Silvana editoriale, Cinisello Balsamo, Milan, 2011.

15 G. Bartolucci, *Testi Critici 1964–1987*, cit., 325.

16 A. Attisani, in *Le forze in campo*, cit., 105.

17 O. Ponte di Pino, *Il Nuovo Teatro italiano, 1975–1988*, cit., 28.

18 L. Argano, *La gestione dei progetti di spettacolo*, Franco Angeli, Milan, 1997; R. De Lellis, *Le regole dello spettacolo*, Bulzoni, Rome, 2009; A. Di Lascio and S. Ortolani, *Istitutzioni di diritto e legislazione dello spettacolo*, Franco Angeli, Milan, 2010; M. Gallina, *Il teatro possibile: Linee e tendenze organizzative del teatro italiano*, Franco Angeli, Milan, 2005; M. Gallina, *Orgnizzare teatro: Produzione, distribuzione, gestione nel sistema italiano*, Franco Angeli, Milan, 2001.

19 S. Chinzari and P. Ruffini, *Nuova scena italiana*, Castelvecchi, Rome, 2000.

20 Interview with M. Martinelli, in G. Guccini, *Prove di drammaturgia*, anno IV, n. 2, dicembre, 1998, 16.

21 The citation is from a brief note made by Paolo Virno in a doctoral seminar at the Università della Calabria during the 2006–2007 academic year, in the FAcoltà di Lettere e Filosofia.

22 M. Foucault, *Moi, Pierre Rivière, ayant égorgé ma mére, ma soeur et mon frère: un cas de parricide au XIX siècle*, Gallimard, Paris, 1973.

23 F. Quadri, Introduction to R. Molinari and C. Ventrucci, *Certi prototipi di teatro*, Ubulibri, Milan, 2000.

24 Cfr. Motus, "Un Manifesto", in *Il Patalogo*, n. 19, Annuario 1996 dello spettacolo, Ubulibri, Milan, 1996, 224–225.

25　Ivi, 224.

26　G. Guccini, "Teatro verso il terzo millennio: il problema della rimozione sto-riografica", *Culture teatrali*, 2/3 primavera-autunno, 2000, 12; in the same issue, see M. De Marinis, "Presentazione", 8. Cfr. also R. Molinari and C. Ventrucci, eds., *Certi prototipi di teatro: Storie, poetiche, e sogni di quattro gruppi teatrali*, Ubulibri, Milan, 2000, 16. See also O. Ponte di Pino, "Le tre onde dell'Avanguardia teatrale made in Italy", www.teatro.it

27　M. Marino, "Nuovi gruppi in scena tra orgoglio di casta e voglia di visibilità", in *Hystrio*, n. 2, aprile-giugno 1998, 23.

28　F. Quadri, "Premessa a un Prototipo", in Molinari and Ventrucci (eds.), *Certi prototipi*, cit., 9.

29　Motus, "Un Manifesto", cit., 224–225.

30　F. Alfano Miglietti, in *Il Patalogo*, n. 19, 1996, 225.

31　S. Chinzari and P. Ruffini, *Nuova scena italiana*, cit., 195.

32　A. Calbi, "Isole di disordine", in *Catalogo Teatri 90: La scena ardita dei nuovi gruppi*, Milan, 1998, 15.

33　D. Haraway, *Cyborg Manifesto*, cit.

34　V. Valentini, *Mondi, corpi, materie*, Mondadori, Milan, 2007, 76.

35　On the concept of "remediation", cfr. J. D. Bolter and R. Grusin, *Remediation. Understanding New Media*, MIT Press, Cambridge, MA, 1999.

36　For an analysis of the work of Ascanio Celestini, cfr. the essay by N. Filice, "Riti e ritmi in Fabbrica di Ascanio Celestini", *Biblioteca teatrale*, nn. 75–76, luglio-dicembre, 2005, 267–294.

37　S. Galasso, *Il teatro di Remondi e Caporossi*, Bulzoni, Rome, 1998, 402–457.

5 Liveness – play – frontality
1999–2013

The Zero Years (the first decade of the new millennium) redefined theater through dispersion, or rather, through a reset that was truly traumatic at the time", Tommaso Ottonieri has declared, adding, "This is the first generation 'born on screen', with television as second nature, the web its window on the world [. . .]; an Acquarian generation that moves as though on screen, knowing that what it sees is filtered by a series of screens.[1]

In Italy, a G8 summit meeting held in Genoa in July 2001 turned violent when the forces of order attacked protesters, resulting in the death of young Carlo Giuliani, who became a martyr for anti-globalization activists.

Internationally, the new century registered an explosive increase in terrorism on September 11, 2001, with the Al Qaeda attack on the Twin Towers of the World Trade Center in New York, killing nearly 3000 people. In reaction, the United States invaded first Afghanistan and then Iraq, after President George Bush accused the government of Saddam Hussein of possessing weapons of mass destruction – a claim that turned out to be false. With Hussein's fall, Iraq descended into a civil war between Shia and Sunni factions.

In Europe, in 2002, 12 countries in the European Union adopted the euro as a shared currency; by 2007 the EU had added ten new member nations.

On September 1, 2004, a group of Chechen terrorists seized an elementary school in Beslan, Russia: The government response resulted in the death of 394 people, including 156 children.

In Palestine, Hamas proclaimed the Second Intifada.

The disaster of the Iraq War and a major worldwide recession, following a market crash on Wall Street, led in 2008 to the election of Barack Obama as the first African American president of the United States. The "Arab Spring" began at the end of 2010, when citizen movements overturned dictatorial regimes in Tunisia, Egypt, and Libya, only to have some of the new governments fall into the hands of Islamic fundamentalists. India and China joined the community of industrialized nations, with China becoming the world's second-largest economy. Osama bin Laden, founder of Al Qaeda and driving force of the World Trade Center attacks, was located and murdered by U.S. troops in 2011.

Technological innovation in the new millennium quickly rendered obsolete inventions which had previously been regarded as cutting edge: photographic film, the cassette tape, the floppy disk, the Walkman, videotape recorders, VHS, and dot matrix printers were tossed onto the dustbin of history, replaced by thumb drives, memory cards, digital cameras, iPods, mp3 readers, laser and 3-D printers, all destined to become familiar, and soon dated technologies. Touch screens began to appear everywhere. Wikipedia, Facebook, YouTube, Flickr, and other social media centered on iPhones and similar tools arose to dominate public communication in the developed countries.

In cinema, spectacular fantasy films produced in series became worldwide sensations, including the Harry Potter saga (2001–11) based on the books for children by J.K. Rowling, and the Lord of the Rings trilogy (1997–2007), by Peter Jackson, based on J.R.R. Tolkien's novels, which won 17 Oscars. The booming film industry in India, nicknamed Bollywood, gained international notoriety, while Chinese cinema produced both popular blockbusters (*Hero*, 2002; *House of Flying Daggers*, 2004) and auteur cinema, such as the work on Wong Kar-Wai.

In Europe, outstanding films were produced by Wolfgang Becker (*Goodbye Lenin*, 2003), Florian Henckel von Donnersmarck (*The Lives of Others*, 2006), Roman Polanski, Michael Haneke, the Dardenne brothers, Pedro Almodovar, Alejandro Amenabar, Lars von Trier, Aki Kaurismaki, and Emir Kusturica.

Performance Art, until now a minority phenomenon, enjoyed a resurgence and entered the larger theatrical marketplace, featuring in particular altered re-enactments of legendary performance works of the Sixties and Seventies, or staged renderings of historical events.

5.1   Tragedy: the end is a beginning

For Italian theater, the new millennium opened with the question posed by Socìetas Raffaello Sanzio concerning tragedy: What form, if any, can tragedy take today? The 11 episodes of their epic work, *Tragedia Endogonidia* (2002–04) immersed spectators in the political and social crises of the global polis while challenging the limits of the medium of theater itself, by dematerializing and transforming the stage with pulsating light and sound that sensorially overwhelmed the viewer.

Endogonidia is a word drawn from microbiology that refers to simple living entities that contain both sexes and reproduce by means of their endocrine system. They reproduce, that is, not through an act of intercourse between two entities, but by self-division. Director Romeo Castellucci's project in *Endogonidia* has analogies with Matthew Barney's *Cremaster Cycle*, which also concentrated on moments of loss of distinction, in which a person might shift between male and female.

The *Endogonidia* cycle attempted to root the ancient form of tragedy in the new century, a project its own authors declared impossible. Life, they claimed, had lost its tragic dimension through the loss of myth, the body of stories universally known and prized by a *polis*, which theater represents in the form of the chorus. To ask what comes after tragedy by interrogating contemporary society meant, for Romeo Castellucci, to question theater's fundamental capacity for representation and its means of doing so. His point of departure was the question, "Can theater establish a contemporary mythology that interrogates vision? Can we re-invent both the visual and the verbal?" Castellucci's idea of tragedy returns us to the source of theater itself as a staged event. Jean-Luc Nancy has argued that the form of tragedy conserves within itself traces of ritual sacrifice, not as imitation but rather in its, "mode of direct discourse, discourse directed at someone".[2] After the tragic ending, after the end of religion and the *polis*, "The word seeks the lost truth, seeks the other; this is the ceremonial word – the poem and song – that restores dignity to humankind". For the contemporary world, the "tragic" no longer exists and there can no longer be "a tragedy that takes place after the sacrifice and before desolation".[3] In Nancy's view, however, the tragic today can proffer a word, an exhortation to humankind, a song of compassion for being itself and for human beings in the present catastrophe. Nancy holds that we must bid farewell to tragedy but reinvent the greatness and dignity of the human.[4]

Democracy and tragedy: One validates and confirms the existence of the other and both have the duty to put the political, the ethical, and the aesthetic to the test. Just as the philosophy of the tragic constructs its own dimension by refusing to limit itself within categories, now that we are "post-tragic", the history of tragedy suffers nostalgia both for something lost forever (the heroic, irrecoverable myths of ancient tragedy) and for the future, disconnected from our present. What can we do, therefore, but bid farewell to the tragic and seek to re-establish truth? Nancy observes that,

> tragedy appears to us as loss itself, and it is senseless to await its return or a substitute. We can recite it, but not reconstitute or reinvent it. Along with tragedy, theater itself has been vacillating and doubting itself for some time now.[5]

In *Tragedia Endogonidia*, the tragic form disconnected itself from the semantic plain in favor of expressive matter: sound was entrusted with the task of expressing the pathos of the events, including the rumbling of an earthquake and the uncoordinated, uncontrollable shaking of epileptic bodies. Sound was the element that created tension, a quivering, unbearable disturbance. Opposite sound stood silence: the tragedy of mutism and solipsism.

To establish its contemporary mythology, Socìetas Raffaello Sanzio constructed a dematerialized setting composed of light, sound, silence, and song, but devoid of words. Castellucci explained that the soundtrack displayed the tragic as an unresolvable dialectic tension between silence and voice, paradox and discourse, organic and inorganic. The stage space was composed of sounds in varied timbres that articulated the far and near through alternating frequencies and amplitude. Sound designed the space by producing a disassociation between what spectators saw and what they heard. With the stage often left empty or dark, spectators were compelled to depend upon sounds in order to orient themselves in space.[6] Most of the dramatis personae were bestowed with sparse movement, but not with speech: unintelligible communication marked *Tragedia Endogonidia*. In ancient theater, the hero was distinguished by his separation from the chorus-*polis*, as expressed in his willful silence, his crushing compulsion for isolation that distanced him from the community, which manifested itself precisely through the word expressed as tragic dialogue.

In Castellucci's cycle, even the chorus was deprived of the word, and thus lost its ability to reflect upon the action taking place around it. The chorus's collective silence mirrored that of the spectators. Stuffed rabbits were positioned in the seating area as a bitter, ironic representation of the mute chorus. *Tragedia Endogonidia* discredited the communicative function of language; rather than reaching out to the other, language was seen as turned in upon itself, directed into the body. Sound became gesture in the form of breathing, stuttering, guttural, and aspirated expirations of suffering. Low-frequency sonorities enwrapped spectators, making them aware of their own breathing, turning the audience into the interior of a body without a face, animated by non-organic respiration. Castellucci's intention was to pass through the voice in order to reach the inner voice, concealed within in the body of the spectator, whose state became the dramatic terrain of the *Tragedia Endoginidia* cycle.

The new millennium thus opened in Italy with a fundamental questioning of the form of theater itself, with *Tragedia Endoginidia* (the last work created by the company as a unified group) asking the question, "What form remains for theater in the new era?"

5.2 Project: producing intermedia

The companies we shall discuss here as exemplary of the first decade of the 2000s are Babilonia Teatri, CollettivO CineticO, gruppo nanou, Muta Imago, Pathosformel, Santasangre, and choreographer Alessandro Sciarroni. The work of these and other artists was described and analyzed in a proliferation of periodicals such as *Teatro e Critica*, *Artribune*, *Alfabeta2*, *Culture teatrali*, and *ateatro*. Many of the new groups came to theater from varied backgrounds in the arts, including visual arts, such as graphics, video art, and set design, but also sound art, architecture, and photography. Their diverse formation can be taken to demonstrate Richard Schechner's concept of "adopted culture", arising from the postmodern crisis of identity, and turning away from the avant-garde models of the previous era, such as Artaud, Grotowski, Brook, Kantor, and Barba. The work of the new companies avoided declarative manifestoes or defined poetics, and numerous productions, such as Santasangre's *Framerate 0* [2009, FOCUS] and *Bestiale improvviso* (2010), Pathosformel's *An Afternoon Love* [2011, FOCUS], or gruppo nanous's *Sport* (2011), drove critics to ask whether what they were watching was theater at all or rather some form of contemporary art.

Our discussion of these companies will suggest certain unifying themes but makes no claim to fix the character of the theater of the first decade of the new millennium. What follows instead intends to provide pathways for investigation.

The "project" serves as an organizing framework for the production process of these groups, which permits open-ended experimentation while also creating a format adaptable to the demands of the theatrical market. The project, rather than the spectacle, became the framing concept for works self-identified as "studies" or as a "trilogy", meaning a line of inquiry elaborated in a sequence of phases. Additional formats, however, were the performance, gallery and trans-media installations, musical productions, DJ sets, site specific works, and video. An example of such work was the 2013 KING project by Strasse, which included a cycle of "laboratories" entitled *Camminare nella frana* [Walking in the Landslide], which analyzed the relationship between bodies and landscape through a constellation of events including writing, video, sound works, and a website-depository (www.casastrasse.org/produzioni/archivio). The phenomenon of contamination of genres depended both on artistic motivations and the multi-faceted composition of the active groups, as well as on the economic fact that sponsors reflected different interests and offered different types of spaces where work could be realized. The members of the Santasangre company came from varied backgrounds, including live performance, video art, body art, and electronic music. The collective's first works took place in so-called underground settings, such as rave parties. *Sei Gradi* [Six Degrees, 2008), the final event of their *Studies for an Apocalyptic Theater* project, was presented not only in a circuit of theaters, but in electronic music festivals and contemporary art galleries.

5.3 Dramaturgies of diffuse bodies

The historic avant-gardes from Craig to Eisenstein had conceived of spectacles as an organic machine in which diverse expressive materials were remodeled in movement, rather than depending solely on the action of the actor or the demands of a written text. The neo-avant-gardes liberated theater from its traditional hierarchies (such as the literary text interpreted by the actor) and added new codes to the predominant linguistic one, including light, sound, space, and image. With the passing of the era of the neo-avant-garde, a significant element in the theater of the new millennium developed a "dramaturgy of diffuse bodies" without setting hierarchies between the organic and the inorganic or between the real and the virtual. The performer and the objects used in performance had equal status with sound and visual elements. New technologies produced a tangible "liveness", as in seminal pieces by Studio Azzurro and Giorgio Barberio Corsetti [FOCUS] in which there was no distinction between the human body, the sound body, and the chromatic-luminous body.

In *Wer möchte wohl Kaspar Hauser sein?* (Studio Azzurro, 2000), darkness was the abode of the wild-child Kaspar, illuminated in his dungeon only by phosphorescent flashes, until the world burst in on his isolation in the form of light. A feather twirled in the air, colored figures took shape, and Kaspar discovered colors, tastes, smells. The boy raised in utter isolation, without language, was suddenly blasted not only by images, but by a choreography of light, luminous chromatics that transported spectators into a dimension of the mind. The sound space enveloped the viewer, intensifying the sensation of collectivity and magnifying total sensorial perception over the merely optical. Images became more than merely visual, accumulating concreteness and density, occupying space through the dislocation of the sources of emission of the sound.

Scholar Enrico Pitozzi dedicated an issue of *Culture Teatrali* to this phenomenon, entitled "On Presence", which he explained in this way:

> The concept of presence can no longer be reduced exclusively to the body of the performer on stage, but must be enlarged to include objective presences – figures composed of sound and light found both in performance spaces and installations [. . .], no presence is privileged over any other; they are expressed in infinite degrees, conceived according to scales of diverse intensity.[7]

As a demonstration of his thesis, Pitozzi referenced the presence of chromatic, luminous figures in the 2004 "Marseilles" episode of the 11-part *Tragedia Endogonidia*:

> Colors and forms follow one another across the screen like sliding magma in a process of continuous transformation of the form of time [. . .]; chromatic materials are re-worked to offer up dynamic forms and architectures of light, objective presences that appear as splashes of color, shadows, masses of organic substances that brush against one another, collide and explode.[8]

The new theater of the 2000s also fabricated simple manual and mechanical devices. The previous decade's emphasis on new technologies gave way to a more fluid combination of the digital with the artisanal and mechanical.

The first spectacles by Pathosformel presented bodies mixed together with machines. In their 2007 piece, *La timidezze delle ossa* (The Timidity of

Bones), the bodies of the performers were hidden behind a white screen made of PVC, like a movie screen, upon which their bodies impressed shapes in relief, in a ghostly play of appearance and disappearance, revealing bones, breasts, bottoms, and abdomens, presence both exposed and negated. In their 2003 spectacle, *La più piccola distanza* (The Shortest Distance – FOCUS), the machine aspect was expressed still more radically: The stage space was entirely occupied with a sequenced movement of colored squares. Behind the scenes, performers worked a pulley mechanism that shifted the position of the squares along six tracks, each independent of the others. In *La prima periferia* (The First Periphery, 2010 – FOCUS), three human-sized manikins, made by the group after months of anatomical study, were composed of yellow ochre metallic bands wrapped around a vertebral column of detachable tubes, constituting a curving science fiction skeleton. The spectacle centered on the osmosis between the animate and mechanical, between human figure and object, granting sentiments and emotions to plastic, luminous, chromatic, and sound material. The organically human disappeared, as attention focused on the humanity attributed to mechanical parts. No one element was subordinate to any other; the sound designer became a live performer, elaborating and varying the sounds produced by the mechanical bodies on stage.

5.4 Reality trend and pop

Under the heading "Reality (television)", Wikipedia defines the term as a particular genre of television series, without a written script, that features melodramatic situations derived from real events, happening not to actors but to regular people. The Wikipedia entry adds that the genre, although born in 1948 with the series "Candid Camera", exploded between 1999 and 2000 with "Survivor" and "Big Brother", serials based on the formula of a game whose winner receives a prize.[9]

In Italy, Pippo Delbono's 1997 spectacle *Barboni* (Derelicts), brought marginalized people on stage, including a man named Bobò, who suffered from brain damage; Armando, a cripple affected with Down's Syndrome; and Nelson, an Italian-American derelict. This "here-and-now non-spectacle" featured a collage of autobiographical statements, such as from Che Guevara, and mystical texts from Ecclesiastes, such as "There is a time to be born and a time to die", offered up in the style of television advertising. Bringing non-actors onto the stage to tell their own stories is a significant feature of theater in the new century. In *Sogni* (Dreams, 2012), choreographer Virgilio Sereni used people from the town of Santarcangelo as part of his "research into the art of the gesture conducted with non-professionals, finding beauty in the power regular people express in the performance of simple actions".[10]

Pinocchio, the 2013 spectacle by Babilonia Teatri, used non-actors and their colloquial speech (reminiscent of reality television) who responded to off-stage questions posed to them. Three men who had recovered from comas after car accidents entered the stage one at a time, half-dressed, stating the essential facts of their name, date, and place of birth, and then proceeded to recount their traumas by answering questions from the off-stage director. The political connotations of the spectacle were implicit in the conviction that the appearance of a person as herself would increase the sense of identification and participation on the part of spectators, as though one of their own had become a lead character in a drama.

Another spectacle by the same company, *Made in Italy* (2007),

> brought on stage, to be exhibited and unmasked, that hypocritical mixture of unfettered consumerism, racism, mortification of the flesh and spirit, quizzes and idiotic announcements, repulsive and ridiculous advertising, nationalism expressed as soccer fandom ('Champions of the World! Champions of the World!') that characterizes Italy at the beginning of this new century [. . .]. Shreds of phrases and expressions are extracted from the flood of communication we are immersed and drowned in, and organized in lists according to themes or keywords. The communication is 'impersonal', 'objective', a cut-and-paste of banality and trite expressions, with occasional gaps of emptiness and waves of hypocrisy: mass media background noise (newspapers and television news) balled together and amplified by 'the people' in their café chatter, on the bus and the train, ever less distinguishable from the shouted vulgarity of certain dailies and weeklies.[11]

The intromission of documentary reality (so termed by Maurizio Ferraris) into new theater in the 2000s also took place in literature. Critic Gianluigi Simonetti observed about Walter Siti's novel *Il contagio* (The contagion) that,

> Not only does *Il contagio* take place entirely on the outskirts of Rome, but the choral structure of the text makes the low-class outer neighborhoods into the novel's protagonist as well as its setting: a dense crowd of simple people, plebeian voices and stories in counterpoint to the single, omnipresent hero we were accustomed to [. . .]. The false mask of autobiography is supplanted by that of social reportage. . . . *Il contagio* depends heavily on the power of documentary, the exact reconstruction of places and situations, and on the multiplication of the labor of narration.[12]

Simonetti attributed this "mimetic" vocation to the influence of mass media: "*Il contagio* pursues the aesthetic of audiovisual flow", comparable to the 2011 television series *Residence Bastoggi*, a "documentary soap opera" filmed in project houses on the periphery of Rome, where the two directors, Claudio Canepari and Maurizio Iannelli, had moved for three months of shooting, together with their crew.

We can ascribe the avant-garde "reality trend" in part to the international influence of popular television, resulting in a pop flavor – using fashion, music, comic books, and web references – in many of the spectacles regarded as typical of the period. In his study, *The Return of the Real*, Hal Foster invited us to reconsider the presence of realist elements in avant-garde movements, despite the avant-garde's tendency to scorn naturalistic evocation.[13] Writing about Andy Warhol's series, *Death in America*, Roland Barthes wrote: "The object of Pop Art [. . .] is neither metaphorical nor metonymic. It offers itself shorn of what came before and what surrounds it".[14] A pop imaginary entered new theater in this era in the form of manga, comics, graphic novels, animated cartoons, commercial song and films, advertising, and soccer. In Babilonia Teatri's 2011 spectacle, the title *The End* comes from the famous song by the Doors. According to Oliviero Ponte di Pino,

> jingles and fragments of live television are inserted as counterpoint or highlights and handled ironically. A jingle can begin with an actor solemnly intoning the first verse of the reprise ("From the skin to the heart"). The live television broadcast of Pavarotti's funeral can be ironically censored with the insertion of a beep whenever the deceased tenor's name is mentioned. . . . The playlist of *Made in Italy* includes hit songs like "Acid acida" by the group Prozac+, "Alzati la gonna" (Raise your Skirt) by Vasco Rossi, "Io sto bene io sto male" (I'm fine, I'm not) by CCCP and the inevitable "Italiano" by Toto Cutugno.[15]

Enrico Castellani, founder with Valeria Raimondi of the Babilonia Teatri company, described their work this way:

> In our spectacles we often use images that everyone knows. A series of windows open up in viewers that include their own life experience. It's as though the spectator has to bring herself into the collective memory we draw from. This generates a personal reflection about what is seen on stage. The same thing happens with music. We use familiar music because we know everyone connects that song to a personal memory. In that sense I go back to the concept of pop, which is not really functional to the spectacle, but creates a sense of shared experience that concerns us collectively, and frees us from the position of having to teach something or give a message to the audience. It creates a real sharing between the stage and the audience.[16]

In *XD. Scritture retiniche sull'oscenità dei denti* (XD. Retinal Writings on the Obscenity of Teeth), by CollettivO CineticO, 2010, the nude bodies of the performers become surfaces

> upon which emerge, in gaudy colors, the trademarks of Marvel superheroes, *Kill Bill*-style Adidas workout clothes, or Japanese manga [. . .].

Francesca Pennini dances with 3D glasses inside her own cartoon frame [. . .]. A naked Spiderman continuously opens and closes his hands as though wanting to spin out his web [. . .]. Superman, also naked except for his red cape, throws himself into the air, held up by two other performers, while children's toys are used to alter voices and create effects typical of animated cartoons [. . .]. Stylized geishas appear in rectangular frames outlined with adhesive tape.[17]

5.5   Narrating by elision and detail

Many spectacles of the period ambivalently combined the need to tell a story with the wish to transcend narrative linearity and the wish to reference great works of literature (Shakespeare, Nabokov, Proust, etc.), with the desire to empty them out. The theater of the Eighties, having recognized the failure of the postmodern paradigm of the end of history and the grand narrations, had attempted to recuperate time and story, re-establishing the relationship of actors and directors with literature and the figure of the author. In Federico Tiezzi's trilogy created with Magazzini Criminali, *Perdita di Memoria* (Loss of Memory, 1984–85), Jean Genet and Antonin Artaud were incarnated by the actor Sandro Lombardi, who appeared possessed by the mythical power these figures exercised in his imagination. In the spectacles of the 2000s, on the other hand, the literary source is little more than an evocative title, a bare outline for the exercises performed by the aspiring Hamlets, for example, in the spectacle of that title by the CollectivO CineticO [2014, FOCUS]. The dismantling of narrative linearity – an obligatory criterion for Italian new theater spectacles since the Seventies – presented itself now as a duty, a program assimilated as an aesthetic norm. Choreographer, dancer, and director Alessandro Sciarroni's productions resort to literary sources as a mere envelope or title to provoke ideas. In *Your girl* [2007 FOCUS], Sciarroni turned canons inside out, mixing the plot of *Madame Bovary* with Giovanni Giudici's poem, "Bovary c'est moi". The choreographer's unconventional fantasy destroyed the frames separating everyday reality from the unusual and the remote, drawing with equal freedom upon the realms of biology, biography, sport, juggling, folklore, and media-soaked society.[18]

In the first decade of the twenty-first century, utopian and visionary stories of the recent past became micro-narrations of forgotten biographical episodes crucial to the construction of the artist's identity. In *Lev*, the 2008 spectacle by Muta Imago, Alexander Luria's report on a Russian soldier who lost his memory during war was staged without temporal or causal nexus, in a score composed of images, bodies in movement, and sound.

The narrative modality proposed in the 2008–11 trilogy by gruppo nanou, *Motel* [FOCUS], recalled the approach of some contemporary literature (works by Abraham Yehoshua, for example) and the audiovisual art of Bill Viola (such as "Observance", 2002). The story was elided, replaced by details: the event itself, with the circumstances that motivated what spectators witness, was removed. Temporal and cause-and-effect relations were avoided; what was supposed to be shown was instead concealed, leaving behind details and objects. Connecting lines were left to be recomposed, headless figures appeared, and action was a simple reverberation of events taking place elsewhere, leaving the performers as observers rather than actors.[19] The space of *Motel* reconstructed a place that generated isolation, turned characters into mere figures, their connection to place mysterious. "The quality of the objects that appear on stage indicate the wish to construct a universe made of recognizable signs, working through a careful selection of details: that couch, that glass, that fabric".[20] This emphasis on objects simultaneously undermined the objectivity that material objects usually enjoy, left the motivating action off stage, and compelled viewers to observe what remained: an intimate but disturbing everyday-ness. The spectacle was built up not so much of fragments, as in postmodern aesthetics, but on details that became a plastic composition, a new unity of meaning unclassifiable in the familiar terms of theater. Fabio Sajiz's light design and Roberto Rettura's sound score referenced not only cinema, but also the painting of Edward Hopper and Gregory Crewsdon's photography.

5.6 Play – event – scene

Play is a free but a serious activity, in that it has specific rules. It is a social activity, but one with no utilitarian purpose. Richard Schechner has argued that play is an organizing principle of performance, a factor that renders performance comprehensible. At the same time, play has links with ritual behavior and with the hunt, a theatrical, dramatic activity that requires group strategies of attack and seizure of the prey, an activity both cooperative and competitive.[21] The tools and procedures that CollettivO CineticO applied to the development of a play-based performance practice formed a systemic interaction of conceptual maps, varied types of games, and random action.

The first section of the company's 2012 spectacle entitled <*age*> [FOCUS] consisted of descriptions of adolescents: "examples taller than 1 meter 80 cm", "cynical examples", "examples who have kissed a boy", "trained examples". If the adolescent performers, chosen through a complex procedure, recognized themselves in the stated description, they would rise to their feet and stand before the audience for a few seconds, until Angelo Pedroni, the onstage figure who established the game's rules, would sound a gong to signal the performers to sit down again. The second section united descriptions with analogous performances: the "vain examples" were directed to act out "rotating behavior", while the "aggressive examples" were commanded to execute "jumping behavior", and so on. Section Three brought all nine adolescents together to perform choreographed actions. To enact "intimidating behavior", for example, they stood in single file waving their arms in a circular motion, suggesting the defensive behavior of a hedgehog.

In response to the call "competition", they played a sort of game of tag, where those who were touched were eliminated. To enact "mimetic behavior", they entered the audience and sat down in empty seats. In each section, the actions continued until the gong signaled the beginning of the next action. <age> was structured like a game in which victory goes not to an individual, but to the whole group. Chance and surprise kept the performers continuously on their toes, awaiting orders. Spectators became more and more curious to guess which of the adolescents would be associated with the exemplary characteristics announced. <age> constructed an unpredictable plot of actions made from the gestures and actions carried out by the teens in response to orders. "From a technical point of view", director Francesca Pennini explained,

> the tempo is marked by Angelo Pedroni. He is the on-stage referee who determines the length of the actions in response to what happens, the attention of spectators, and how the actions take place as the spectacle unfolds. The fact that he sets the tempo amplifies the tension in the performers: they risk everything because they have no margin of choice within the system of rules.[22]

The presence of the "demiurge" function, as enacted here by Angelo Pedroni and his gong, whether visible on stage or audible from off-stage, is no longer in the manner of Tadeusz Kantor, the legendary avant-garde director who would appear on stage together with his actors during performances, walking among them and guiding them like an orchestra conductor. Rather, the new method is more similar to that of a wizard breathing life into inanimate presences, as in Babilonia Teatri's *Pinocchio*. In Alessandro Sciarroni's *Lucky Star*, of 2010, the demiurge director works like a sculptor who shapes the elastic bodies of his identical-twin performers until they assume the shape he wants.

CollettivO CineticO's *Amleto* (Hamlet) also worked on the principle of a collective game. In this one, spectators were called upon to choose who to designate Hamlet until the next performance. Performers competed with physical exercises, improvisation, and recitation, with a finale in which audience applause would choose the winner.

> Actors, professionals, dilettantes, passersby, timid intellectuals, directors, hairdressers, exhibitionists, dancers, bored insurance salesmen, last-minute substitutes, critics, the virtuous and unlucky, all compete to play the spectacle's leading role. Real candidates who don't know what will happen on stage. Their only reference point is an instruction manual sent out two weeks before the performance. Each candidate prepares alone, and as soon as they arrive at the theater they are ordered onto the stage. Guided by a disembodied off-stage voice and aided by mute assistants, the candidates compete in a series of tests

that synthesize the formal principles of Shakespeare's play. Left alone with only the instructions and their skills to guide them, they all find themselves *per excellence* in the situation of Shakespeare's Hamlet. Suspended between desolation and entertainment, the spectators at each performance elect the winner, the sole survivor among the bodies and remains of adversaries left on the ground, victims of irony and tragedy.[23]

In his classic study, *Homo ludens*, Johan Huizinga argued that, "Play is above all a free action. Commanded play is no longer play". But the relation between liberty and constraint is ambiguous, because the child and the animal play for pleasure, out of natural instinct, and thus develop their psychophysical faculties, while for the adult, "play is superfluous. Play is no longer 'ordinary' or 'real' life".[24] This dimension outside of daily life makes play similar to the theatrical event, another game played with extreme seriousness.

With its staged play on Hamlet, CollettivO CineticO configured new frames and contexts that created a performance event liberated from dramatic tradition; unprejudiced, free of ideological accretions (in the sense that it was disinterested in tearing down traditions, past masters, and conventions). The essential element was the live encounter of the sharing of a task: the emphasis was on the event, a mechanism that favored the unexpected and unpredictable. Silvana Borutti has made a pertinent observation concerning the "here and now" of the role of the spectator in the interactive installations of Studio Azzurro, stating that the need for presence – the direct action of the spectator – becomes an element that cannot be symbolized; it is a "liveness" that has less to do with theatrical representation and more with ritual, especially the aspect of shared experience: "contemporary art makes itself present to compel (participants) to feel [. . .]. The artwork becomes its own execution, an action in the present moment".[25]

Many of these groups choose theater – rather than the spectacle – as a performance paradigm, because theater is a place for liveness, where presences come into play, including that of the spectator, and not necessarily that of the actor. Theater is a place for purposeless physical effort, like a sport without competition, involving the acceptance of rules to be carried out seriously and with discipline. From this perspective, the reality trend converged with liveness to shape theater in the 2000s. There was less representation and more play, an occasion for sharing "here and now".

5.7 Engaging the spectator frontally

The need to leave the stage, to appear "without script, with plain people in front of other people who are there to watch", as expressed by Codice Ivan in *Pink, Me & the Roses* (2009), and as seen in *The End* by Babilonia Teatri, takes shape in the cutting away of the conventions of stage conduct.

In the digital era, with its interactivity and social networks, theater has surpassed the confines between public and private space. It has even surpassed the meta-theatrical dimension, the tendency of theater to "stage itself", to analyze, self-reflexively, its own conventions, by inserting actions that shatter stage illusion. Meta-theatrical approaches reveal the fictional, conventional character of theatrical representation through a process of doubling, a back-and-forth shifting between convention and its often ironic reflection. All the elements that compose stage action are based on convention, including the role of spectators, who can now be directly engaged and summoned to serve as witness and accomplice, sharing the same space as the actors. A defining characteristic of the meta-theatrical is the condition of liminality, the threshold state between two dimensions, the stage and the meta-stage: neither can exist without the other, while together they reinforce the representation, re-establishing the framework that sets it off from surrounding reality. This condition, little analyzed in a theatrical context, becomes deactivated in the new century, because the threshold between the opposite axes is removed. Instead, actors and performers relate directly to the spectators, engaging them frontally, an act that implies both the abandonment of the game of representation and the back-and-forth movement between stage behavior and its meta-theatrical reflection. Engaging the spectator is prohibited in the conventions of classic cinema but permitted in television, where communication pretends to be direct, so as to break through the frame of the monitor in an effort to attract viewers.

In the later twentieth century, in both theater and visual art, the neo-avant-gardes considered the linearity and verticality of single-point perspective to be a paralyzing, coercive aesthetic and conceptual trap. In its place, they imposed the concept of environment, as expressed in the horizontality of minimalism, Land Art, and certain video installations. For theater, the crisis of perspective space was announced by Richard Schechner in his *Six Axioms for Environmental Theater*, and put into practice in Europe and the United States with simultaneous actions and multiple viewpoints.[26]

How, then, are we to interpret the new century's impulse toward direct engagement of the spectator in a two-dimensional space without scenic elaboration, with a single-axis rapport between performer and spectator? The change undoubtedly arises from impatience with the conventions regulating theatrical representation, and conversely, from a wish for empathic, unmediated contact with the viewer.

One possible explanation for this change might be found in myth. The Gorgon Medusa exists as a mobile object between one term and its opposite, incapable of indicating a direction; she represents what is instable and incomprehensible. Thus she paralyzes whoever looks at her: "Staring at the Gorgon means losing one's own eyesight into her eyes, transforming into blind, opaque stone".[27] By forcefully imposing the frontal dimension, the theater of the new millennium stigmatized the destructive and paralyzing "Gorgon-stage" of the late twentieth century, which had disoriented the spectator because it was devoid of directionality.

For the New Theater, just as for the visual arts of the later twentieth century, central perspective, linearity, and verticality were considered coercive dimensions for the spectator, to be counteracted and substituted by minimalist horizontality, the kind of orientation toward process found in video installations, simultaneous actions, and multiple viewpoints. The goal was to safeguard the imaginative, cognitive, and emotional resources of the spectator, rejecting both the narrow vision of Plato's image of the cave, where enchained prisoners could see only what was directly before them, and the disorienting vision of the Gorgon.

Notes

1 A. Cortellessa, ed., *L'Illuminista: Narratori degli anni Zero*, Pontesisto, Rome, 2011, pp. 51–51. The citation refers to *Un po' di"latte" a rappresentare I nuovi linguaggi*, "carta", December 13–19, 2001 (republished in *L'Illuminista*, 237).

2 J. L. Nancy, *Corpo teatro*, Cronopio, Naples, 2010, p. 63. J. L. Nancy, "Humanidades", *Corps-théâtre*, n. 57, Editora Universidade de Brasilia, 2010 – French original in *collettivo* n. 330.

3 Ivi, 57.

4 Ibidem.

5 J. L. Nancy, *Corpo teatro*, cit., 48.

6 C. Reggio, "Ipotesi di un ascolto tragico: La Tragedia Endogonidia della Societas Raffaello Sanzio", in V. Valentini (ed.), *Dammaturgie sonore*, Bulzoni, Rome, 2012, 315–340.

7 E. Pitozzi, "Figurazioni: uno studio sulle gradazioni di presenza", in Id. (ed.), *On Presence*, "Cultural teatrali", n. 21, 2012, 107–108.

8 E. Pitozzi, cit., 121.

9 See M. Ferraris, *Il manifesto del nuovo realismo*, Laterza, Rome-Bari, 2011, and https://nuovorealismo.wordpress.com/rassegna/2011-2/); and M. Ferraris, *Documentalità: Perché è necessario lasciar trace*, Laterza, Rome-Bari, 2009.

10 Program of the Santarcangelo Festival, Coedizioni Santarcangelo dei Teatri-Maggioli editore, 2012, 38.

11 O. Ponte di Pino, *Un teatro divertente per un paese disperato: Made in Italy: Popster e Pornobboy* by Babilonia Teatri, in "ateatro" (www.ateatro.it) and on the company's website: www.babiloniateatri.it/sudinoi/

12 G. Simonetti, *Romanzo e morale: Una discussion su 'Resistere non serve a niente' di Walter Siti*, www.leparoleelecose.it/?p=11253

13 H. Foster, *Il ritorno del reale: L'avanguardia alla fine del Novecento*, Postmedia Books, Milan, 2006 (*The Return of the Real: The Avant-garde at the End of the Century*, MIT Press, Cambridge, MA, 1996).

14 R. Barthes, *Miti d'oggi*, Einaudi, Turin, 1974, p. 198; *Mythologies*, Editions du Seuil, Paris, 1957.

15 O. Ponte di Pino, *Un teatro divertente per un paese disperato*, cit.

16 Cfr. www.gruppoacusma.com/art/t-74-categoria-interviste-ini-P/conversazione-di-mauro-petruzziello-e-enrico-castellani-babilonia-teatri.html

17 Cfr. M. Antonaci, www.teatroecritica.net/2010/12/collettivo-cinetico-riflessioni-coreografiche-fra-denti-osceni-ed-immaginario-pop/

18 Cfr. A. Sciarroni in G. Graziani, "Quaderni del Teatro di Roma", n. 8 October 2012, in https://grazianograziani.wordpress.com/2012/09/20/your-girl-alessandro-sciarroni-tra-fisicità-e-sentimento/

19 M. Antonaci, *Si chiudono le porte del Motel di gruppo nanou a Drodesera*, "Artribune", August 26, 2011, www.artribune.com/2011/08/si-chiudono-le-porte-del-motel-di-gruppo-nanou-a-drodesera/

20 Cfr. C. Pirri, *I molteplici altrove del nostro quotidiano*, AlfaDomenica, January 5, 2014, www.alfabeta2.it/2014/01/05/i-molteplici-altrove-del-nostro-quotidiano/

21 R. Schechner, "Drama, script, teatro e performance" in V. Valentini (ed.), *La Teoria della Performance 1970–1983*, Bulzoni, Rome, 1984, pp. 77–112, 109.

22 F. Pennini, "Il marchingegno performativo di *age*", interview with I. Vinella, *Artribune*, December 27, 2012, www.collettivocinetico.it/amleto.html

23 www.collettivocinetico.it/amleto.html

24 J. Huizinga, *Homo ludens*, Einaudi, Turin, 1972, 10–12. (*Homo ludens: Versuch einer bestimmung des spielementest der kultur*, Pantheon Akademische Verlagsanstalt, Amsterdam-Leipzing, 1939).

25 S. Borutti, "Divenire figura: Le immagini fra memoria, desiderio e sublime", in D. Guastini, D. Cecchi and A. Campo (eds.), *Alla fine delle cose: Contributi a una storia critica delle immagini*, Usher Arte, Florence, 2011, 213–215.

26 Cfr. R. Schechner, *Six Axioms for Environmental Theater, La cavità teatrale*, De Donato, Bari, 1968.

27 L. M. Napolitano Valditara, *Platone e le "ragioni" dell'immagine. Percorsi filosofici e deviazioni tra metafore e miti*, Vita e Pensiero, Milan, 2007, p. 105. The author compare the deceptive vision of the shade with specular and frontal vision, "face to face", noting the ambivalence between visual, specular, and frontal (85). Napolitano analyzes a passage from Euripides' *Bacchae*, in which Dionysus creates the world using the reflection in a mirror, and the myth of Narcissus. The Gorgon represents a negative frontal vision, in contrast with the myth of the androgynes in the *Symposium*: the latter represent a positive frontality because – in contrast to the prisoners in Plato's cave – they could look in all directions, but they could not see one another. "Between these opposites, nature would position that visual and cognitive capacity of man himself. This capacity, to operate, must recuperate that which was denied to the prisoners and to primitive humans: the vision, horon horonta, of the visage and the eye of the person facing us" (11). Euripides's *Helen* is proposed as an example of the possibility of knowing oneself through dialogue with others, different from us, who think differently of us than we think of ourselves.

6 Dramaturgies of the spectacle and the literary text

6.1 Continuous and discontinuous in new theater

6.1.1 The new theater tradition

In Italy, Naples represents an exemplary case of a tradition whose robust local roots – anonymous poetry, Bourbon civilization, popular theater – regenerated themselves through contacts with national and international sources of inspiration, as in the way Neapolitan playwright Eduardo De Filippo drew upon his Sicilian forebear, Luigi Pirandello, and France's Jean Genet influenced Enzo Moscato. Theater in Naples and its surrounding region of Campania exemplified a line of continuity between tradition and innovation, between the local and the global, based upon the central figure of the actor/playwright, who unified the production process around a single individual, and upon bilingualism, which grafted the city's spoken dialect onto the literary tradition of written Italian.

According to Gilles Deleuze, an innovative relationship with tradition is possible as long as the minority alternative builds itself around a majority's nucleus, which applies in our case to the theater system. Becoming minority, in Deleuze's sense, is not a steady state, but a practice of continuous variation: changing position to avoid self-formalizing, constant shifting.[1] From Artaud to Foreman, from Brecht to Wilson, from Stanislavski to Grotowski, relations of continuity do not lack fractures, but allow us to see New Theater as heir to the tradition of the historic avant-gardes. We can trace ideal itineraries connecting the works of Robert Wilson to the Surrealists, or analyze Wilson's composition in terms of the principles laid out by Eisenstein in his theory of montage. "Brecht", wrote Richard Schechner,

> paved the way for highly formal, aestheticized contemporary theater. Brecht is a precursor of Wilson, of Pina Bausch, of Richard Foreman, of Mabou Mines. These modern masters learned two things from Brecht: how to insert their own conscience between the character and the spectator, and to look toward Asia to grasp concretely how to achieve this result.[2]

It was Giuseppe Bartolucci who republished the manifestos of the Futurist movement of the early twentieth century as a first step in establishing what soon became a canonical link between the historical avant-gardes and New Theater. The new generation of creators made rich and continuous use of, and reference to, historical models, drawing in particular from the avant-gardes of the early twentieth century. Among the figures, schools or phenomena who served as direct sources of inspiration and guides, both technical and spiritual, for New Theater, a partial list must include the following: Bauhaus, Russian Constructivism, the revolutionary Russian Poets, Italian Futurism, Italian vaudeville, Schoenberg, Stravinsky, Eduardo De Filippo, Surrealism, Mayakovski, Meyerhold, Gordon Craig, Artaud, Commedia dell'Arte, and Neapolitan popular theater, along with ancient models such as Piero della Francesca and Commedia dell'Arte, and recent influences such as Lucio Fontana, Andy Warhol, and American cinema.

While in Eastern Europe there had been an uninterrupted line of teaching and transmission between the historical avant-gardes of the early twentieth century and the neo-avant-garde that emerged in the second half of the century, in Italy the transmission was less direct. Without direct contact with preceding generations, Italian New Theater mythologized and idealized key early-century founders of modern theater such as Gordon Craig, Antonin Artaud, and Meyerhold.

The rediscovery of the early avant-gardes in Italy sprang from specific practical problems confronted by New Theater creators as they took up the instruments of theatrical art. The arrival of the Living Theatre in Rome in 1965 revitalized the response to Brecht, pushing the reception of the German dramatist beyond the narrow borders of political ideology, joining his example to that of Artaud, whose *Theater and Its Double* exerted widespread influence in art and literature, well beyond the bounds of theater. The Sixties generation sought to establish a new statute of postmodern aesthetics. The Gaia Scienza company made significant use of visual art models such as De Chirico, Duchamp, Malevic, Picasso, and the Constructivists, finding in each a means to reveal the strange in the seemingly normal. Gaia Scienza constructed its own "poetic memory", inventing its own "oral tradition" from which to draw instruction. This familiar, intimate assimilation of past models provided creative energy and permitted free invention, without demanding homage to masters or requiring young artists to tear down father-figures. The historical avant-garde provided a matrix of inter-textuality, favoring the formation of an original voice, allowing young artists to hear themselves and recognize what was new in their own subjectivity. Rather than blindly accepting the idea of linear transmission between the historic and neo-avant-gardes, we need to look now at how the postwar generations invented a past composed of multiple influences that allowed them to develop autonomously.

6.1.2 *Cultures of adoption and orphancy*

"We have no family, despite our desire at times to find one. We are uncomfortable everywhere. Condemned to many loves and many farewells. The force that pushes us to search for roots of belonging, the force that keeps us away from them and the sense of lack belongs to us almost genetically, and are the salient traits of a destiny, of a life".[3]

New Theater fled from theater schools and did not privilege the culture and traditions of theater, preferring instead to find models in visual art and cinema, jazz, rock, literature, poetry, anthropology, psychoanalysis, and other sources. It was international and intercultural: Peter Brook traveled to Africa, Eugenio Barba to deep southern Italy, while Americans traveled to Europe, and Eastern European companies traveled west in search of support and sustenance.

Music, dance, and visual art came to the fore, overcoming barriers of language. This did not mean refusing to identify with an inherited culture; on the contrary, Robert Wilson found success in Europe precisely because he carried on the tradition of the American neo-avant-gardes. Grotowski fascinated spectators with the spirituality of his theater, which emerged from a culture rooted in ideas of self-sacrifice. The intercultural dimension of the theatrical culture in the Seventies meant the integration of elements extraneous to traditions and cultures of one's birth, such as Japanese theater and Balinese dance.

The epistemological rupture with concepts of continuity and spatio-temporal linearity led each company to form its own "adopted culture", choosing from a much vaster repertory of influences than what could be absorbed by the standard genealogy of Italian theater. Forming an elective tradition implies an act of choice rather than inheritance. When Marco Solari of the Gaia Scienza company was asked by Giuseppe Bartolucci about the influence of "great masters", such as Grotowski and Barba, on his spectacle *Cuori strappati* (Torn Hearts, FOCUS), he answered,

It's obvious that we have a lot of differences with Grotowski and Barba, because we are a group of individuals, of individualities. In their work, despite emphasis on the actor, there is the figure of the director [. . .]. In our case, on the other hand, there is no director, nor does the collective direct; there is no staging [. . .] because our origins are very different. Rather than being born from the theater, we are tied to the experience of performance, the visual arts, dance, or American postmodern dance. Our first works had a high degree of improvisation.[4]

In *Santa Sofia Teatro Khmer*, by Socìetas Raffaello Sanzio, in 1987, the character of Pol Pot, played by Chiara Guidi, declaims,

I hate tradition. The real is all tradition [. . .]. Believe me, there is an Other living in your place: tradition, chains of the real. Chains of evil. Chains of political power. You are no one, believe me, you are the meteor of tradition [. . .]. I hate tradition/I hate literature and any other art/Art is a temptation of the devil. Art makes us believe we are fighting against tradition/While it re-exhumes it continuously.[5]

In this spectacle, the plan of Khmer theater, the theater of Pol Pot, is precisely that of wiping out representation, destroying all images, and with them the tradition of optical realism itself. This was the plan of an iconoclastic theater, one which intended to reduce the form of theater to zero, along with history, tradition, language, and the subjectivity of the self. Thus an artist such as Yves Klein, with his *antropometrie*, appealed to Socìetas Raffaello Sanzio: he invaded a setting, the white walls of the gallery, with his own spiritual presence. Without touching paints, he emptied himself like the makers of icons once would have. The spectacle and theater were seen as real actions in present time, the only place where things really take place. The theater was the place of truth, the full instant.[6]

To profess oneself "without roots" was characteristic of the identity of the New Theater, a condition accepted "with torment and as a law that saves us". The groups constructed their own adoptive family rather than accepting the one given by nature, and within the new family, the dead continued in intimate dialogue with the living. The word "adoption" meant two things: to create an individual palimpsest of skills developed freely and experientially from a wide range of disciplines, and to simultaneously share one's artistic process with a community, through lively and intense exchange among diverse disciplines. Feeling part of a context, developing a community, being in collectives that shared the tension of striving for change, powerfully characterized the Seventies, both in Italy and internationally. But the interdependence between the movements that challenged the existing sociopolitical and artistic systems had already unraveled by halfway through the decade, replaced by the "strategy of tension" and by terrorism. In the Eighties, theaters constructed their own worlds, their own language (such as the *generalissima* proposed by Socìetas Raffaello Sanzio), independent of any larger social movement, with an isolationist attitude about their artistic practice, shorn of links with either the past or the present, "without fathers or teachers".[7]

The homologous face of the poetics of living without roots is the refusal to leave behind an inheritance through the transmission of knowledge and awareness. "My experience", Romeo Castellucci of Socìetas Raffaello Sanzio has written,

passes on nothing to the younger generations because it must not. I don't like reasoning in terms of generations, justice, or pedagogy: I have never done that, not even when I was young, when I could have complained about adults. I never did that. I only paid attention to my own work and looked out the corner of my eye at the work of others, mostly to establish my distance from it. In reality, I think it's about kidnapping awareness, knowledge and techniques, as long as this theft runs in two directions. Adopting the antonymic opposition between the two generations reduces the discourse to the stereotype of the "gap" between adults and young. I don't feel that to be true: the history of theatre is no longer one of progress; there are segments, autonomous one from another, parallel lines that will never cross. And this is because contemporary theater is being weaned away from the breast. There are no longer any schools, God forbid. And so, it happens that what seems dated is in reality two steps ahead.[8]

The many variations that manifested the genealogical relations between the historical avant-gardes of the early century and the neo-avant-gardes of the Sixties and Seventies seem to scatter and disperse during the Nineties and the first decade of the new millennium, leaving the new era with the sensation of being "posthumous".

6.1.3 *The workshop as a means of production*

"In industrialized societies both east and west, the workshop originated as a means of recreating, at least temporarily, some of the contexts and certainties that supported the small autonomous groups. It is a way of playing with reality, a method for examining behavior, re-ordering it, fragmenting it, recombining it. The workshop is a protected time/space where relations within the group can grow without being threatened by the aggressiveness of the group".

"In the workshop. A particular gestuality takes shape, special subcultures emerge. It does not belong exclusively to theatre, but can be found everywhere to some degree.

In science, this is the experimental method, the laboratory team, the research center, the forward outpost of field research".[9]

One of the first discussion sections in the Ivrea conference was entitled "Laboratory Theater and Collective Theater", with the explanation that, "research and experimentation, in their most extreme forms of individualization or collectivization, find wide justification".[10] Doing theater by adopting the production strategy of the laboratory entailed forming a group to work together and to be recognized as such by the outside world, a stable microcosm inside of which to share diverse abilities (rejecting the hierarchical criterion of the director, who lays out a spectacle that others must enact). The collective creation of the spectacle through improvisation corresponded to the method of the Living Theatre, described by Julian Beck in *The Life of the Theatre*, in which an anarchist political ideal served as the basis and ideological glue for the construction of a group culture with a shared vision both of the world and of art.

The space-time of the workshop was the production mode that characterized New Theater. Pina Bausch's TanzTheater in Wuppertal began to
compose its spectacles without a pre-established plan that the director/cho-
reographer handed to a mostly stable group of actor/dancers to carry out.
The first spectacles of Gaia Scienza, such as *La rivolta degli oggetti* (The
Revolt of the Objects, 1976) were group elaborations, in which each participant integrated the text, choosing what to do and say on stage, when
to do it, and to whom to direct their speech or action, beyond any defined
roles or pre-established sequence of actions. The movements and dramatic
trajectories of the actors were improvised, and every performance was different from any other. The spectacles of Sosta Palmizi, such as *Il cortile* (The
Courtyard, 1985) and *Tufo* (1986) were similarly composed by the group,
with each participant as much author as actor.

This method of construction, contrary to the demiurgic idea of directing
as the staging of a literary text with a fixed point of departure and a focused
destination, became widespread in New Theater between the Sixties and
the Eighties. It meant applying the experimental principle of trial and error,
opposed to the linear procedure implied in a dramatic text stamped on a
page, of which the director is the custodian and exegete. In Italy, the role of
the director coincided historically with the modernization of theater and the
single figure's function as mediator among all the elements of the spectacle.
The invention of the director served to reconcile the actor with the playwright, the text with the stage action, and to find an equilibrium between
conflicting roles both on and off stage. In contrast to the pre-existent literary text, the New Theater of the second half of the twentieth century did
not presume to impose a critical interpretation, but let itself be guided by
experimental method. Cesare Ronconi said,

> There is a basic idea, but normally on stage I never do what I think
> I want. The elements that comprise the work are already there, but they
> aren't in the right place [. . .], neither the words, nor the movements,
> nor the images. But there is a point at which everything locates its place
> [. . .]. It's all already there, I just have to listen, let myself be led by an
> exploratory instinct. This is theater: the destruction of the plan.[11]

Giorgio Barberio Corsetti was another practitioner who turned upside-
down the idea of the director who conducts the actors toward a destination
fixed in advance by the literary text. He posed the matter in these terms:

> What does directing mean? You don't direct anything. You let yourself
> be directed. A director is not someone who directs; a director listens,
> lets himself be shaped by the drama. He does not construct; he lets
> himself be mounted by the drama, even in a sexual sense, he lets him-
> self be penetrated, he lets the actors course through him, he listens to
> them. The worst thing you can think is that the director is someone who

creates. The director doesn't create anything; he lets the actors do it, he listens. He speaks not as an oracle, not as a seer, as someone who sees. A director has his hands tied, his feet tied; he is nothing but eyes and mouth, ears and skin.[12]

In the Seventies, the necessity to form groups came from the search for an identity, as individuals and as a collective, in a process that included the plurality of single individuals and the entire social context. The idea was to re-form the world starting from the person-actor and the surrounding environment of the stage. Composing a spectacle was like building a world. Connected to this practice was the diffuse idea that the functional formalization of the completed work – the spectacle as product – was considered limiting compared to the research process. Because the final product was unforeseen, it may not even need ever to be seen. Each component of the theatrical group considered him- or herself an artist who participated in a work to be composed all together, but starting from one's specific individuality. Later, in the New Theater of the Eighties, the varied skills involved in composition of the production once again separated out one from another and the various roles again became distinct.

The theorization and most convinced practice of the theater group as tribe can be definitively ascribed to Eugenio Barba, along with the demand to discover something new in human relations, something even beyond the confines of the artistic process. This theatrical-tribal group was something to be studied with the same ethnographic criteria an anthropologist might use to study Bantus in Zambia, with the goal of better understanding the mechanisms that ordered the "trade" of public performance. Barba followed in the wake of Grotowski, who believed that, "rehearsals are not only the preparation of the spectacle, but the terrain in which to discover ourselves, our possibilities, the field in which to overcome our limits".[13]

A production model based on the "project" corresponded to the concept of the group as a collective author. The project format offered the possibility of controlling the phases of the elaboration and execution of the work (which acquired, in this way, the character of a continuous process of activity) by musicians, writers, painters, and actors, all drawn to the idea of transforming the processes of art into a scientific method.

Forming a group that could share the same vision of the world and of theater, rather than hiring people to fill the roles required for each new spectacle, characterized the identity of many different kinds of Italian New Theater groups, including Leo De Berardinis and Perla Peragallo, Gaia Scienza, I Magazzini, Socìetas Raffaello Sanzio, Teatro Valdoca, Teatro delle Albe, gruppo nanou, and Teatrino Clandestino, but also companies that might at first be thought to be more traditional, such as the company of Eduardo De Filippo and the collective of Dario Fo and Franca Rame. Very often, these groups involved families, couples, and other forms of affective relations who cemented the creation of a theatrical aesthetic, especially during the years when the group was founded and took shape. Remarkably but by no means coincidentally, this defining characteristic of New Theater in the Sixties and Seventies, notwithstanding the different historical context, could not fail to recall the model of family-based Italian theater companies that had survived in Italy from the eighteenth to the mid-twentieth century.[14]

6.1.4 Scrittura scenica: new means of composing spectacles

Along with transforming the idea of theater itself, New Theater radically altered the ways in which theater was produced and the ways actor-authors, spectators, and technicians collectively and individually lived in relation to theater.

In the document "Discussion Topics for the New Theater Conference" [FOCUS], in section II, "Acquisition and Experimentation with New Stage Materials", we find a description of *scrittura scenica*,

> a type of composition for the stage in which the various elements that contribute to its actualization (dramaturgical writing, directing, acting, set design, music, lights, stage space and architecture) are redeveloped [. . .] without one element predominating over any other.[15]

The term *performance text* (a concept denoting a practice and production model widely followed in the world of theater, but lacking a fixed lexicon) signified independence from the traditional domination of the pre-existent dramatic text over all other creative elements. It meant taking texts from many different literary sources, recognizing the autonomy of the various theatrical languages and mixing them together, outside familiar hierarchies. This primarily oral dimension clashed with the standard function of the director to rationalize and universalize all the elements of production into a linear furrow determined by the literary tradition of dramatic writing. The first step in this change came during the early postwar period in Italy, with the emergence of a practice of "critical directing" that modernized the production cycle according to the principle that the task of the director was to actualize the spectacular potential of a text, although even here, the operation still consisted in interpreting a literary text. In practical terms, to realize a spectacle in this way meant exalting not so much the imaginative faculties of the director, but the figure's organizational ability to furnish new product for the theatrical market.

For the theatrical groups who identified with the Ivrea Manifesto, however, the term *performance text* indicated the new method of production which came to be identified as New Theater. Elaborated by Giuseppe Bartolucci, the concept and practice of New Theater entailed a radical change in direction: in place of the literary text, theatrical languages came to the fore. Instead of interpreting a literary text, creative production came to be modernized in light of the theories of Lukács and the post-Brechtians. Rather than depending upon ingrained habits of translation and transcription, the new spectacle should "mediate nothing, lead back to nothing; must be autonomous, alive".[16] In a spectacle devoid of established hierarchies of theatrical codes, not only must each element in a production speak its own language, but each language must be produced independently of the others, de-constructing each single code. In doing this, the neo-avant-gardes radicalized an approach found in the historic avant-gardes, such as the example of Meyerhold and the Russian Constructivists, who treated the dramatic text as not only a material, but as though it were matter, to be taken up and remodeled according to the needs and wishes of creators and their spectators. In this vein, Richard Schechner evoked the authority of John Cage and Grotowski in what he called his Sixth Axiom: "The text is not necessarily the point of departure [. . .] the text is a map marked with many roads. Whoever wants to work on it must decide where to go".[17]

Carmelo Bene was a guiding example of an author/performer who no longer presented a text (in his case, often one by Shakespeare) but rather rewrote it, completely re-inventing the stage action, eliminating characters and inserting selections taken from other authors. He explained his method in these terms: "(My) process radically opposes the stubborn dramaturgy of the a priori which refuses to understand once and for all the concept of *scrittura scenica*, a thrilling theatrical language in its self-creation (the alternation of sound-darkness-light-song-silence-music-voice-gesture-phoneme-etc.)".[18]

The theatrical practice of New Theater is rooted in this procedure. Giorgio Barberio Corsetti declared,

> I never consider the work I am doing as staging a text, but rather as *performance text*, writing on stage, in the sense that I work on texts created through a geography of bodies, a geography of movement, and a territory that has to do with myths and ancient stories. I also resort to contemporary writing, Kafka or Barker, but in this case, I also think of what I'm doing as *performance* text, which does not use only the words of the author – to which I seek to be as faithful as possible, to the point of obsession – but also other words and another language, that of the stage, which I always try to activate through all the possibilities offered by contemporary language.[19]

A correlate of *performance text* is the process of montage, which Eisenstein formulated as a binary process of decomposition and recombination that imagined the spectacle as an "organic machine". In dramatic literature, the montage process served to condense a series of episodes into a narrative framework, but in the dramaturgy of spectacle in the later twentieth century, montage was exploited for its anti-dramatic function, breaking up the linearity of the story and introducing into the dramatic moment elements widely distant in space and time, thus eliminating the opposition between static space and dynamic time. These practices became canonical in the work of Jerzy Grotowski, Eugenio Barba, Robert Wilson, and Pina Bausch.

Between the Seventies and the early Eighties, the space of the stage became a place for assembling the most heterogeneous materials, a place where objects, both material and imaginary, were torn from their familiar contexts, broken into pieces, and recomposed in a way that represented the variety and deformity of the world. Montage works by caesura, with ruptures in perceptual flow exposed to open view, highlighted by contrasts in dark and light, loud and soft, slow and fast, following an aesthetic that recalls television advertising (as seen in Falso Movimento's *Tango Glaciale*, 1982). Suddenly alternating acceleration and slow-motion contradict our habitual perception of movement, forcing us to note miniscule details and focus on time itself, observing how it functions.

The characteristics identified with New Theater were group composition without fixed roles, the workshop as a place for experimenting with languages and their contact with reality, and composition through montage. These factors developed in various ways in each of the many groups. In some, for example, montage functioned to interrupt narrative flow, while in others it dilated and stratified the layers of visual presentation, and in still others a "polyphonic" montage created dialogic exchanges among languages of light, color, sound, words, space, and actors.

From the perspective of stability and persistence in time, ruptures and crises led to change. In the mid-Eighties the distinction of roles between actor, director and writer returned, with a redefinition of the meaning of "workshop" or "laboratory". The principles of group-as-family and work-as-vocation, in the image of the Living Theatre, gave way to temporary groups that assembled for the creation of a single spectacle, and then dissolved.

We see from all this the ways Italian theater followed paths different from those of other nations, which were staging scripts by Sarah Kane, Harold Pinter, Peter Handke, Tom Stoppard, Mark Ravenhill, Juan Mayorga, and Rafael Spregelburd, among others. New Theater in Italy developed a dramaturgy of spectacle that existed outside the literary market and beyond the familiar concept of text embodied in and reproducible on paper; it never sought a writer to legitimate its dignity. At the same time, however, in several notable cases, the various theatrical languages, envisioned by New Theater as autonomous one from another, often came together in a single individual, as in the cases of Eduardo De Filippo, Dario Fo, Enzo Moscato, Franco Scaldati, and Giovanni Testori, figures in whose work playwriting and stage practice were so intimately interwoven as to be practically inseparable.

6.2 The theatrical vocation of Pier Paolo Pasolini

6.2.1 Experience

To understand Pier Paolo Pasolini's relationship to theater, it is not enough to limit ourselves to the period 1966–68 – during which he wrote his series of tragedies and the Manifesto for a New Theater – because some of his earliest writings were theatrical texts, and he continued to concern himself with theater throughout his life. During his university years in Bologna, he met leading actors and directors (such as Ermete Zacconi, Memo Benassi), read periodicals such as "Il Dramma", sketched out plans for a company, and absorbed the ideas of Bragaglia, Orazio Costa, and Enrico Fulchignoni, for whom theater was not only a pillar of humanistic culture, but an instrument of social communication. As a youth in 1938, he wrote *Gli alati* (The Winged Ones) and *La sua Gloria* (His Glory), which joined dramatic writing to poetry. Between 1943 and 1949, as a middle-school teacher in Casarsa in the far northeastern region of Friuli, for and with students he wrote and staged plays veined with themes that later become central to his art. A theatrical text of this era, written in his highly poetic interpolation of Friulan dialect, *Turcs tal Friul*, promoted the cause of regional autonomy. His incomplete play *Rappresentazione profana* (Profane Representation) attempted to give form to his experience of being fired from teaching and consequent banishment both from the communist party and the regional autonomy movement for inappropriate conduct with the minors in his care. His *Storia Interiore*, severely criticized by Italo Calvino, attempted to project the inner dimensions of the individual psyche into theatrical space. In the postwar era, he developed contacts with Giorgio Strehler, Paolo Grassi, and Giovanni Testori, artist-intellectuals for who theater served as an instrument for the moral and cultural reconstruction of Italy.

Still more essential to Pasolini as an artist was the fact that his use of the word, whether written or spoken, always entailed a fertile relationship between poetry and theater. All his poetry speaks in a distinctly rhetorical voice that a reader seems to hear as much as to read. His rarely-performed tragedies were composed in verse. For Pasolini theater was by no means a marginal practice with respect to his poetry, cinema, and critical and narrative prose, and his writing for the stage should not be dismissed as awkward and unsuccessful. On the contrary, it represents a crucial node in his overall production.

Pasolini's discovery of the theater of Brecht impacted his thought in ways that went against the current of the political-cultural context in which he found himself. For most on the left, Brecht simply represented the use of theater to advance left-wing ideology, whereas for Pasolini, the German poet-playwright pointed a way for intellectuals to confront the crisis of Marxism. Like Roland Barthes, Pasolini stood apart from the avant-garde, always preferring critical analysis to group-think. From Brecht, he learned that theatrical spectacle – hybrid, heterogeneous, and popular, like cabaret – deals simultaneously with a plurality of communicative codes. In the *Italie magique* project written for actress Laura Betti, (1964), Pasolini took up Brecht's example in a parodic key, combining cinema, theater, and marionettes.

Among the stage performers of his own era, Pasolini admired both the traditionalist Eduardo De Filippo and the transgressive Carmelo Bene, but above all Laura Betti, who he considered a phenomenon of plurilingualism. He generally eschewed professional actors and accused the leading stage directors, including Luchino Visconti and Giorgio Strehler, of academicism. He charged Strehler in particular with having "codified a sort of theatrical kitsch, a totally external modern taste, where everything is stamped with a predictable beauty, as though licked to a shine, in a way that surprises nobody".[20] The mutual dislike between Pasolini and the intellectual avant-garde poetry movement that called itself Gruppo '63 was ascribed by the group to what they called his cultural conservatism, while he accused them of excessive formalism. Pasolini saw Grotowski's *The Constant Prince* at the Spoleto Festival in 1967 and recognized its innovative force, but soon, in his *Manifesto for a New Theater*, he grouped Grotowski's Polish Theatre Lab together with Artaud and the Living Theatre as negative examples of "theater of the gesture and the scream". Pasolini's *Manifesto*, presented publicly on the occasion of the debut performance of his verse tragedy, *Orgia* (Orgy) in Turin in 1968, demonstrates the key role played by theater in the lifelong development and formulation of Pasolini's political and aesthetic theory. Rereading the text today, we cannot fail to notice the ways it anticipates not only the debates around theater that were soon to come, but also the way it identifies the unresolvable problems and contradictions that were to plague New Theater as it tried to apply theory to practice. The avant-garde's repression of Pasolini's prophetic *Manifesto* betrays the movement's fatal tendency to shun complexity in favor of the non-dialectical oppositions which were articles of faith for political theater, laboratory theater, and Third Theater in the Seventies.

6.2.2 Towards an effective theater

Pasolini's theatrical vocation cannot be enclosed within the frame of the texts he wrote for performance, and the six verse tragedies he composed in a concentrated period, conceived rather for publication rather than for staging, waited some years to come to the light. Working on the model of the Platonic dialogue, between 1966 and 1969 (the same era as his films drawn from Sophocles's *Oedipus Rex* and Euripedes's *Medea*), he wrote the plays *Calderón*, *Affabulazione*, *Pilade*, *Porcile*, *Orgia*, and *Bestia da stile*, in each of which he attempted to combine poetry with ritual. Their intended audience was more the community of highly literate artists and spectators than the general theater-going public. Although sharply opposed to Pasolini, in the same period, the avant-garde poets and writers of Gruppo '63 had also taken upon themselves the cultural task of renewing theater.

At this point, there is little to add to the discussion of Pasolini's conception of history and the world. It is important for our purposes to highlight the fact that his theater and cinema in this period arose from his effort to overcome the ideological and artistic crisis he faced concerning his poetry and narrative prose, which can be expressed essentially in the question, "Why write anymore?". Through cinema he sought wider contact with society. In theater, he theorized the reciprocity between creator and spectator, their unity in a community joined in sharing a cultural rite. At that time, there was widespread effort in the world of theater to rediscover ritual at the core of theater practice, in order to restore meaning to art and the role of the poet. In Pasolini's vision, cinema and theater become a "poetry of action", utilizing the concrete elements of reality, rather than mere signs, linguistic codes, and symbols. "One can write or read poetry simply by living", he wrote in "Res sunt nomina".[21] Theater must reinstate its authentic foundational dimension as ritual, restoring efficacy to art, with all the expression of irrational impulses and passion that true ritual encompasses.

With declarations such as these, and with the kind of aesthetic militancy expressed in his *Manifesto for a New Theater*, why then did Pasolini largely reject theater? There were two overwhelming motives. The first was his disgust for the reigning systems of Italian theater, which he excoriated in his introduction to *Bestia da stile*, the last of his six tragedies:

> Italy is a country that becomes ever more stupid and ignorant. It cultivates a rhetoric that is ever more unbearable. There is no conformism worse than that of the left, especially when the right also adopts it as its own. In this context, in which protest is the official form, Italian theater stands at the lowest level of culture. Old traditional theater is ever more nauseating. New theater – which consists of nothing but the slow rotting-away of the model of the Living Theatre (except for Carmelo Bene, autonomous and original) – has managed to become just as nauseating as traditional theater. It is the shit of the neo-avant-garde and of 1968. Yes, we're still stuck there, with the addition of the regurgitation of the slithering restoration of the ancien régime. Conformism of the left. As to the ex-fascist Dario Fo, nothing could be uglier than his playwriting. I couldn't care less about his thousands of spectators, despite their flesh and blood presence, or about his audio-visuality. All the rest, Strehler, Ronconi, and Visconti, is pure gestuality, stuff from the popular weeklies. It's natural that in a situation like this my theater can't even be perceived".[22]

The second reason Pasolini spurned theater might be found in an observation he confided to Jean Duflot: "I become ever more aware that doing theater cannot be improvisation; it's an undertaking that requires the commitment of a whole life".[23] Having set aside the project of a "Theater Forum" that would join poetry with direct political action, and having renounced any relation with the stage, his texts for theater become a purely literary exercise for him, the total opposite of his original faith in it.

The themes that Pasolini confronted in his writings for theater were virtually the same as those found in his giant unfinished novel, *Petrolio*, and in his films derived from theatrical sources, such as *Oedipus Rex*, *Teorema*,

Medea, and *Porcile*: his conviction that the advancing technological revolution was leading to regression, a new barbarism, "a new fascism", causing an anthropological mutation in Italian society. For Pasolini, a kind of cultural genocide was underway, one which would wipe out the nation's linguistic dialects and in which the writer would no longer serve any function. The cultural project born during the anti-Nazi Resistance to involve the populace actively in politics and culture had collapsed. Pasolini devoted intense thought to the problem of language in his *Manifesto* because he foresaw the process of cultural homogenization that would result from the combination of neo-capitalism with social technologies. The humanist roots of the Italian language were being cut away even as the dialects died, leading to a middle-range Italian language that eliminated regional variation in the name of national unification. Pasolini's theater was totally dedicated to rebellion against this outcome [CONTEXTS '60].

The most active characters in Pasolini's theater are the bourgeois; they are the ones who trigger abnormal situations, generated out of the conflict between bourgeois utilitarianism and the reality of the world. The reactions of the bourgeois characters are stamped by their resourcefulness, their drive to overcome limits, which renders them at once terrifyingly powerful and terribly clumsy. Facing religious crises in the absence of religious faith, they perform acts of perversion, cruelty, imbecility, and so on. The logics of rationalism, the marketplace, and power generate madness in those who cannot abide their restrictions. In *Affabulazione*, the Father follows an apparition that appears in a dream, driving his upper-middle-class life off the rails and toward suicide. The character of Rosaura in *Calderón* cannot look at the world without weeping and vomiting, as she suffers the trauma of being unable to escape the oppression of her social role, as she seeks an authentic relationship with others.

Pasolini's theater is a-dramatic, in that it is based on a pseudo-dialogic skeleton: the original impulse to write in the genre of tragedy came not from a rereading of the Greek classics but rather from Plato's Dialogues. The texts resort to excursus which deviate from a central plot, drawing in disconnected times and places. *Orgia* unfolds in flashback: A man who has committed suicide looks back over the most significant episodes in his life; his "here and now" is death, with existence confined to memory and dream. Pasolini applied the montage technique of cinema to theater, to represent actions that in conventional dramaturgy would be represented as taking place in the present. *Orgia* is a tragedy in which the protagonist, given the generic name "Uomo" (Man) hangs himself, then reconstructs the motives that led him to suicide, which consist of the unresolvable clash between respect for norms, deference to power, and the individual's essential otherness. In the final scene of *Calderón*, Rosaura recounts a dream in which she finds herself in a death camp which is liberated by workers who beat down the doors, singing and waving red flags.

The hortatory nature of Pasolini's dramaturgy comes from the urgent drive to communicate directly with the spectator. His characters are ideas whose function is to express the author's thought. Rather than developing individual voices, all the characters are the same: They are the writer speaking. Typical of this oratorical style are profuse verbalizations by a single character, which are then reinforced by the irruption onto the stage of a figure who takes the place of a classical chorus (for example, one denominated the Shade of Sophocles) who enunciates, *coram populo*, what the author thinks about theater, Italy, communism (as in *Bestia da stile*), the death camps (as in *Porcile*), the Franco dictatorship and the Inquisition (*Calderón*), or father-son conflicts (*Affabulazione*). Speaking directly to the spectator is motivated by the need to convince, to persuade, to actualize a community of exchange between the author, the actors, and the spectators – a dimension that presupposes the autobiographical element in the material and carries more an elegiac mood than a tragic one.

For Ferdinando Taviani, it was precisely its conceptual nature that decreed the failure of Pasolini's theater, making it ill-adapted to stage presentation; it was a "mental theater devoid of theatrical effects but full of visual effects and ideas".[24] In the *Manifesto*, in fact, Pasolini had written that theatrical space exists in our heads, not on the actual stage.

Scholars of Pasolini's literary production have pointed out certain structural devices that recur in his texts, and some of these are common to his theater as well: the series of oppositions, linguistic and not, that reveal the domination of the affective over the rational realm, and a mechanism of accumulation and repetition that dissolves the claim of language to logically, correctly define reality, without confusion, without enigma".[25]

But if everything is also its opposite, and if opposition derives from division of a unity, then there is no real conflict that can lead to a synthesis. These oppositions, instead, are binary, and maintain their separateness by pursuing different strategies, including the presence of the author-poet who gives voice to the individual characters. The mechanism of the self-division of the author stands at the base of Pasolini's theatrical writings, and it is this self-division that provides for the pseudo-dialogic form that impedes dramatic conflict and sets up instead a pattern of repetition, rather than a process of dramatic unfolding leading to resolution. An intimate, uncertain, self-reflective dimension and a sense of the suspension of traditional dramatic canons determine the critical judgment of the spectator of these plays. Along with the couples of opposites, Pasolini also represents the ways opposites become neutralized: the body, eros, and sex are uncontrollable, primordial forces; the instinctual sphere of fantasy clashes with the logic of reason and power, which transform eros into perversion, defusing their originary clash. Children begin by rebelling against their fathers, but then the role inverts: in *Affabulazione*, the father kills his son and returns to his "animality".

The play *Calderón* is structured by a recurrent device of dream episodes, but there is no strong distinction between waking and dreaming, just as there is no explosive rupture of realistic settings into settings representing dreams or other states of alterity, such as disease or madness. *Affabulazione* begins with a dream, but then seems to proceed like a normal bourgeois drama until the realistic structure cracks, with the entrance, first, of the Shade of Sophocles and then of a Necromancer who perceives the two simultaneous, co-existent realities of the Father. In the final scene, the Spirit of the Dead Son appears. The perverse bourgeois figure in *Orgia* begins to speak after his own death. In *Bestia da stile*, the character Jan speaks with the dead and with spirits.

The contradiction in Pasolini's conception and handling of theater, embodied in his six tragedies, is found in his wish to make theater both into a ritual and into a public forum; he wants it to be both Artaud and Brecht, the two dominant models for New Theater well into the 1970s. In the effort to restore poetry to its primordial function, the expressive materials available to theatrical spectacle come to be seen as an obstacle to reaching the critical consciousness of the spectator, which is the primary object of the theatrical experience. Pasolini wants to dialogue with the spectator in a close-up exchange, totally different from the kind of communication offered by television and mass media.

Two spirits inhabit the thought and practice of Pasolini, one self-reflective and the other not at all. His dramaturgy in fact contradicts the original motivations and objectives that led him to theater in the first place. He wanted a theater that would guarantee him a space for reality, and in particular that zone of reality impenetrable to the word, whose limits he had plumbed. By attributing to words the pragmatic force of action, he negated those margins of alterity that he so craved to embrace and comprehend, and for which he had abandoned literature for cinema and theater. Like silence itself, *phône*, the pre-logical and pre-verbal (as in Rosaura's aphasia and linguistic confusion in *Calderón*), turns out to be overrun by verbality, the traces of reality and its conflicts. His bodies are overrun by logos.

In Pasolini's theater, word and action, saying and doing, names and things, all coincide, producing characters who embody ideas and whose dominant activity is reasoning, leading to a "paradox within a paradox": "the language of bodies, so insistently announced and verbalized, is never exhibited on stage. As in ancient Athenian theater, all action takes place off-stage, far from the view of the audience, and then is summarized in omnipresent, omnipotent words".[26]

This is where his theater fails: the expressive capacity of reality, things, bodies, and the scream are all aborted: "The voices remain to speak of the flesh (distant, cursed, imperious) and of the world (lost, like Eden, or too-present, like a death camp)".[27] The theater of Pasolini therefore is not a pacified genre of literature, but a tragic disagreement that becomes suffocated by a conceptual apparatus both too sophisticated and too ingenuous. As Luca Ronconi observed,

> Pasolini's writing for the theater always requires the voice, because it follows a rhetorical path: what appears to be lyrical effusion turns out to be a rhetorical structure that presupposes vocality. By vocality, I mean the transgression of the flatness and uniformity he called for in his *Manifesto*. Summoning the voice means ambiguity, equivocation, and the possibility of misunderstanding.[28]

6.3 Testori: in the Belly of Theater

6.3.1 The word becomes flesh

Giovanni Testori (1923–93) entered the debate over the renewal of Italian theater in June, 1968. His manifesto, *Il ventre del Teatro* (The Belly of Theater, published in *Paragone*) made explicit his ethical-aesthetic vision: a theater based on the word, capable of "verbalizing the clot of existence; making flesh (as it takes shape in history) become word, to comprehend its inexplicable reasons for violence, passion, and blasphemy, and to fall again into its shadowy blind mud".[29]

In her chapter on the criticism of Testori's work in her book, *Invito alla lettura di Testori* (Invitation to Reading Testori), Annamaria Cascetta writes,

> The impossibility of reducing Testori to conventional schemes, forms, and ideological prejudices, especially with regard to his position as an oppositional catholic, have made Testori a repressed figure in Italian culture, often dismissed with vague formulas, categorized as an expressionist experimenter, or tagged hastily as maximalist, fundamentalist, or counter-reformationist.[30]

For Annamaria Cascetta, Testori's production, including theater, poetry, novels, and art criticism, has a substantial unity, because it "directly interrogates God, demanding definitive answers about the meaning of birth, evil, and death", and finds its belonging most of all in theater, where word and body, dramaturgy and liturgy coincide.[31]

Until 1973, Testori's work was staged in traditional theater spaces by established companies and directors: *Maria Brasca* was produced by the Piccolo Teatro in Milan in 1960, directed by Mario Missiroli; Luchino Visconti directed *L'Arialda* in 1961 for the Morelli-Stoppa company. In 1973, Testori founded Teatro Pierlombardo, with Franco Parenti, in an old movie theater in Milan, and debuted the following year with an adaptation of *Macbeth*, directed by Ruth Shammah. The *Scarozzanti Trilogy* consisted of *L'Ambleto* (1972), *Macbetto* (1974), and *Edipus* (1977). From his hospital bed in 1992, Testori wrote the three Lays: *Cleopatràs*, *Erodiàs*, and *Mater Strangosciàs*, published posthumously in 1994; three funeral laments. spoken by three female figures, which follow Dante's scheme of Inferno-Purgatory-Paradise.

The writer-director-actor collaboration of Testori-Shammah-Parenti continued in a vein distinct both from established prose theater and from New Theater. In *The Belly of Theater* [CONTEXTS '60], Testori wrote, "we aim for a group work process; or better, a family (with the right of each to divorce, at the right moment). By work, I mean what happens between writer, actor and director".[32]

Sandro Lombardi has stressed the similarity between Pasolini and Testori: "the two authors are only apparently distant, but in reality united by a similar artistic-historical background under the guidance of Roberto Longhi (and the shade of Gadda), as well as by an analogous, irreducible resistance to homogenization".[33] For both, the center of their poetic world is occupied by marginalized people and places, the scrubby outskirts of cities, anger, and scorn for the bourgeoisie. Testori's imagination is rooted in violence and the flesh, against an urban background populated by human refuse.

In *In Exitu*, 1988, Testori put himself on stage in the figure of the scribe, with the power of granting voice to a human being; in this case a drug addict, who is rejected by a society which he in turn rejects. This is the power of theater, to open a curtain on a stage animated only by the presence of the actor who gives a body to words, to exhibit a wound reverberating with anger, prayer, insult, and supplication, "a place that enucleates the primary questions of existence, destiny, and everything else. It is the place where the lamb's throat is cut".[34] In Pasolini, the conflict between nature and social rules defined the period of the economic boom that rapidly transformed Italy from an agricultural to an industrial nation. In Testori, instead, we live in the ruins of disordered capitalist expansion, and the ceremony of theater produces no change of state. The writer affirms his impotence and solitude; the chorus, in fact, is absent, and the only possible action is to affirm the theater that, "all my drifting comrades have betrayed, perverted, and cuckolded, but that exists and will always exist, against everyone and everything, until the end of all ends".[35]

Testori's theater-world is inhabited by degraded victims. "I think, or rather, I believe", he wrote,

> this is where Christ lives. In fact, I believe I have become aware that perhaps in the demented, in those who we consider to be deprived of speculative capacity, resides the maximum intelligence, because they are the true depositories of Christ, the poor in spirit and, with them, all who suffer for passion, for lack, for liberty, for disease . . . victims of a deaf, blind condition of life, or a society that strangles any demand for liberty, and seeks to cancel out the meaning of birth and the meaning of sin.[36]

Characters in Testori's theater do not themselves take action; instead they are recounted in a flow of words that unravel the story that evokes them.

In *Edipus* [FOCUS], the *scarozzante* (drifter) is the *dramatis persona* who brings to life the literary characters Jocasta, Laius, and Oedipus, who unfold the familiar tale. The storytelling deflects the dramatic dimension into epic and transforms the setting from a concrete location into a ghostly scene, making it impossible to distinguish the limit between thought and action, the continuous back-and-forth between actor and spectator. The theatrical space is the place of sacrifice, immolation, and purification, through the word that passes through the body of the actor and is reborn, sacred, as *verbo*.

Pirandello, Manzoni, and Shakespeare are visible presences in *Promessi sposi alla prova* (The Betrothed Put to the Test), *L'Ambletto*, and *Macbetto*, which take the form of parodies, expressing a reflection on theater conducted by the maestro-director-writer who guides the group of actors to discover the truth about theatrical art, safeguarded in the word. Both Pasolini and Testori favor a theater in which the literary text becomes flesh in the voice-body-presence of the actor, and the text absolves the function of overcoming the artificiality of "standard spoken Italian" that Pasolini so abhorred. Testori too wrote,

> the necessity of inventing a language to express certain things, events, thoughts, sensations, derives also from the fact that the Italian language, in the form in which it circulates today in daily life, in newspapers and on television, no longer serves any purpose on the stage of a theater. I want to express everything instinctual, atavistic, primitive, and degraded to the very limit of animality, in terms of dialogue, on stage. I could not make this pass through normal Italian; it would be senseless. Thus, I once said that we must have an apocalypse of words, twisting them, dismembering them, shaking them.[37]

In Testori, the plurilingualism invoked by Pasolini includes archaic and foreign expressions, borrowings from French and Latin, sacred liturgy, a mèlange in which the word becomes the actor's gesture, body, and action.

> My language is a spontaneous language that gushes out from within, almost a re-flowering of my ancestors. The words we use evoke only death; they do not tremble, do not vibrate, they arouse no sensation. But language must be physiological, must create tension between the one who speaks and the one who listens.[38]

6.3.2 Oedipus and Cleopatràs: theater's latrine

On the topic of the monologue, Carmelo Bene observed,

> The 'monologue' has always been considered the noble form of dramatic art, with 'dialogue' as its dialectical, didactic vulgarization [. . .]. The actor of illness takes care not to deprive himself of the ranting and

raving the monologue offers. The need to monologue is congenial to
him, even if in dialogue form, to restore it to the nullifying weave of its
essential delirium.[39]

In the same vein, Giovanni Testori makes a similar statement in his manifesto:

> It seems almost certain to me that the point of departure of theater
> (and therefore its point of collapse and arrival) is the character solo, the
> character in monologue. The terminal point of tragic tension and com-
> pression is not out of necessity a second character, but specifically that
> particular quality of flesh and movement (splitting, screaming, flushing
> out, yelling) within the word in theater. A movement that, because of
> its origin, becomes possible only when the interlocutor is not a created
> character but a creating force. The free monologue . . . today can do
> nothing but render more crude and visceral (pre-natal) the situation of
> a character in a determined moment of his existence.[40]

For Testori, Elizabethan theater was a model of "monologue in many
voices" and also a model of immobility, which derived from "an accumulation of motive forces" whose destination was death. In *In Exitu*, the young
drug addict Gino Riboldi gives voice to his desperation, calling upon the
scribe (Testori) to witness his agony, as he describes friendships, affections,
blasphemies, episodes of his life, slogans, and repeated phrases that explode
from the actor.

If the actor's interpretation and staging can be considered a form of critical reading that contributes to the comprehension of a theatrical text, this
assumption is particularly relevant to the texts of Giovanni Testori as performed by Sandro Lombardi and directed by Federico Tiezzi. The difficulty
of reading the written flow of Testori's texts finds here a point of access in the
vocal-gestural expression of the actor. The epic narrative density entrusts to a
single stage presence (the actor, as an absolute character) the responsibility to
bring to life the other figures who populate the literary landscape of Testori's
Edipus.[41] In this work, the varying sentiments and passions reveal themselves
through a mixture of literary speech and slang, Latin and Lombard dialect,
French, Spanish, and invented words. The grammatical and syntactic construction of the sentences comes from the prose sentence and from the rhym-
ing couplet, weaving in lyrics from pop songs and learned citations. The text
also employs poetic devices such as iteration, anaphora, chiasmus, phonetic
and rhythmic assonance, anacoluthon, and plays on words.

Oedipus, alone on stage, animates the tale cut from his memory. He is a
guitto, a poor provincial actor, who carries on verbal battles with the ghosts
of Jocasta, Laius, and the Sphynx, in an ageless Lombardy. Collapse and
the actor's solitude, his sense of the uselessness of his trade, scar the noble,
timeless rite of theater.

His is an art in decline: Oedipus is the last one to bear witness to it,
throwing out invective against those to reject theater in favor of bourgeois

consumerism (the lead actor leaves early on to play a cabaret transvestite, while the lead actress marries a lame furniture dealer). The conflict develops in the text between the mediocre actor who plays Oedipus, and the characters of Dionysos and Laius: In his solitude, Sophocles's king is a condensate of desperate rebellion, ineffective, and devoid of a future, who instinctually resists the power represented in Laius.

About this play Ferdinando Taviani wrote,

> Testori's down-at-heels actor is a double negative that does not constitute an affirmative but multiplies the negativity: he opposes the bourgeoisie but also the people, who he sees as examples of degradation that contemplates and represents itself, far from humility and any social dialectic.[42]

Sandro Lombardi's Oedipus transforms himself into Jocasta, dressing in her wedding gown, putting on her diadem, fur, and pearls, describing as he does so the actress who should have played the role. Once the transformation is complete, he sits down on the bed and speaks in the role of Jocasta, taking pleasure in her incestuous love for Oedipus ("Only now has my flesh awakened"). And as she cries for incest and reacts with horror at the vendetta of the Furies, she introduces a register both grotesque (an advertising for the Motta confectionary company) and sentimental (a pop song by Mina, "A Year of Love'). Rather than climaxing, her peroration declines into a mumble. When the actor removes the costumes of his characters, his tone becomes aggressive, bitter, angry: "On this roller coaster, I can't tell anymore if I'm Oedipus or Jocasta".

In the character of Laius, the father-king's distance from the people is expressed in Latin words, but his attempt to appear regal, dressed in papal vestments, is undermined by the actor's struggle with the prompter, who fails to whisper Laius's pompous lines on cue, forcing the actor to resort to making gestural sounds, gargling, stuttering, and playing with syllables, like a child imitating the rumble of an engine. As is typical for Testori, Lombardi's speech ranges from the pulpit to the gutter, from intimate to declamatory, between irony and poetry, sacred music, and pop songs. The Oedipal conflict, the link between virile power and otherness (in the form of a rejection of society in favor of the maternal) are all anaesthetized in favor of the actor's self-reflexive performance, which brings literary phantoms to life. In Testori's *Edipus*, these phantoms still reference a public dimension of crisis and defeat, while in his late works, it will be the private dimension of memory and loss that predominates.

6.4 Franco Scaldati: an enchanted garden where no one dies

6.4.1 *Fluid texts without genealogy: eternal becoming*

The first career of actor and writer Franco Scaldati (1943–2014) was as a tailor, a trade that Walter Benjamin allies with the art of storytelling.

Beginning in the Seventies, working primarily in Palermo, he wrote more than 60 texts for theater, performed in films, and animated the theatrical life of his city in a series of independent performance spaces. For many young people, he represented an exemplary artistic itinerary. His theater texts have still not been published in definitive edited versions, and during his life they were in a continuous state of mutation, changing every time he took them up. His work process involved a period of writing in the morning, in his tiny studio, and the choral work of staging in the evening, working with actors to give voice to his words and action, to his figures and imaginary situations in often improvised, temporary spaces. The weaving together of writing and staging shaped his composition: *Il Pozzo dei Pazzi* (The Well of the Crazies) and his recurrent characters Totò e Vicé would never have been born without the improvisational collaboration of Franco Scaldati with Gaspare Cucinella. The interdependence between solitary writing and its immediate verification through the voices and bodies of actors in space lend his texts that particular trait of seeming always in process that characterizes stage work generally. Viviana Raciti, who has closely analyzed Scaldati's work, has written, "It is very complex to talk about a completed work in Scaldati's theater because he never stopped re-touching words, shifting scenes and refining the dynamics between characters, rewriting, correcting, using White-Out".[43]

Although his production has been vast and varied, we can mark out three phases in Scaldati's career. The first goes from the late Seventies to the end of the Eighties, followed by a second, "nocturnal" period, when he abandoned dialogue and characters to feature solos in dialect by female voices recounting a truculent repertory of violence, incest, sadism, etc. The dominant components were sex and death, orgasm and agony, blood and sperm, and the actions presented a scenario of splatter combining Eros and Thanatos. Nature and lyricism disappeared. Creatures from beyond the tomb spoke of earthly life, evoking monstrous humans fighting with rats and cats over the garbage they fed on.

The third period, beginning in the early 2000s, and mostly written in Italian, returned to stories with a bittersweet quality, almost like scripts for television.

Throughout his theater, lyric and epic traits prevail over dialogue, in a way that many have erroneously associated with Beckett. In Beckett's theater, life is withdrawn, rarefied, and the threshold between the self-excluded character and the world of life cannot be crossed. In Scaldati's world, by contrast, colors, passions, tender gestures, and amorous sentiments circulate in cascades of flowers, moonlit nights, and dawns bright with stars. The beauty of nature is sensually savored, with descriptions of fragrant foods, and bodies attract one another, even though they are mutilated. Scaldati's is not a theater of fleshless bodies, even when the creatures who inhabit those bodies are ghostly beings of uncertain, multiform identity. A character named Lucio in the play of the same name, for example, is a double of Illuminata, the Enlightened One, who is a poet-comic actor and at the same time the shadow of creation and the light of beauty.

On stage, the actor-author reclaimed a primordial voice and gesture, summoning up the speech of diverse characters. Speaking in first person and direct discourse, he brought into existence a phantasmagoria of events and places that seemed stitched by hand. Beating time with his feet, he expressed a sacred feeling for nature by employing strange, guttural sonorities in a narrator's voice, both lyrical and epic. His stories recounted episodes suspended in a dimension in which high and low are reversed, the sky below and the sea above. Paradise changed places with Hell, the reign of the living – with their biological needs and desires – with the reign of the dead. Like an epic bard, Franco Scaldati dramatized his stories without the pauses typical of stage dialogues. The rhythm of his body made listeners follow the story as though it were a fable, evoking a world both terrestrial and primordial. As an actor, Scaldati seemed absolutely extraneous to any rules of theater, and at the same time he affirmed the primacy of the epic singer who would evoke a whole world with a quick gesture and with the changing timbre and tone of his voice, making all the standard trappings of theater seem superfluous.

6.4.2 A sensory theater-world

Without a principle action as such, the structure of Scaldati's theater texts typically consists of blocks which are neither episodes nor fragments, and could thus be added or removed at will. The succession from one block to the next is not motivated by the familiar Artistotelian sequence of recognition and change, but rather by an alternation of voices. The two characters Totò and Vicé, for example, are wanderers who appear and disappear with no motive, seemingly emerging from a distant eternity. The blocks out of which the spectacle is constructed establish a sense of coherence in the repetition of thematic and spatial elements: The characters make increasingly frequent references to their location, a cemetery, and the other figures they speak about all exist, but *in absentia*. At the beginning of the spectacle, Vicé falls asleep and, never waking again, weeps for his own death. As he describes this to Totò, he insists on being accompanied to the cemetery, where he begins to describe the dead. The compositional structure of the work consists of the erratic apparitions of the couple, Totò and Vicé, between the earth and the beyond, their conversations marked by digressions, showing off their vocal abilities (imitating animal calls) and telling tales of amazing lives and prodigious personages, such as "Pupeddhu", who helped anyone in need and was dressed as an angel when he died. The forms of the piece's building blocks are varied and quite diverse: there are ballads of love and death, gardens of death, black fables, dreams (told in a pre-logical language rich with sonic gestures), weeping, sing-song assonance and onomatopoeic phrases, animal calls, silences, pauses, repeated words and phrases, echo effects, and so on. Each of these elements determine the rhythm of the written page. The vowels are the music of the world.

Franco Scaldati's texts are outstanding for their high level of literary and theatrical quality; the words embroidered onto the page impress themselves on the body-mind of spectator and reader, summoning from silence the voices that pronounce them, leading back to the root of *pneuma* (spirit-breath) and its sources in the body. Scaldati's vocal writing includes an extremely rich sonic universe that encompasses nature, the city, and the sphere of emotions, and that is graphically rendered on the page with punctuation marks (commas, periods, spaces), or by onomatopoeic expressions, with interruptions and silence. The sounds take form on the page, letters seem designs: Words are spatialized, transmitted like sonic bodies and mental images. Light and voices, words and space, are matter that the writer manipulates and transforms, passing from page to stage, from letters to the alphabet of bodies. On stage the voices become song, inviting listeners to repose, like lullabies.

In the earliest texts, from the late Seventies, the presence of song and music has a salvific function. In soothing dialect, the character Lucio sings for wine: "You have to understand, Lucio/can't sing without a voice/ . . . it takes a glass of wine. Just one/ . . . and then, he'll sing you/every song in the world".[44] In *Il cavaliere Sole* (The Sun Knight – 1979), song structures the spectacle. A drunk plays the harmonica and sings in a trio; a young man in love sings a serenade; the Wind travels with its instruments, finds the young lover dead, and invites the dead youth to join him in a moving song.

The vocal and sonic registers compose a score of accentuated chromatic timbres, echoing with the cry of babies and the laments of the old, the sighs of lovers and the screech of cicadas, the sounds of rain and a ringing telephone, the tinkling of bells and the cries of traveling vendors, or the sound of a violin. In *Totò e Vicé*, "every noise is a sound". The duo amuses themselves by imitating the call of donkeys, sheep, nightingales, sparrows, chickens, turkeys, cats, frogs, chicks, mice, ducks, and crickets. The *Libro Notturno* (Nocturnal Book) is also full of onomatopoeic expressions: "toc toc toc death knocks at the door; the bells ring to give you away".[45] The theatrical world of Scaldati arouses the sensorial sphere, transmitting odors, irradiating light and color, enwrapping us in shadow. Light marks the passing of the day, with a peculiar poetic melancholy when dusk turns to dark. Preparing for sleep is a ritual in *Assassina*, as is the moment in *La gatta rossa* (The Red Cat) when children playing in the street turn toward home, called by their mothers at end of day. The everyday actions carried out by the characters have something ritualistic and sacred about them, their gestures are free of "naturalism", "realism" or "minimalism": they wash themselves, dress, urinate, prepare to eat, and anticipate the pleasure of drinking fresh water, or drinking a glass of wine to clear their vocal chords before singing a serenade to their beloved.

Food and hunger, placated by the imagination, are a recurring topos in Scaldati's texts, which could almost be turned into a recipe book. In *Lucio*, a character named Crocifisso (The Crucified One) dreams in dialect in extreme detail about appetizing plates of food. The list itself makes a spectator's mouth water. Nature in all its animal and vegetable forms, down to its primary elements, permeates all Scaldati's writing: there are flowers, the moon, the sea, fish, and animals who live with humans (Totò keeps flies in his pockets). In *Assassina*, a mouse converses with an old lady; *Indovina Ventura* features talking cats and mice, and there are fairies in *Le Fate* who play instruments, laugh, and sleep under rose bushes and jasmine trees. The fairies are like drops of dew; they travel on wisps of air, disguised as flower sellers who slip into people's houses, making them happy. The deformation of human bodies – the character of Lucio has no arms – makes them prodigious, closer to the animal world, inseparable from nature as a whole. They live in a choral dimension that implies the unity of all living things, suspended between sky, earth, and sea.

The characters have a propulsion to regress to their primordial elements, fuse into the cosmos: the human body tends to come apart, dissolving into light and voice. Everything in this universe is in a state of blending ("I am learning to speak like the animals, and then I will teach them to speak like me") and assimilation ("I've been drinking only water for a week, now everything looks transparent to me".) To meld into other things means belonging to everything ("I spent a whole night staring at the fire, and there were so many eyes in the middle of the fire".)[46] Scaldati's figures are inscribed in a cosmogonic setting composed of primary elements: water-sea, air-sky, fire-earth. The sea – animate, vital, beneficent – is forever calling, the place where things happen. Together with the cavern, an abyss where opposites coincide, these elements present archetypes of life and death, dark and light, but they are not symbols, because everything is constantly transmuting, in an unstoppable process of becoming. The flirtatious moon, in fact, is a principle *dramatis personae*, performing diverse actions, and death is a living creature. The power that attracts the characters in Scaldati's theater toward high (an apotheosis in the sky) and low (plunging into the bottomless darkness of the cavern) recall the baroque described by Gilles Deleuze as a regime of color and light: "we can think of light and shadow as 1 and 0, the two planes of the world separated by a thin watershed. The blessed and the damned".[47] But the two regimes are not opposed one to the other, because both figure and shadow emerge from the same dark background. They represent a spreading-forth of light that penetrates the darkness, such that "the clear never stops immersing itself in the dark".[48] Matter (body) descends and Spirit (light) rises, and the fold marks the line between the two.

As in the Gospel of John, there is no conflict between light and shadow, but rather interpenetration between water and fire, demons and saints. Humans cross borders with angels on one side, demons on the other. The sensorial world of Scaldati envisions a lost paradise of Eden, where everything was once both unique and indistinct, before names: "In ancient times, roses smelled like jasmine, and jasmine like roses . . . in ancient times roses and jasmine wound one into the other", until an eye and a hand shattered this amalgam of flowers, colors, and perfumes.[49] In this cosmos, writing came before history as the original act of creation ("they wrote my book with fateful ink/but I don't know how to read").[50] Writing comes from a high source that reveals a world seen from below ("his theater represents the shadow . . . and me? I construct shadows".)[51]

The theme of light (fireflies, eyes, moths, moon, sun, lightning, or simply the color yellow) is braided into the theme of shadow, the theme of the house as a dark cavern, that of the abyss, and that of the voice:

> How did the jasmine see? Eyes like roses in the/gardens. A great fire and there's the full moon. Like a dream that vanishes/in the morning. The sun is . . . light of the eyes/What light is it? Light like a woman Who is it? . . . the night asks the day . . . the sky asks /the moon Who are you?[52]

6.4.3 Picture cards, marionettes, shadows, doubles

The characters in Scaldati's theater appear with the light and vanish with the coming of dark. A couple named Lella and Emanuele wash the stairs in their old building, sleep in the ruins, and struggle to survive hunger, living in the street or in collapsing buildings, huts, grottoes, and desolate interiors. They live in uninhabited, crumbling apartments (like many in Palermo, after bombing during the Second World War) or, in *Assassina*, "in a pile of rags in the rubble of an old palace".[53] In *La casa abbandonata* (The Abandoned House), "an impoverished old woman abandoned in her stuffed chair lives the last instants of her earthly life; nothing else breathes in the entire building. The old woman dies; as her eyes close, the whole house darkens".[54]

Scattered among detritus, the sick, deformed, mutilated, and suffering seek the light. They listen to old songs: a Chopin nocturne or the Neapolitan songs of Aurelio Fierro. They count the day's take, putting coins in a tin can hidden under a brick (*Un angioletto vestito di giallo* – An Angel Dressed in Yellow). In *Il Pozzo dei Pazzi* (The Well of the Mad) Aspano and Benedetto gather cigarette butts and fight over a stolen chicken. Pupa and Regina are "crazy women, and therefore witches, holding on solely by instinct".[55]

The characters are often doubles who cannot be distinguished one from the other and who have virtually the same names, such as Cecchino and Cecchina in *La guardiana dell'acqua* (The Water Guardian). Like the andro-gynes described by Plato in the Symposium, before they became separated they were one: a child and a schoolteacher, a little girl and an old woman. Scaldati's theater does not display the familiar stage relations between tor-turer and victim or master and servant, but figures who coincide one with another, "each is mirror and shadow of the other". They are interchange-able with the personified animals: a couple of mice in *Lucio* speak in rhyme, talking about when they lived on the moon and fed on milk. In *The Sun Knight*, Salomone is a rooster who reads comic strips and gets so drunk he forgets to announce the dawn. Every morning he has to be woken up and made to put on his comb and tail. Another chicken appears in *Luciana buffa gallina* (Luciana the Silly Chicken), who crows for an entire page.

A similar presence is the Shade who recites a litany of his life in an empty house during a night interrupted by lightning flashes. In *Lucio*, angels save people at the moment of death. They are possessed voices, like the Sibyl; someone is speaking through them. It becomes impossible to distinguish people from ghosts, who function as a chorus, detached observers standing close by, who observe the bloody phantasmagoria of earthly affairs. All the voices breathe the same air, and the ghosts have a vitality equal to the gabbing people who tell terrifying tales; although ethereal, these ghosts have corporeal presence. The ghost named Shade in *Totò and Vicé* tells the story of a woman who asked for alms, performed miracles, and sold little cards with images of saints on them. Later, she is found dead under the stairs, with roaches swarming over her.

Scaldati's characters are inclined to mutation: one becomes a cat, another a mouse, and each can switch back as well. Life and death change places ("the dead is alive and the living is dead; and some are neither alive nor dead".).[56] Women become men and men become animals ("Totò, last night I dreamed I was a hen, I woke up and I'm still a hen".).[57] Totò and Vicé pass from shadow into light, from the cemetery to heaven, from suffering to joy. We can tell Totò from Vicé only because one keeps asking questions that the other must try to answer ("If someone walks and never stops, where do they end up?").

The state of constant becoming produces uncertain identities ("I don't know who you are and who I am".)[58] For these characters, having names guarantees that they exist; it is the name that establishes identity, but they continue to wonder whether they are human beings or beasts. One of the couple's favorite occupations is to imitate animal sounds, such as sheep or roosters, and they get confused as to what is animal and what is vegetable ("A flower is confused, he doesn't know if he might be a butterfly".).[59] They pass through different material states, taking on shapes according to whether they are made of breadcrumbs, tissue paper, or snow; or perhaps they are projections on a wall, or portraits, or drawn in pencil on paper. Finally, they turn into air and vanish.

Because Scaldati's characters, such as Totò and Vicé, are stupefied, it seems logical to them that the world should turn upside-down, like the Carnival realm described by Michail Bachtin. Vicé is always late, but walks backward; to the couple it seems possible and unexceptional that the moon might descend to the earth. They laugh, play, sing, or dance, trying out the entire gamut of human language and animal sounds; barking or crowing are as much a part of their vocabulary as human speech. They are similar to the children described by Jean Piaget who ask themselves about how the universe works and try to understand themselves, but in this case Totò and Vicé only have one another to ask and answer ("Do you know who put the salt in the sea? [. . .] who invented names? [. . .] if I was named Vicé and you were named Totò, would we still be Totò and Vicé? They play at "what if" and "let's pretend" ("If you were a pig and I were a chick, would you eat me?").[60]

Their worlds are woven with light and shadow and seamed with comic lightness, close to nonsense verse. Love and pleasure clear away pain and lack. The one who has suffered, who has passed through perdition, is the one who is saved. In *Occhi* (Eyes), Uncle Saverio, a cripple, offers money in exchange for sex. Couples stab one another, threaten to kill one another, but they are inseparable, out of fear or being left alone. Being deprived of love makes them howl with pain.

Scaldati's world is different from Pasolini's subproletariat Rome and from the Milanese hinterland of Testori. In Scaldati's Palermo, the property holder and the poor soul with nothing mix together in the ruins of an inexorably collapsing city. In this state of dissolution, an old man in pyjama and tie, a trash scavenger, a prostitute, a transvestite, and a madman make their way between imagination and reality, death and life, theater and daily life, knowing that each can change into the other at any moment.

Notes

1 C. Bene and G. Deleuze, *Sovrapposizioni*, Feltrinelli, Milan, 1978, 89.
2 R. Schechner, *The Future*, in «Biblioteca teatrale», *La crisi della critica teatrale*, n. 54, April-June, 2000, 155.
3 E. Dallagiovanna (ed.), *Teatro Valdoca*, Rubbettino editore, Soveria Mannelli (CZ), 2003, 170.
4 Conversazione di Marco Solari con Giuseppe Bartolucci, 1984, unpublished, Valentini archive.
5 C. Castellucci and R. Castellucci, *Il teatro della societas raffaello sanzio*, Ubulibri, Milano, 1992, 21–25.
6 V. Valentini, "Per una nuova cartografia del teatro", in A. Attisani (ed.), *Le forze in campo. Atti del convegno di Modena, 24–25 maggio 1986*, Mucchi, Modena 1987, 203–212.
7 E. Dallagiovanna (ed.), *Teatro Valdoca*, Rubbettino editore, Soveria Mannelli (CZ), 2003, 170.
8 Letter from Romeo Castellucci to Valentina Valentini after *The Four Seasons Restaurant* in «Alfabeta2», November 30, 2013, www.alfabeta2.it/2013/11/30/Castellucci-Valentini correspondence. Cfr. V. Valentini, "Avanguardia, tradizione e scrittura scenica: Rifondare il teatro/alimentare l'utopia, in *Biblioteca Teatrale*, n. 48, October-December, 1998.pp 11-32
9 R. Schechner, "Drama, script, teatro e performance", in V. Valentini (ed.), *La Teoria della Performance 1970–1983*, Bulzoni, Rome 1984, 77–111–112.
10 F. Quadri, *L'avanguardia teatrale in Italia*, Einaudi, Turin, 1977, 138.
11 C. Ronconi in A. Pirillo, "Comporre in scena è come stare dentro una partitura musicale, intervista a Cesare Ronconi", in *Biblioteca Teatrale*, Bulzoni Editore, nn. 91–92 July-December, 2009, 305–313.
12 G. Barberio Corsetti, "Il teatro oggi ha a che fare con l'ignoto", in *Biblioteca Teatrale*, Bulzoni Editore, nn. 91–92, July-December, 2009, 279.
13 J. Grotowski, "Dalla compagnia teatrale a L'arte come veicolo", in T. Richards (ed.), *Al lavoro con Grotowski sulle azioni fisiche*, Ubulibri, Milan, 1993, p. 126.

14 R. Ciancarelli, *Appunti sulla famiglia comica*, contribution to the conference *Paradigmi dell'attore fra 800 e primo 900, Fonti Database e metodologie di ricerca*, Sapienza Università di Roma, Facoltà di Lettere e Filosofia (unpublished), Rome, March 27, 2015: "The theater family, as a producing organization and matrix of knowledge, stage and dramaturgical skill, has a central/crucial role in the theater of its era".

15 In F. Quadri, *L'avanguardia teatrale in Italia*, Einaudi, Torino, 1977, 141. Cfr. also G. Manzella, "Prologo a un discorso sul metodo di produzione del Nuovo Teatro", in O. Ponte di Pino (ed.), *Il nuovo teatro italiano, 1975–1988*, La Casa Usher, Florence, 32–35.

16 Giuseppe Bartolucci, "La materialità della scrittura scenica", in *Testi critici 1947–1987*, cit., 97.

17 R. Schechner, *La cavità teatrale*, cit., 71.

18 C. Bene, *La voce di Narciso*, Il Saggiatore, Milan, 1982, 25.

19 G. Barberio Corsetti, "Il teatro oggi ha a che fare con l'ignoto", in *Biblioteca Teatrale*, Bulzoni Editore, nn. 91–92, July-December, 2009, 279.

20 P. P. Pasolini, *Il sogno del centauro*, Jean Duflot (ed.), Editori Riuniti, Rome, 1983, 130.

21 P. P. Pasolini, "Res sunt nomina", in Id. (ed.), *Empirismo eretico*, cit., 260.

22 P. P. Pasolini, "Bestia da stile", in Id., W. Siti e S. De Laude (eds.), *Teatro*, Mondadori, Milan, 2001, 761–762.

23 P.P. Pasolini, *Il sogno del centauro*, cit., 130.

24 F. Taviani, *Uomini di scena uomini di libro*, Il Mulino, Bologna 1995, 211.

25 F. Fortini, *La contraddizione*, cited in in E. Liccioli, *La scena della parola: Teatro e poesia in Pier Paolo Pasolini*, cit., 235.

26 E. Liccioli, *La scena della parola: Teatro e poesia in Pier Paolo Pasolini*, cit., 199.

27 R. Schechner, "The Future", *Biblioteca teatrale, La crisi della critica teatrale*, n. 54, April-June, 2000, 155.

28 L. Ronconi, "Introduzione in forma di appunti", in S. Casi (ed.), *I teatri di Pasolini*, cit., 14.

29 G. Testori, *Opere 1965–1997*, ed., F. Panzeri, Bompiani, Milan, 2003, cit., 1541–42.

30 For an introduction to the work of Giovanni Testori, cfr. the two volumes by A. M. Cascetta, *Invito alla lettura di Testori*, Mursia, Milan, 1995.

31 A. M. Cascetta cit., 130.

32 G. Testori, *Il ventre del teatro* in G. Santini (ed.), cit., 40.

33 Program distributed during performances of *Edipus*, 22.

34 G. Testori, "La parola, come?". *Tre conversazioni con Giovanni Testori*, in "Comunicazioni Sociali" Nuova Serie n. 3, September-December, 2002, 372–394, 70. Cfr. *Le fibre lignee della 'parlata' valsesiana*, in *Artisti valsesiani. Artisti del legno: La scultura in Valsesia dal XV al XVIII secolo*, eds G. Testori and S. Perrone, Società per la Conservazione delle opere d'arte e dei monumenti di Valsesia, Valsesia editrice, Borgosesia, 1985.

35 Giovanni Testori, cited in S. Lombardi, "Diario e appunti delle prove", in *Edipus* program, Florence, Teatro di Rifredi, January 13, 1994, 21.

36 Conversation with Gianfranco Colombo, 1988, cit. in Elena Ferraro, *Il teatro di Testori: temi, personaggi, linguaggi*, degree thesis, DAMS Facoltà di Lettere e filosofia, director V. Valentini, Università della Calabria, aa. 2001–02, 168.

37 G. Testori, *Opere 1965–1997*, F. Panzeri (ed.), Bompiani, Milan, 2003, cit., 1541–1542.

38 Ivi, 1541.

39 C. Bene, "Il monologo", in *Opere*, Bompiani, Milan, 1995, 1000.

40 G. Testori, *Il ventre del teatro*, in G. Santini (ed.), cit., 36.

41 On Sandro Lombardi and Federico Tiezzi's work on the four spectacles by Testori, cfr. O. Ponte di Pino, *Il corpo della parola, Il Testori di Sandro Lombardi e Federico Tiezzi*, «ateatro» link: ateatro 19.4 www.trax.it/olivieropdp/mostranew.asp?num=19&ord=4

42 F. Taviani, *Uomini di scena, uomini di libro*, Il Mulino, Bologna 1995, 195.

43 V. Raciti, *La produzione drammaturgica di Franco Scaldati*, cit., 11, 106.

44 F. Scaldati in V. Valentini, *Franco Scaldati*, Rubbettino, Soveria Mannelli (CZ), 1997, 21.

45 F. Scaldati, *Libro notturno*, ERSU, Palermo, 2005, 77.

46 F. Scaldati, *Totò e Vicé*, cit., 30, 27, 179.

47 G. Deleuze, *La piega: Leibniz e il barocco*, Einaudi, Turin, 1990 (*Le pli: Leibniz et le Baroque*, Les Éditions de Minuit, Paris, 1988), 48.

48 Ivi, 49.

49 F. Scaldati, *Totò e Vicé*, cit., 151.

50 Ivi, 187.

51 F. Scaldati, *Ombre folli*, unpublished, Archivio Scaldati *OF1a*, 1999, the picture "*Tutti i cosi lairi i stu tintu munnu*", 22. Cfr. V. Raciti, *la drammaturgia di Franco Scaldati*, cit., 93.

52 (Archivio Scaldati, *PROF 2*, 2) apre una versione precedenze all'edizione Ubulibri, Milan, 2005; cfr. V. Raciti, *La drammaturgia di Franco Scaldati*, cit., 36.

53 F. Scaldati, *Assassina*, cit., 62.

54 Undated, in the unpublished text, *Dieci piccole pallide storie* (2001), Scaldati Archive, *Casa Abbandonata 1A bis*, 1.

55 Cfr. Scaldati Archive, *L2*, luglio, 2006.

56 F. Scaldati, *Totò e Vicé*, cit., 63.

57 Ivi, 156.

58 Ivi, 46–47.

59 Ivi, 23.

60 Ivi, 162.

7 The dramaturgy of space

7.1 Sensory-motor rupture

From the late Sixties to the present day, stage space has undergone enormous transformation. The prevalent drive of New Theater was to declare the continuity in space between stage and house, to disrupt the division between the place for acting and the place for spectating. At the same time, there was a movement to theatricalize settings such as factories, schools, prisons, and hospitals, to open up enclosed spaces to festive gatherings and street parades. This shift permitted the reinvention of theatrical practices and ways of life. Conventional formats were dismantled in favor of new ones. In place of static theater halls with fixed seats, audiences gathered in studios, for performance actions and installations. Theaters, art galleries, and concert halls were substituted by swimming pools, garages, boats, rooftops. Sound, light, and visual technologies created three-dimensional, virtual, immersive, multi-sensorial spaces (touch and hearing were especially privileged), freeing up the possibilities for staged representations of psychic, memorial, and imaginary space. The construction of new types of space for theater, in order to purify it of its stagnant cultural stratifications, took diverse forms: rites of initiation, protected spaces (where the tribe of theater might find solace), and experience-as-process. Alongside the stage with a traditional set, a cage to enclose action, there now appeared a dematerialized stage made of light and color. Architecture became liquid, "an animistic entity, animated, metamorphic".[1] Different ideas of space-time were elaborated in response to what was being discovered in physics during that era, driven by technological transformations.

Observing the changes in the art of painting at the beginning of the twentieth century, the poet Rainer M. Rilke, in *Worpswede* (1902), had observed that the human figure no longer inhabited the landscape, and the landscape no longer allowed space for the human. Combining ethics with aesthetics, Rilke hypothesized a relation between this vanished relationship and the advent of abstract art, warning that this detachment would lead to the fading away of the moral sense and the beauty of art. The unhinging of the connection between subject and setting, which had begun with the Impressionists, who absorbed the figure into the background, and had continued with the reduction of the figure to a mere ghost (as in De Chirico's long shadows in deserted piazzas), and the Futurist mechanical man sucked into the gears of a machine-world, became more and more pronounced, leading to a fluid, moving space without limits. A kind of anti-space split open or narrowed to a slit, sharing the cosmic qualities both of the living and the inert. People began to look at planet Earth as though from a satellite, projecting themselves beyond, into cosmic space. The coordinates of terrestrial orientation slipped, blurring the confines between outside and inside, high and low, centrifugal and centripetal.

Within this new conception of space, the subject became simultaneously errant and clairvoyant: lacking destination, the single subject moves incessantly, repeating trajectories, gestures, and pathways. Another may freeze in place to observe a world of shadows that never cross paths. Still more often, the individual turned inward to examine the self, one's own mental landscape.[2]

For the purposes of the itinerary we are tracing here, we shall describe the utilization of space in theater as a kind of writing, a dramaturgical device, a place where events occur, where the body is deformed, compressed, suspended in a void, absorbed into color, dematerialized; a place where objects become "actant figures" in disproportionate relief to their actual size.[3] The stage space is no longer a container for an action that unfolds within a circumscribed frame, a *boîte* of Euclidean geometry. Just as painting had crossed beyond the picture plane and the frame, and visual art no longer meant only painting (but also performance, Body Art, Land Art, installation, site specific event), the theatrical event constructed its own space, beyond the two-dimensional pictorial backdrop and three-dimensional quadrilateral.

Environment is the common denominator of experiences that pertain both to the visual arts (intermedia, Land Art, Performance Art, installations) and to performing arts in this period.[4] Beginning with the contestation of the stage and the spectacle, categories such as "environment" and "event" became fundamental to the new theatrical epistemology, formalized as theory in Richard Schechner's definition of "environmental theater" (1968).[5]

In his *Six Axioms for an Environmental Theater*, Richard Schechner described a theater free of central perspective and scenic illusion, one that might generate a continuity between theatrical representation and real life, where multiple actions might take place in different points in the space. By multiplying stage locations and actions simultaneously, slicing the space vertically and horizontally, and framing the momentary points of focus, a totality is reduced to pieces, so as to give new vitality and energy to the detail. Setting aside the immediate glance that grasps the world as an interrelated unity, creators experimented with new means of watching, including obstruction, visual disturbances, and blindness. The spectator became conscious of missing something, that not all can be seen, and that he or she stood within, rather than in front of, the spectacle. There was no longer any separation between the stage space and the space of observation; in its place came an actor-spectator continuum. "The theatrical place is thus, at the same time, the place of the stage and the house, and the elements that compose it constitute the precise formal and conceptual reason for the dramatic action".[6]

The hypothesis that Giuliano Scabia started with for the text of *Zip Lap Lip Vap Mam Crep Scap Plip Trip-Scrap e la Grande Mam* (1965) is similar to that of Beckett's *Act Without Words*: "identification of theatrical language with theatrical space [. . .], in a certain sense is a matter of preparing theatrical scores not limited to the writing of dialogue, but inventing the inhabited space already housed in the text".[7] In fact, the literary writing of Samuel Beckett is put into form by a spatial device. Beckett's theater "stages" abstract categories (time, space, memory, perception) in a profound self-reflexive metalinguistic action. *Zip Lap Lip Vap Mam Crep Scap Plip Trip-Scrap* . . . utilized space in its entirety: ten clowns who were masks of contemporary society (divided between those with power and those subject to it) spoke in phonemes and banal commonplaces. The stage was extended with walkways halfway into the house, so as to include spectators in the theatrical action, which had simultaneous focal points.

After 1968, the status of the artwork as merchandise with exchange value in the art market entered into a deep crisis. The artist put himself or herself into action in first person (Performance Art, Body Art). Architecture became radical, attributing value to project design and to the utopian aspects of metropolitan living, without concern for whether the architectural work could ever be realized in material form. Theatrical space no longer required theaters and visual art no longer needed galleries. Artists chose non-institutional settings, preferring socially and historically charged spaces such as factories. These places thus became a single body with the gesture of the artist who intervened to modify it. The goal was to render it impossible to discern between the "found" (the natural) and the "constructed" (the artificial), between art and reality. In this way living and ephemeral materials entered the world of art – like the parrots (1967) and horses (1969) exhibited by Jannis Kounellis – as did the human bodies of Body Art. Raw materials such as earth and water, or everyday objects like rubber, plastic, clay, glass, cotton, and coal came into use (Michelangelo Pistoletto's *Orchestra di stracci*, 1968; Kounellis's *Cotoneria e Carboneria*, 1967–68), as did immaterial substances such as fire and breath (Yves Klein).

I testimoni (The Witnesses, 1968) [FOCUS] directed by Carlo Quartucci, with scenic design by Jannis Kounellis, transported the aesthetic of *arte povera* to the theatrical stage, with a conception of the image of the set as living, authentic action, and a handling of the set as a visual-sonic installation in the act of becoming, without defined form. The intention was to bring down the spectacle as merchandise, and theater as institution, just as *arte povera* had worked in the context of the visual arts. Ettore Capriolo described *I testimoni* this way:

> On a bare, brightly illuminated set, Jannis Kounellis has created an installation with more than 'a hundred cages of chittering multicolored birds and raw materials of life scattered here and there': cactus, octopus-egg bowls, heaps of carded wool, moth balls, piles of coal, burlap sacks [. . .]; the stage refuses its function as a static, elegantly framed picture [. . .], to become protagonist of the theatrical fact, in a space that never achieves a definitive arrangement, but transforms uninterruptedly before our eyes.[8]

In the effort to break down the form of spectacle, other formats were experimented with in spaces not created for theater. Like the artists of *arte povera*, theater groups attributed meaning to places, interacting without prejudice with natural, artificial, constructed and found settings.

Presagi del vampiro (Omens of the Vampire, by Il Carrozzone, 1976) presented itself as a series of "studies for an environment", a practice characterized as an analytic "inclination", more existential than conceptual. The "studies" were unique, unrepeated events set in non-theatrical spaces for a limited number of spectators, with the goal of revitalizing the relationship with the spectator, transforming observed event into lived experience. The "Study" thus was a flexible format charged with diverse contingencies, such as the space in which it was produced; the number of actors (for director Federico Tiezzi, the word "actor" could apply just as well to non-human elements in a spectacle); the socio-cultural context; and the attitudes of the individuals present. "Studies are not sketches for a hypothetical final canvas, nor means to an end, but ends in themselves, that is, analytical instruments, hypotheses of re-foundation, measurements of unrooted space. The theatrical operation consists in synthesizing these instruments".[9] The Carrozzone group's Studies often took place in art galleries, lasting from 15 to 30 minutes, and were named with the English word, "performances".

Breaking through the frame of the stage space raised issues about the relationship between subject and space, inside and outside. The use of cinematic and video images projected on monitors introduced other spaces and times, doubling and mirroring what took place on the stage. In *La Camera Astratta* (The Abstract Chamber, by Studio Azzurro-Barberio Corsetti, 1987) [FOCUS] there was no longer a "here" and a "there", a distant and a close: There was an immaterial-mental space that received the interpretive work of the spectator. Space was no longer expected to contain and circumscribe the event; rather, it generated and constituted the event. Space was dynamic, breathing together with actors and spectators, open to the unpredictable; a four-dimensional space, unhooked from linear time.

In the twentieth century, with the affirmation of the theories to relativity, the connection between space and time revealed itself to be inextricable, constitutive of the world.

7.2 Dynamic simultaneous space

Even before staging his version of the kaleidoscopic Renaissance epic poem *Orlando Furioso* [FOCUS], Luca Ronconi's spectacles upset the single-point perspective space of the traditional Italian stage set by multiplying the locations where performances took place (including the simultaneous presence of all the actors, who were, however, concealed one from another but not from the view of the spectators). The spaces he constructed were dynamic but sometimes cage-like, claustrophobic, and impervious.

In the same year that Richard Schechner published his *Six Axioms for an Environmental Theater* in New York, Ronconi's staging of *Orlando* practiced and confirmed those same maxims. We can thus take Ronconi's spectacle as an important example, not so much of the influence of the United States on Italy, as of the pervasive presence of New Theater practice on an international scale. Schechner's theses coincide with *Orlando*'s staging techniques, especially the principals of the simultaneity of actions and the sensory stimulation of the spectator. The concept of the reversibility of space and time shifted the linear story line, putting real time in its place, including its banal repetition, the absence of a beginning, and a destination; actions took place not in sequence but contemporaneously. There was no single focal point, but many; rather than having the gaze of all spectators converge on a single action, their eyes shifted from one scene-place-action to another, without a predetermined itinerary.

Like a reader, the spectator was compelled to choose at each moment which aspect of the story to follow; the entire space was open both to performance and to the spectator's participatory gaze.[10]

As in multimedia installations in which a visitor enters an environment unaware of its governing rules, the spectator in *Orlando Furioso* "faced two choices", as Ronconi explained, "whether to participate in the game we propose, or stand aside and observe. But in the latter case he or she will get bored, because this spectacle must be lived, not merely watched and judged".[11] As Franco Quadri observed, spectators at *Orlando* regained the infantile sensibility and spontaneity of play, surprise, and participation, in an occasion where "without retouching, a sophisticated spectacle became a popular festival (in the piazzas) [. . .], a saraband for seven thousand flushed, frenetic people".[12]

Orlando removed spectators from the protective rituals of the theater hall and stage, projecting them into an unpredictable open space (the piazzas of the cities where it was performed), where the rules were unwritten and the viewer was subjected to acoustical aggressions (the confused voices of the actors in motion simultaneously in different parts of the performance space) and spatial disorientation. Spectators were compelled to let themselves go into an overwhelming flow of action, deciding on the spur of the moment which dramatic thread to pursue. This took place, for example, in the scene representing the Siege of Paris: on opposite sides of the performance space, on one side stood Charlemagne's castle, while on the other, riding on carts, the enemy army bristled with long wooden poles. The dynamically violent battle surrounded the king's tower, simultaneously attacked from above, by Rodomonte on horseback, and from below, by Rinaldo with his foot soldiers, in hand-to-hand combat, using poles which were swung and waved perilously close to the spectators.

The space of the action was articulated in four distinct locations which corresponded to four thematic motifs (the grotesque, the erotic, the epic, the fantastic), with two mirroring stages and carts carrying actors, which were maneuvered either by stagehands or the actors themselves.[13] The carts could be either very simple or fitted up to serve as horses, a pyramid, a hippogriff, a whale, or like the palace of the wizard Atlante in Paris, with stairs, platforms, and a maze.

The autonomy of this spectacle derived from a political strategy of participation conceived as an intellectual and sensorial stimulation. The Ronconi-Ariosto-Sanguineti *Orlando* represented an ideal type of new Theater spectacle, an avant-garde reinterpretation of popular festivals, of the *sacra rappresentazione* and the epic storyteller, but one that made no claim to restore to life any of these antique forms. Rather, it showed a way to combine experimentation with a commitment to the social virtues of theater, a juxtaposition that would soon split Italian theater into two mutually distant paths, with the political opposed to the experimental.

7.3 Audio-chromatic space

Light, noise, sound, object, actor, set: in a few short years (a decade, more or less) the futurist critical vocabulary was enriched with a prodigiously modern inventory.[14]

The aesthetic of the Seventies was dominated by the "environment" and by the materials of *arte povera*, with an "explosion, with a 'physicalized' stage space, of images and sounds, both 'surrounding' and 'shattering'".[15] Light constructed the stage space, taking into its embrace both the spectators and the actors. The light came from images projected onto multiple screens, accompanied by fragmented sounds composed of noises, syllables, and actual words.

The image-oriented spectacles of the "Roman School", as Bartolucci termed those groups, formed in within the New Theater scene between the end of the Sixties and the early Seventies, shared in common the use of cinema projections and high-volume sound effects. The binomials of visuality and sound (light-color-image and sound-noise-vocality) were dominant compositional devices, directed toward an abstract, non-linear representation. An aesthetics that privileged the perceptual and sensorial dimensions put the sound score into high dramaturgical relief: Sound was a physical element that increased the involvement of the observer-spectator, producing the sensation that the listener was not merely watching, but was in the same space as the event.[16] Angelo Maria Ripellino attributed the origin of this development quite rightly to Carmelo Bene, saying, "He was the one who began the acoustic dissection of the verbal weaving, the pulping of texts [. . .], in sum, the invasion of confusion and the scream onto the stage".[17]

In his description of the version of *Macbeth* produced in 1973 by Leo de Berardinis and Perla Peragallo, Ripellino manifests an extraordinary ability to render for the reader the materiality of the spectacle, the sensorial aspect of the languages involved:

> Like rock singers with microphones at their lips, Perla and Leo translate the hallucinations and ravings of two ruffians and their birdlike clamor into an oratory of unbearable shrieks and cackling, groans, foreshadowings of death, and screeching owls that ornament the night when Duncan was slaughtered. They turn bellows and cries into hymns of vespers and compline. Leo screams like a clawed pig, he mews, tearing his throat in harsh rooster calls. Perla passes from diseased wheezing to vampire-like whispers, then breaks out in gasping, retching, and ululations.[18]

De Berardinis and Peragallo's spectacles made use of microphones and neon, screens and projections, tape recorders, transistor radios, stage lights, and various adapted musical instruments. In *La faticosa messa in scene dell'Amleto di Shakespeare* (The Laborious Staging of Shakespeare's Hamlet, FOCUS), muttered words of text were submerged under "brawls of words at maximum volume [. . .]. Except for an acoustic riot, nothing happens".[19]

In *Sudd* (1974), Perla mumbled her "solos" while immersed in a bathtub positioned center stage alongside a cooking plate, a toilet or bidet, garbage cans, and a transistor radio. Leo rummaged in the dark with a flashlight to rouse his comrades, beat on the garbage can as though it were a drum set, and set string instruments into vibration with the copper handle of the purpose-built flashlight. In *Avita murì* (You Have to Die, 1978, FOCUS), anti-fog lights were pointed at the spectators. In *Chianto e risate, risate e chianto* (Tears and Laughter, Laughter and Tears, 1974), in a landscape suggesting the Gulf of Naples at night, Perla, a resuscitated spirit, wandered among tombs, her body bent, crooked, and made clumsy by a squalid sack, carrying a harmonica and various rubbish.[20] The objects represented (flower bushes, cemetery lanterns, red glass spheres for streetlights, neon tubes, multicolored stars projected on a screen), the materials used (formica, polystyrene), and the objects on view (lighted store signs, advertising posters, letters of the alphabet) all recalled pop art. The artificial and natural coexisted with non-functional found objects (the trash can), leftovers of affluent society, now reactivated and put to use to scar the shiny surfaces of consumer merchandise. Hi-tech instruments coexisted with everyday objects.

In Memè Perlini's spectacles (*Pirandello chi?* – Pirandello Who?, 1973; *Otello*, 1975), bodies, the faces of actors, and the furnishings became sources of light that composed and decomposed images, varying their colors. Objects (canvases, mattresses, lights, wooden sticks) created halluci-nations in combination with the bodies of the actors under the play of stage lights, candles, and other light sources of every kind, skillfully maneuvered. In *Otello*, sharp-edged beams of light cut through the dense shadow, reveal-ing objects and bodies, as in a dream: a paper boat standing for the Moor's flotilla, a stairway, a blackboard, dinner plates, and sheets to evoke Othello and Desdemona's wedding celebrations, with the sound of a dog howling in the night.

In his 1979 *Morte Funesta* (Baleful Death), Simone Carella visually inscribed a text by poet Dario Bellezza about the death of theater onto the walls of a room in the Modern Art Gallery in Rome. Using a calculator keyboard in place of a lightboard, she struck keys that made a band of light outline each single letter of the poem. Although the projected phonemes derived from the original literary source, the text was incomprehensible to spectators because the velocity of the appearance of the letters made read-ing impossible. Instead, viewers experienced the text physically; the verbal phonemes were transformed into luminous phonemes that immersed the spectator in a Babel of signs. The words were inscribed onto the stage space in light, and the act of inscription constituted the spectacle. The light and geometric designs were the protagonists of the script, dynamic vectors that scoured and measured the space.

7.4 Analytic space

Analytic space has no perspective; it is horizontal. It contests the canonical relations of Italian theater, recreating for each new spectacle a new perfor-mance zone and a new perspective for the spectator's gaze. It is space in the act of becoming that continuously transforms the point of view, which can be crossed diagonally or from above, or can thrust itself upward into space.

In Il Carrozzone's *Ebdòmero* (1979), the movements of the actor in space were directed at measuring it out, at defining its geometric coordinates (similar to what took place in Richard Foreman's spectacles). The space was analytically measured and laid out on a horizontal plane, like many minimalist sculptures. In *Presagi del Vampiro* (Omens of the Vampire; Il Carrozzone, 1976) images of Renaissance architecture (regulated by the proportions of the human figure in space) were projected onto the walls, only to then unhinge the rules of the harmony of body in space through impulsive, destructive actions by the performer. The analytic space thus transformed into a place of obsessive disarticulation provoked by repeated movements, gestures, sounds, and chromatic-luminous material.

In *Theatre functions critical* (Beat 72, 1979), the exterior and interior, theater and street were connected only by sound. Charlemagne Palestine's music and the noises produced by spectators were captured by microphones and mixed, to construct a pathway which moved with spectators from one room to another within the theater, finally reaching the doors and then pouring out into the street, its forms distorted. The actors in Gaia Scienza's spectacles [FOCUS] interacted with the space, whether on a stage set or in the city street, allowing themselves to be absorbed by their surroundings while impregnating the space with their own presence, constructing a space identified by the individual components of the group. The goal was to transfer to the performance space itself the same charge of energy produced by the performer's body as it followed indeterminate spatial trajectories and responded, as subject, to different motor dynamics, including running, falling, and jumping to the point of exhaustion. In their *Cronache Marziane* (1977), the stage space was divided into three zones where separate actions took place simultaneously, including slide projections, colored light, a puddle to walk in, a palm tree, sand, and foam rubber that bodies ran and threw themselves against. There was a surface scattered with blocks of tufa from which poked lighted neon tubes. The principal action of the actors in a piece entitled *Una notte sui tetti* (A Night on the Rooftops, 1978, FOCUS), was to run heedlessly and without stopping, climbing up walls, balancing impossibly, using broken movements and rhythms, combining contact improvisation, acrobatics, the subjective dimension, and risk, including chasing one another over rooftops, with a real danger of falling. This group's interventions fit somewhere between installation art and environmental studies, aimed at reaching beyond the walls of the theater. In the final scene of *Gli insetti preferiscono le ortiche* (Insects Prefer Nettles, 1982, FOCUS) the backstage wall opened onto the park of the Villa Borghese at night. The stage space – conventionally metaphorical, symbolic, a mirror of the world – suddenly blended into the real one, in a continuous flow.

In Simone Carella's *Esempi di lucidità* (Examples of Lucidity, 1978), an ephemeral architecture of inflatable plastic tubes occupied the entire space of the theater, seeming to dilate the walls outward. The interior opened out toward the exterior, cancelling out the demarcation between the public (the world) and the private (the house), similar to the way the American artist Dan Graham experimented in the same era with electronic devices to unite architectural and social environments.[21]

7.5 Monitor space

After the darkness and the black-and-white design motifs of the Theatre of Images, the chromatic element exploded in spectacles produced in the early Eighties by Falso Movimento (*Foresta Nera*, 1980; *Rosso Texaco*, 1980; *Dallas*, 1983; *Tango glaciale*, 1983, FOCUS). *Dallas* was designed on models taken from cinema, television, comic books, and photography, bringing the urban media universe onto the stage, using artisanal instruments to transform the theatre space into a television monitor across which images would scroll. The perceptual effect was still more sophisticated in *Rosso Texaco* and *Tango glaciale*. In the first, the theme of the voyage permitted the introduction of a series of images of cities taken at night from the viewpoint of a moving automobile.

> The city is no longer conceived as a sedimentation of history and identity, but as a place of interchange whose totems are luxury hotels, motels, road junctions, supermarkets, the highway, truck stops, all places that indicate transit and rapid movement. The city is constructed out of the remnants of an imaginary experienced through the media and urban agglomerates that are no longer definite places but *all* places, including their negation (the desert).[22]

The composed landscape places objects and human figures on the same level, while also dematerializing them, reducing them to shadow and a luminous flash. *Tango glaciale* told the story of three inhabitants who walk through a house, from the living room to the kitchen, from the roof to the garden, and from the swimming pool to the bathroom. The spectacle portrayed a domestic adventure in continuous transformation, projecting itself in time and space, plunging suddenly into ancient Greece or the New York in the 1940s, full of Argentine tangos and classical melodies.[23] The space was an architecture of light composed of slides, films, paintings, drawings, and cartoons, articulated across 12 different environments. The scene changed every five minutes, adding up to one hour. Real space and designed space were equal, equally synthetic. In the absence of a dramatic text, only music linked the actions together, with a collage of diverse numbers that carried the spectacle forward, serving a narrative function.[24]

Crollo nervoso (Nervous Breakdown, by Magazzini Criminali, 1980, FOCUS) was enclosed in a cube with walls made of venetian blinds, rendered bluish by neon lights that alternatively indicated a beach in Mogadishu and Los Angeles International Airport, in a historical framework that oscillated between July, 1969 (date of the moon landing) and a then-still-distant 2001 (Kubrick's *Space Odyssey*). On stage, accompanied by a mixture of Brian Eno music and the voice of Billy Holliday, a science-fantasy-style platoon of figures armed with toy pistols moved, shifting in time from the remote past to the present. The verbal register was an indirect communication with a strange interlocutor, with questions and illogical answers reiterated and mediated by transceivers. A voice that preferred English over Italian yelled in an effort to overcome the noise. The impersonal verbal amalgam coming from unidentifiable sources was as anonymous as the spaces it echoed in: airports, icons of interculturalism that represented the globalized world. Stratifications of words, voices, and radio stations constructed the simultaneous space of cities in a still more incisive way than the kaleidoscope of actions, making *Crollo Nervoso* into the manifesto of de-subjectivization, of the nomadism of postmodern theater, where fashion, advertising, language, object, and banality reign supreme. The spaces were zones of nomadic transit, like airports, highways, subways, the Olympic Stadium in Munich (with

Hanna Schygulla, *Ins Null – Verso Zero*, Il Carrozzone, 1980), the beach at Rimini, amusement parks, a highway service station – places of mass assembly, a world that surpassed avant-garde elitism. In these contexts, ambient music became a diffuse sonority, a total synthesis of mental and physical space.

7.6 Landscape and errancy

Landscape can no longer be configured as "city" or "country", two dimensions that belong to a phase of human habitation now left behind. We now face instead a transfinite space in which the confines that identify and connote space appear indistinct, intermittent, evanescent. Space now consists of "small communities", an expression taken from urban planning but equally or more applicable to the realm of emotion and the psyche; "a fractal geometry of stones, cement and asphalt", as Arminio has put it, that renders "the intimate fragility of everything" ever more visible.[25]

The spectacle thus became an event designed to resonate in harmony with its chosen place, as in a ritual enactment. An imaginary, mythological, dream-like form of theater took shape, representing mental landscapes. The heroes of this dramaturgy were space and open-ended, unlimited time, where the terms "far" and "near" lost their meaning, and where landscape (whether mental or natural) and journey were recurrent figures. In a philosophy characterized by relativism, *errancy* was considered an indispensable quality in a type of work that spatialized time and temporalized space, in which the spectator journeyed, both concretely and psychically. This same dimensionality was common in minimalist sculpture, but derived also from the ordered, organized set designs of Robert Wilson. The spectator was compelled to become *errant*, to wander among the pieces of the work that the artist had scattered around the space. Errancy meant the impossibility of stopping in any fixed point; "being always at the point of departure for distant lands", like the characters in Peter Handke's novels, corresponding to a philosophical topos marked by conceptual relativism and the loss of certainty and identity. The spectacles put viewers in a condition of perennial nomadism, exalting a dimension of statelessness.[26]

The city as a site of interconnection functioned as a paradigm for art in the Eighties, which regarded architecture as an ordering device that could offer models for linking into a new system different from that of the previous decade, which had conceived architectural systems as spread across a surface. The new concept imagined the city as space organized by stratifications of time upon time, an interrelation of diverse parts. The interrelation consisted not of fragments on a vast surface, along which each spectator chose a path; rather, the system was now to be experienced as an organism, within which the spectator must follow certain indicators.

The *topos* of the voyage and the landscape as an absolute stage set are inscribed in the increasingly complex, mid-Eighties spectacles of Giorgio

Barberio Corsetti, in which myth and science fiction, remote past and future, ancient cities of the dead and cities to come, blend in a journey that led the author back from where he came. The city of his ancestors transformed into a voyage into consciousness, a mental landscape where thought wandered in solitude. The tone of these spectacles suggested the contemplative state of a person writing a diary, a rhythm of unhurried rumination that allowed deep exploratory penetration.

The continuous transformation of the stage space distinguished the emotional geography of a spectacle such as Gaia Scienza's *Cuori Strappati* (Torn Hearts, 1983, FOCUS), a narration of spatial events. The itinerary of this surprising spectacle consisted of movement through ever-changing landscapes (atmospheric, terrestrial, aquatic, fissures opening in the walls), reacting to each in term, with constant changes in rhythm provoked by *coup de théâtre*, such as chairs that came to life and rocks that turned into human bodies. The text of *Cuori Strappati* consisted of a score of movements enacted by the stage space itself: The walls themselves moved, composing new spaces, accompanied by environmental sounds such as rain, ringing telephones, car horns, and the sounds produced by body-sculptures in movement.[27]

The inversion of *animate* and *inanimate*, hard-rigid and soft-flexible, living body and inert matter, combined to reinforce the effect. In the spectacle, the unexpected was a chair reaching out its arms to crush, rocks that moved by hopping, houses that bodies passed through and, vice versa, bodies that became houses, walls, chairs, rocks, etc. The space was organic, punctured, practicable, open to crossing – a body-city, body-abode, inhabited in its interstices and crevices.

The problem that Eisenstein found unresolvable in theater, that of integrating the person into an environment in space and time, became a privileged field of experimentation in Barberio Corsetti's spectacles.

> If I have to think of a family relation, I think of Meyerhold's process or Eisenstein's montage. We were interested in the body as part of a landscape or a whole. For that reason, it was always being interrupted, like in certain Futurist paintings where there is a split between the movement and the body. The idea was that the materials, and the whole stage, were a prolungation of the movement of the actor and, vice versa, that the movement of the actor was a prolungation of the stage.[28]

In Barberio Corsetti's *America* (1992), the spectator experienced the journey of Karl, the protagonist of Kafka's novel of the same name, by following the spectacle on foot through the different places in the city where the "itinerary" stopped; mental voyaging was thus also a real voyage. The spectacle made loitering, the wandering of the *flaneur* characteristic of the twentieth century, into a concrete compositional form, where the natural ties between subject, setting, and event were broken. The distinction between inside and outside (rendered, for example, by a window connecting the landscape with the person observing it) disappeared, as did that between the physical (the landscape) and the psychological (the person watching).

Sorger, the geologist character in Peter Handke's *Langsame Heimkehr* (The Long Way Round, 1979) must regain the ability to suffer and love because he has been abandoned by language, become deaf, afflicted by an internal mutism. His slow voyage entails a transformation in his way of looking at and perceiving the world. He must stop merely describing the visible landscape in order to rediscover the inner mystery of the world, and then reinvent the world with the aid of people who are able to hear, within silence itself, the voices ready to burst out. A similar story takes place in Barberio Corsetti's autobiographical *Prologo a Diario Segreto Contraffatto* (Prologue to a Counterfeit Secret Diary, 1985/86), which recounts a passage from outside to within, from the quality of plastic, visual space, to the space of thought. Barberio Corsetti's *La Camera Astratta* (The Abstract Chamber, 1987, FOCUS]) presented an electronic mental space as it took form with the speed of thought, a place where the physical and the psychic could finally be recomposed, where bodies were exempted from the laws of gravity. Matter became light, bodies became transparent, with constant leaps between here and now, inside and outside, present and absent.

7.7 Constructing space

> "The concept of *oikos*, 'place where life is rooted', stands at the center of the compositional process of Teatro Valdoca. Creating a spectacle is the process of constructing the *place* (which may also be 'found spaces' outside theaters) where the actor may feel at ease, inhabiting it, caring for it, observing it".[29]

The two founders of Teatro Valdoca, Mariangela Gualtieri and Cesare Ronconi, were originally architects, for whom the stage space was both a surface upon which to trace lines, like a sheet of paper, and a space exploded by light and darkness, inhabited by essential objects made of living, natural materials, such as reeds, branches, water basins, stones; vegetable and animal nature. In *Lo spazio della quiete* (The Space of Quiet, 1983), the actions of two female figures mark out a *templum* where they can practice their perception of space and measure the trajectories of their gaze. The inhabitants are part of a tribe with its own rules and shared rituals that build participation and solidarity.

The idea of this spectacle was to delimit a space and mark paths through it, trajectories of movement, transported by words of poetry that – during the process of development of the spectacle – function to produce disorientation, a field of resistance that motivated the actor to turn her or his gaze inward. The space of Teatro Valdoca's spectacles was chromatic and luminous: *Fuoco Centrale* (Central Fire, 1995) washed over the spectator with the light and heat of myriads of candles burning on gigantic candelabra and lightbulbs waved by the performers. The *dramatis personae* were living sculptures, enhanced bodies, and spots of color; predominantly red (the color of tragedy) and white (the color of divinity).[30]

In the theater of Rem & Cap, the theatrical performance coincides with a ritual of foundation, the preparation of the place where the event will take place, a process of marking out the sacred enclosure of theater, demanding a long, effortful ceremony. The world-theater in *Mendel* (2013) was designed by the dramaturgy of the space, set up and brought to life by the dynamic of the actions that animated and transformed it, over the course of a spectacle that continued to assemble and disassemble itself, in a state of continuous becoming. At the beginning, books gathered into blocks formed a cross, which then become motors of the actions of six young actors, dressed as waiters, who passed them from hand to hand, composing sculptures and installations. They transformed the stage space, bestowing diverse forms upon it, making the books themselves the true protagonists both of the story and the set.

7.8 Installation and digital space

In the decade after the end of the millennium, we again find in New Theater the traits of installation art, a practice which expanded rapidly in the Sixties as part of a trend of "theatricalizing" visual art, which stepped beyond its known spatial limits to take on temporal dimensions. This format was common to the specific artistic practices Raymond Bellour (2012) identified as a "*querelle des dispositifs*", the phenomenon of overflowing the borders within which each separate art discipline had heretofore been confined.[31]

Space exists on its own, even without a spectator. It is thus similar to sculpture, like the display cases in *Catrame* (Tar, by Motus, 1996), which contained cerebral, individual space rather than the actions of characters in relation to the world.

> They are cages, display cases, transparent containers, self-referential worlds [. . .]. In the theater of the Nineties, stage space [. . .] stopped representing the collective demands (political and moral) of society, making appeal instead exclusively to the dimension of the individual, in a one-on-one relation.[32]

James Graham Ballard was the writer, Francis Bacon the painter, and David Lynch the film director who were repeatedly referenced in New Theater spectacles during the Nineties, where constant themes involved shifts in consciousness, neuroses, post-human mutations, and mediatized people living in cage-like high-rises, without past or future, exposed to view rather than subjects in action. The *Twin Rooms* project, by Motus, set up the stage like an art installation of a minutely realistic film set (with lights, objects, props, and decor all extraneous to classical theater set design) and editing equipment employed in real time. Like an installation, it appeared self-sufficient, presupposing a gaze more like that of a visitor to an art exhibition than a theater spectator. The room in *Twin Rooms* was inspired by the motels described by Don DeLillo in *Americana*, simultaneously public and anonymous, intimate and pregnant with living presence.[33]

The space in Fanny & Alexander's *Ponti in core* (1997) was claustrophobic, isolated from the spectator and the external world. Twenty-four spectators were positioned in individual niches, like statues. In *Idealista magico* (Magic Idealist, by Teatrino Clandestino, 2004), the set looked like a giant box, inside which were projected sequences of actions onto a thick black scrim, each in its own setting.

> The Sacher house interiors are typical of a soap opera: everything studiously matched. The objects recall Mattel doll houses, where every single detail is controlled. Everything immobile, ascetic, and 'dead' – think for example of the "incredibly yellow" vase of flowers in Sequence X (*Il mattino seguente Maddalena prepara la colazione ai bambini;* The next morning Maddalena prepares breakfast for the children) – as though for inanimate beings rather than people in flesh and blood.[34]
>
> [FOCUS]

Anticamera, by gruppo nanou (2012, FOCUS) was set not in a theater but in an art gallery, confirming its installation format. A woman whose face was concealed came forward in slow motion, arriving at a wooden cube with an opening in front: a box that surrounded the performer in a wallpapered room set with an easy chair, similar to the motel rooms in Motus's *Twin Rooms*. The design was photographic, framed by light that put details of the body into relief, but obscured objects and the full human figure, which flattened and seemed to vanish. The constricting, claustrophobic space of the cube offered the human body a new measure by which to reinvent itself, setting aside verticality in favor of horizontality or transversality, or broken lines. The world was absent, and in its place were details, shoes, ankles, legs – a reified universe, vision in a box, like a series of digital snapshots seen in sequence.

Romeo Castellucci's 2010 spectacle, *Il velo nero del pastore* (The Shepherd's Black Veil) was presented in a theater but might just as well have been given in a museum, because it was configured as a succession of visual-auditory images which were seen by the spectator from a distance and position typical of the separation between a theater's seating area and the stage. This same separation was nullified, however, by the acoustic space surrounding the viewer. In Castellucci's *Four Seasons Restaurant* (2013), the second part of the spectacle transformed into a sound installation. No live actors were present – only a violent turbine of crashing water, leaving a silver, shining, deafening liquid vortex at center stage, astonishing in its material and acoustic aggression.[35]

To comprehend the phenomenology of theatrical space during the period crossing into the new millennium, we must also consider the concept of digital space: a sensate environment which is not set apart, does not divide but mixes together, and which demands not only visual observation but multisensorial exploration on the part of the spectator.[36] Useful in this context is the list proposed by Derrick de Kerckhove that describes cyberspace in terms of oppositions: Static-Dynamic, Explosive-Implosive, Visual-Tactile, Frontal-Immersive, Fragmented-Integrated, Abstract/Desensitized-Multisensorial, Spatialized/Actualized-Virtualized.[37] These polarities help us understand the passage from analog to digital, but the qualities listed need not be regarded as strictly oppositional, just as the virtual and the real need not be seen as mutually exclusive.

> Virtualization is not a de-realization (the transformation from one reality into a gathering of possible realities), but a change of identity, a shift of the ontological center of the gravity of the object in question [. . .]. Virtualization is one of the most important vectors for the creation of reality.[38]

We find this coexistence inscribed in the dramaturgy of spectacles that demonstrate the non-existence of the fracture between the tangible and the intangible, the virtual and the real. In Santasangre's *Framerate* (2011, FOCUS), the living quality of a sheet of ice as it melts models the stage space, homogeneously, toward the assimilation of diverse expressive materials (light, sound, body) without cancelling out the differences between the body of the performer and the auditory-luminous body.[39] The stage is devoid of human bodies: in their place are sonic, luminous, chromatic bodies endowed with presence.[40]

Notes

1 M. Novak, *Architetture liquid nel ciberspazio* in *Cyberspace: Primi passi nella realtà virtuale*, Muzzio, Padua, 1993.
2 V. Valentini, "La figura umana nel paesaggio elettronico", in(ed. V. Valentini), *Le storie del video*, Bulzoni, Rome, 2003, 81–93.
3 Cfr. L. Mango, "Drammaturgia dello spazio", Chapter 3 in *La Scrittura scenica*, which considers the issue in relation theater historiography; cfr. 171–228. Cfr. also H.-T. Lehmann, *Dramatic and Postdramatic Space in Postdramtic Theatre*, Routledge, London and New York, 2006, 150 (*Postdramatisches Theatre*, D-Frankfurt am Main, 1999).
4 In Europe, and especially in Italy, happening and performance blend one into another, overlapping, such that only in the second half of the Seventies do people begin to use the term performance. In 1969, Renato Barilli proposed the loose term *comportamento* (behavior) to cover an extended sematic area including Body Art. Cfr. R Barilli, *Informale, oggetto, comportamento, la ricervca artistica negli anni cinquanta-sessanta*, vol. 1 and *negli anni settanta*, vol. II, Feltrinelli, Milan, 2007 (First edizione 1975. See the programming of the Attico of Fabio Sargentini in Rome. Cfr. Sargentini, R. Lambarelli and L. Masini, *L'Attico 1957–1987*, Mondadori, De Luca, Milan-Rome, 1987.

5 R. Schechner, "Sei Assiomi per l'Environmental Theater", in Id. (ed.), *La cavità teatrale*, De Donato, Bari, 1968, 23–125 (*Six Axioms for an Environmental Theatre*, "TDR", Spring, New York, 1968.

6 AA. VV., *Elementi di discussion per un convegno sul nuovo teatro*, in Giuseppe Bartolucci (ed.), *Testi Critici 1964–1987*, Bulzoni, Rome, 2007, 119.

7 G. Scabia, "Nota a Zip", in *Zio All'improvviso*, Einaudi, Turin, 1967, 47–48.

8 E. Capriolo, "Un funerale per il vecchio teatro", *Sipario*, n. 73, January 1969; cit. in S. Margiotta, *Il Nuovo Teatro in Italia 1968–1975*, Titivillus, Corrazzano (Pisa), 2013, 33.

9 *Ombra diurnal*, at the Pastificio Cerere, Roma, for *La citta de teatro*, 1978. Cfr. G. Bartolucci, L. Mango and A. Mango, *Per un teatro analitico esistenziale*, Studio Forma, Turin, 74.

10 Cfr. R. Schechner, *La cavità teatrale*, cit. 39–44.

11 Cfr. Luca Ronconi, in F. Quadri, *Il rito perduto*, Einaudi, Turin, 1973, 91.

12 F. Quadri, Ivi, 109.

13 Cfr. C. Longhi, *Orlando Furioso di Ariosto-Sanguineti*, ETS 2006, 8.

14 Cfr. G. Bartolucci, "Per un nuovo senso dello spettacolo", in Id. (ed.), *Scrittura scenica*, cit., 164–169. Cfr. also Bartolucci in "La luce-movimento-rumore in de Berardinis-Peragallo", in Ivi, 50–57.

15 G. Bartolucci, *La scrittura scenica*, cit., 164.

16 The recorded work of visual artists such as Joseph Beuys, Terry Fox, Jan Dibbets, Christian Boltanski, and Mimmo Rotella merits fresh investigation: cfr. G. Celant, *Offmedia, Nuove tecniche artistiche: Video Disco Libro*, Dedalo, Bari, 1977.

17 A. M. Ripellino, "Mezza Napoli nel tritacarne", in *Siate Buffi: Cronache di teatro, circo e altre arti* ("L'Espresso" 1969–77), cit., 119–120.

18 A. M. Ripellino, "Pirandello a testa in giù", in *Siate Buffi*, cit., 141–143.

19 A. M. Ripellino, "Chi ha visto passare Amleto", in *Siate Buffi*, cit., 521.

20 A. M. Ripellino, "Lazzaro fa il marameo", in Ivi, 410–412.

21 Cfr. Dan Graham, "Il video in rapporto all'architettura", in *Le pratiche del video*, (ed. V. Valentini)Bulzoni, Rome, 2003, 43–68 ("Video-Architecture-Television", in *Writing in Video and Video Works, 1970–1978*, University Press, New York, 1979).

22 M. Petruzziello and W. Paradiso, "'I Want to Be a Rock'n'roll Star': Pratiche ed estetiche nel suono nel Nuovo Teatro dei primi anni Ottanta", unpublished, 2014.

23 M. Martone in AA.VV., *Falso Movimento*, 77–82, Taide, Salerno, 1985, 71.

24 M. Martone on *Tango glaciale*, ibidem, "Then there is the music, the "wall" of compact sound, continuous a long trace that cuts the image, now taking it full on and guiding it, now crossing subtly across it on a diagonal. A geometric work, composed of many puzzle pieces of very different types of music, chosen and re-elaborated by me and Daghi: Debussy, Penguin Cafè, 007, Piazzola, Peter Gordon, and, finally, the tango composed for the show by Bisca, along with rap by Topmas and many other things".

25 A. Cortellessa, "La terra della prosa", the Introduction to his *Narratori degli anni Zero*, "L'Illuminista", nn. 31–32–33, gennaio-dicembre, 2011, 42. Cfr. Anche F. Arminio, *Viaggio nel cratere*, Sironi, Milan, 2003, 38.

26 The idea of nomadism has been thematized in music by the Italian singer-songwriters of the Seventies and Eighties, for example Enzo Jannacci, in *Messico e nuvole* (1970) and Paolo Conte, in *Sud America* (1979).

27 M. Cacciari, *Icone della legge*, Adelphi, Milan, 202. Cfr. V. Valentini, "Sulla costellazione", in AA.VV. (ed.), *I Quaderni di Odradek*, 48–51. Cfr. Anche V. Valentini, "Figure dello spazio e del tempo", in Id. (ed.), *Dopo il teatro moderno*, cit., 97–121.

28 G. Barberio Corsetti, *La Camera Astratta*, Ubulibri, Milan, 78–79.

29 Cfr. V. Valentini, *Mondi, corpi, materie*, cit., 27.

30 Ivi, 143 and sgg.
31 Cfr. R. Bellour, *La Querelle des Dispositifs*, P.O.L., Paris, 2012.
32 S. Chinzari and P. Ruffini, *Nuova scena italiana: Il teatro dell'ultima generazione*, Castelvecchi, Rome, 195.
33 V. Valentini, *Mondi, corpi, materie*, Mondadori, Milan, 2007, 87; Motus, "Vacancy rooms", in *Art'o*, Aprile 2001, 61–69.
34 A. Pirillo, *Fenomenologie attoriali negli spettacoli di Pippo Delbono, Societas Raffaello Sanzio, Teatro Clandestino e Teatro Valdoca*, MA thesis in Saperi e TEcniche dello Spettacolo Teatrale, Cinematografico e Digitale, University of Rome "La Sapienza", a.a. 2008–09, 215–216.
35 Cfr. M Petruzziello, 'The Four Seasons Restaurant", *Alfabeta2*, 16 novembre, 2013. www.alfabeta2.it/2013/11/16/the-four-seasons-restaurant
36 Cfr. S. Colonna, *Definizione critic-estetica di Archittettura Liquida*, BTA, Bollettino Telematico dell'Arte, 16 giugno 2014, n. 715. http://wwwbta.it/txt/aO/07/bta00715.html. In his essay, Colonna cites Salvatore Rugino, *Liquid Box*, Roma, Arachne, 2012 (1.a edizione 2008), which references Derrick De Kerckhove's table, *L'Architettura dell'intelligenza*, Testo&Immagine, Turin, 2001, 7.
37 Derrick de Kerckhove, *L'architettura d'intelligenza*, Testo&Immagine, Turin, 2001, 7.
38 Pierre Levy, *Il virtuale*, Raffaello Cortina, Milano, 1997, 8–9.
39 See Chapter 5, *Liveness-Play-Frontality:1999–2013*.
40 Cfr. on the concept of presence, E. Pitozzi, "Figurazioni, uno studio sulle gradazioni di presenza", in Id. (ed.), *On Presence*, "Culture teatrali", n. 21, 2012, 107–108.

8   The plural modes of the actor

8.1 Actor and theme: critical and methodological issues

The twentieth century proposed and elaborated diverse ideas about the actor, from the elimination of his presence from the stage (Gordon Craig), to imagining a body without organs (Antonin Artaud), to the epic, didactic theater of Bertolt Brecht, to the voice without body in the late work of Samuel Beckett, to puppets who double the actors in the theater of Tadeusz Kantor.

Starting from the premise that we cannot separate the phenomenological analysis of the actor's presence from the subject who brings it into being historically,[1] it must be observed that thought about the actor in Italy, at least up until the Seventies, was marked by the conflict between "immersion" and "alienation". It was precisely New Theater that transformed the paradigm of the actor as interpreter of a literary text, proposing in its place the sciences of the body, non-verbal languages, and movement in space, along with the use of vocality as expressive matter.[2]

Just the same, during the *Le forze in campo* (*The Forces at Play*) conference in 1986, Claudio Meldolesi criticized the way New Theater had dealt with the figure and role of the actor, saying,

> Group theater, despite its different sensibility, has not treated the actor much better than normal theater. Today, in general they possess the culture of their group but do not possess the culture of their profession. Which renders them weak and, in certain cases, it imprisons them.[3]

The New Theater, Meldolesi charged, had grown up spontaneously, outside the institutional structures of training, leaving aside the encounter with specific methods and techniques. At the same conference, Attonio Attisani brought to light the authorial dimension of the New Theater actor, observing for example,

> Looking at the cases that have defined a way of being on stage (think, for contrasting examples, of the particular presence of Claudio Remondi

and Riccardo Caporossi, on one hand, and Leo de Berardinis on the other), we find a problem that remains to be resolved. The experimental theater groups are often formed by self-trained performers, from a theatrical point of view; it's logical that there is something missing, especially on the level of the acting [. . .]. But it's ridiculous to hypothesize a resolution to the problem by substituting what we see in experimental theater with solid professionals drawn from the market. First of all, the actors are the authors as well as the performers of what we see. Eliminating them would destroy the essence of the group itself. Furthermore, those actors possess many qualities that are extraneous to a standardized formation.[4]

Oliviero Ponte di Pino, in *Il Nuovo Teatro italiano, 1975–1988*, attributed the reduction of the actor to an object to New Theater's expulsion of the literary text from the spectacle. In this way, he seemed to presume a type of causal nexus between the present of a literary text and the presence of an actor as a central subject in the theatrical event; an "actorial subject". But opposing the concept of an actor capable of integrating mind and body to that of an actor manipulated by a director does not resolve the problems associated with the actor during the later twentieth century, since both the historical and the neo-avant gardes pursued the goal of an ideal integrity of the person-actor (in an ethical-political sense), by redefining the actor's technical-expressive parameters.

The actor is formed with a specific training, neither scholastic nor generalist, which is intended to produce a figure congenial to the aesthetic vision of a given director. This training takes place through laboratory workshops aimed at creating a spectacle resulting from a project. This is a model different both from that of the actor-author and from the master-student nexus.[5]

The New Theater does not diminish the actor, because the paradigm of stage composition means that all possible aspects of the spectacle have the same value and an analogous function, without a pre-constituted hierarchy that privileges either the actor or the dramatic text. The centrality of the actor in New Theater was defined within new parameters, which were shaped around each performer's specific practices. In the *Perdita di memoria* (*Loss of Memory*) trilogy, Federico Tiezzi affirmed the centrality of the actor as the figure who measures and regulates the physical, psychic, perceptual, and imaginative space. The actor, that is, is not so much a sonic and gestural vehicle of the written word, but a figure who re-integrates the word through the rhythm of his or her body. The New Theater is therefore an actor's theater, in that the actor is also the author of the spectacle, and is exonerated of the task of having to transport a character, with that character's affect and psychology. Rather, Tiezzi's actor, in *Perdita di memoria*, imposes his or her presence as a type of energy, with all the physical and psychic electricity of the figure's existence in space. This type of actor appeared in New Theater spectacles in all of the following ways: flung like a projectile;

set off like a bas relief; framed in a tableau (*Diario Segreto*); immobile as a vegetable; a nocturnal phantom capable of evoking other phantoms (Marion D'Amburgo in *Ritratto dell'attore da giovane* – Portrait of the Actor as a Young Man, FOCUS); a mysterious, anthropomorphic figure, a cross between animal, vegetable, and human (Barberio Corsetti in *Diario segreto contraffatto* – Counterfeit Secret Diary); a narrating voice that creates images and presences. In the spectacles of Rem & Cap, the actors appear in continuous mutation, passing from animate to inanimate, from puppet to phantom, to shadow; from a costume element (a metonymic part standing for the whole) to a bundle (a bunched-together costume that takes the place of a character, denoting the character *in absentia*).

The rupture of the harmonious relation between the stage and the character, a relation expressing a model of the dialectic unity of an "I" with its surrounding world, led to the disappearance of the character and an interruption in the sequential chain of stage action. Instead, the body and its postures, the voice and its sounds, took center stage. The word cohabited with and penetrated a body that itself became a stage, a space, and an object. No longer were only stage characters endowed with voice, but vocal modulations – mumbling, breathing, the whole gamma of sonic gesture – became themselves characters. At the same time, the character was broken down into corporeal attitudes, like certain rock singers or figures in Andy Warhol's movies. Spectators heard pure voices, pure postures, without consequential or motivated actions to perform; vocal expressions of a dismembered organism, a sound invading the body from outside (hetero-direction), the body imploding in on itself. Discussing the function of the actor meant investigating the relation between body and voice, returning to the roots of *pneuma* – pure breath – and its corporeal sources, revealing the scission between them due to the forms of mediation, and the efforts at reintegration.

The territory of this analysis includes the presence of characters split between verbal and gestural languages, rendering impossible any conciliation between time and space, between verbal flow and physical action. New technologies gave stage expression to interior voices (for example, in Carmelo Bene's technique of being alone in public). The various modalities of psychic – rather than physical – space were represented in the division between the disembodied, acousmatic voice and visible subject. Actors were dispossessed not only of their voice, but also of their capacity for thought and action, becoming dismantled body-machines, with prostheses or grafted parts. The actor-presence embodied figures of the living and the inert, the animal, and the still life. Bodies dissolved into light, dematerialized.

Rather than describing abstract models of performance, New Theater actors should be analyzed according to the modes in which they manifested their presence, in their multiple forms, through the description of the effectual actions they carried out on stage. Effectual action depends upon a triangulation including at one point *ethos* and *pratton*; that is, the actions the actor performs and the abilities such actions demand. At another point of

the triangle stands the actor's function within the dramaturgy of the spectacle. At the third point stands the implicit visions of the world to which the
actor gives shape.[6] Against the historical background of the macro-systems
invented by the founders of modern theater, the paradigm of the actor of the
later twentieth century is a plural one, in tune with the practices and visions
of the theater-world of the various authors of each New Theater spectacle.

8.2 Actor as collective body

New Theater centered discourse about the actor on the body, a platform
upon which to build a rapport between diverse cultures (west and east),
between disciplines (anthropology and theater), and between languages
(dance and theater).

In his *Manifesto* of *arte povera* (1967), Germano Celant wrote, "among
living things, the artist discovers also herself, her body, her memory, her gestures".[7] Celant evoked a relation between the organic and the inorganic,
between subjects belonging to the vegetable, animal, and mineral worlds, and
described life as a flow which the human being may also blend into, simplify-
ing her intentional actions. Celant claimed that artists must disempower their
technical and intellectual know-how, privileging instead the sensorial sphere.

The emphasis Celant placed on the artist as a new type of human being
was not dissimilar from what Jerzy Grotowski was claiming about the actor,
and Grotowski's convictions in this regard drove him to abandon the practice of theater. The central concern was to change the human being, a far
more urgent priority than training actors, because the new actor could exist
only alongside a new man.[8] Just as theater in those years privileged non-
verbal languages as a way to regenerate itself against the domination of
the literary text, the visual arts of the era zeroed-out "discourse via images,
structures that imposed regularity, behavior, syntax",[9] in favor of the dimension of the living organism (as in the "I am the work" principle in Body
Art), favoring the combination of action and experience, artist and spectator together. The political drive of *arte povera* was to transform society,
starting from the subject who discards the burden of history and culture,

> a movement toward de-culture, toward regression, toward the primeval
> and the repressed, toward pre-logical, pre-iconographic states, elemen-
> tary and spontaneous behavior, a preference for the primary elements
> of nature (earth, sea, snow, minerals, heat, animals), life (body, mem-
> ory, thought), and politics (the nuclear family, spontaneous action, class
> struggle, violence, environment).[10]

These ideas found an effective confirmation in the work of Jannis Kounellis, who conceived space as a theatrical cavity in which the spectator was
projected into the center of the action, and reciprocally, in the conception
of the stage space as a picture frame. In a statement entitled *Del corpo, del*

comportamento, del "natural", del "vivo" come autenticità teatrale (On the body, on behavior, on the "natural", on the "alive" as theatrical authenticity), written for a 1968 spectacle by Carlo Quartucci, *I testimoni* (The Witnesses), Kounellis called for a radical paradigm change:

> We can and must start over, beginning with our own body, the actor and the spectator in parallel, on stage and in life. And we can and must start over with an alternative behavior, for the actor, for the spectator, performing and living. In this way the body and behavior are no longer disjointed, one moving in one direction, the other in another. What is old in theater, what is definitively dead, is precisely this existing, persistent contradiction on stage and in life between what we assume physically and the way we react to this physicality. Instead, this "corporality" must be understood not as a need to achieve an expressive form "technically", but rather to assimilate a moral "authenticity". From this is born the extraordinarily "active" demand for concord between what happens on stage and the way we react, since only a fundamental authenticity can today at least correct, if not transform, the old way of doing theater, which is that of remaining within the "product" and never wanting to demolish it.[11]

This ideal was at the base of the aesthetic revolution of New Theater in the Sixties and Seventies, as manifested in different ways by the Living Theatre, by Grotowski, by Quartucci, and by many others, many of who worked collectively with experimental methods and technologies of the self. The historical avant-gardes and many twentieth-century theater communes were marked by utopian politics and spirituality, including the belief that changing society is possible by modifying individual behavior, both in daily life and on the stage.

From the end of the Sixties until the mid-Seventies, numerous experiences were stamped with these ideas. In the spectacle *I Testimoni*, (The Witnesses), Kounellis and Quartucci [FOCUS] aimed at creating a crisis in the product, in technical knowledge, and in the bourgeois architecture of theater, substituting them with something living, true, natural, authentic. The political and aesthetic drive was to eliminate the separation that traditionally opposed producers and consumers, bringing in the inhabitants of the provincial town of Marigliano, where Leo de Berardinis and Perla Peragallo went to live in search of a new sense of theater.[12] *Prova del Woyzeck* by Büchner (Carlo Cecchi, 1969) chose a non-theatrical space to bring to life stage actions with spectators very close, adopting the dialect of the inhabitants of a working-class neighborhood (Lingotto in Turin), presenting itself as a permanent open rehearsal, outside the traditional Italian theatrical sphere, invading the space of the spectator and making fixed social roles more flexible.

The ethical dimension of the actor (*ethos* as thought and vision of the world) emerged as a device and attitude to be privileged over the technical dimension and professional actor training. The behavior of the subject-actor outside the theater (that actor's life as an individual in society) should dictate the conditions of his or her action (*pratton*) on stage.[13] The words "collective" and "laboratory" expressed an effective synthesis between experimentation with languages and political-social commitment (speaking of a people's revolution, in 1968!) in a dimension separate from the radicalism of North American experimental theater.[14]

One important change in the practice of artists was *doing* in place of *observing*. This "doing" led to cancelling out the distance between the subject and the world, and was synonymous with "participation". "Doing" also tended to abolish the role of the spectator, who was summoned to participate in a community, setting aside bourgeois individualism.

8.3   Without language or subject: from the monologue to the solo

Carmelo Bene is at the origin of our investigation into how New Theater redefined the actor's functions, roles, and practices. Bene was convinced that the actor who enunciates a literary text must not, to begin with, understand it. Rather, he or she must make the words sound good and produce a rhythmic reading, with neither thought nor interpretation, until the process comes to a word that wounds; from that word, the meaning of the entire text will disclose itself. In this way, the text becomes transformed into a score, where every single letter in a word is given color. The actor who occupies a stage and faces an audience must not limit herself to proffering a text, but must swallow it, chew it, and tear it to pieces.

In this dimension, the actor is "anti-performative" and must never render a "character", but rather exercise control over her body, using gesture and voice in relation to the stage space. The voice must be utilized not according to the modulations and clichés of traditional acting, but as an exercise of distancing from standard diction, inventing new phonetic aggregations. From this viewpoint, we can understand Carmelo Bene's use of the sound-noise, bound to his gesture-body-word, and his mode of rewriting the stage text as autonomous with respect to the literary text, which becomes unrecognizable. Bene pronounced sequences of syllables, masticated words, interrupted phrases with hysterical laughter, and overlaid voices with echo effects: "speaking to oneself *sottovoce* in a public piazza [. . .] Hearing one's own language as though it were foreign, using continuous tonal variations".[15]

As actor, Carmelo Bene stood radically apart from the actor-speakers who memorize the literary text and

> present the text, ignorant of the fact that "the text" is the actor; the *text* is the *voice*. External to the text, they address another external (listener). Galactically distant from *Greek amplification*, it is a certain destiny that the heavenly beings prohibit them from approaching, except

grotesquely, the *sonic instrumentation* that alone consents an *inside* to
transmit itself into another *inside, cutting the thread of communication.*
An *inside* "breathes" into another unmediated, demonic *inside* [. . .].
And the voice itself listens to itself speak [. . .] In *vocal writing, poetry
is the voice.* The *text is its echo.*[16]

Taking off from Carmelo Bene's theater writing and performance as actor
(speaking as though alone, eradicating "the other" from the stage and, with
it, the dialogic form), from his way of introjecting his own voices into the
world, the theater stage became populated with soloing actors representing
an imploded world. Dialogue disappeared from contemporary texts composed for the theater. In its place, actors pursued their own thought in a
space-time that led them beyond the stage. At most, dialogue persisted as a
mere residue, masked within an empty frame (as in the senseless conversations of Samuel Beckett, or in the concert-form voices in Robert Wilson's
work, which exploited only the abstract form of dialogic interaction). Characters no longer exchanged information, but alternated lines on stage without effectual dialogue; each character speaking to him- or herself.

In a form of theater with no room for dialogue – as an expression of inter-
personal relations between subject and world, or of conflicting positions
that move toward synthesis – there were no longer monologues, but solos,
in a musical or choreographic sense. The solo became a form of monologue
going off the rails, because it manifested an egocentric form seeking not
debate (through which diverse notions of the world may be confirmed or
refuted) but an epiphany of one's own existence, through a verbal-gestural
flow. The solo stages a language made partly of actions and partly of words,
a language not directed at others, but like that of an infant making sounds
for itself, which resembles less the realm of language than that of action.[17]
The impossibility of dialogue in dramatic literature in the later twentieth century manifested itself as the impossibility of separating the object
from the subject, because the subject, having introjected the world, is no
longer capable of "holding it in front of his eyes". The interlocutor becomes
an ever-mobile point of view, articulated by the subject itself, who simu-
lates diverse presences with the mimicry of her own voice. The distinction
between self and other, between question and answer, is shrouded in fog,
and the actor is no longer a unity of thought and action, or of the spoken
and its consequent action.

Carmelo Bene's theater represents this tragedy of the divided self, the crisis of theater based on roles:

> The actor of illness takes care not to deprive himself of the wavering
> that he consists of. Rather, he even needs to use the dialogic form in
> his monologues, so as to restore the essential delirium of the nullifying
> plot [. . .]. The omnivorous voice is the temporal sunset of the senseless
> protagonism of the roles [. . .]. Finally, the monologue is no longer one

moment among others in the theater. On the contrary, it is the entire spectacle.[18]

As stated earlier, in Carmelo Bene's case the traditional definition of the monologue is not appropriate. Literally, the monologue is the rendering in direct form of the thought of a character (without comment on the part of the writer), distinct from the mere flow of consciousness, due to a lesser intrusion of the unconscious. It is a suspension of the temporal flow of the drama and the spectacle, during which the character gives voice to her thought. Bene's modality is also different from the soliloquy, where the character stands alone on stage and supposes that his words are not heard by anyone else. It is also different from the solo, a modality in which the character reveals her feelings, something like an operatic aria.

Romeo Castellucci's observation may help us to distinguish the solo from the monologue:

> The monologue still has a strong literary structure, closely linked to a narrative and illustrative structure. The monologue inevitably alludes to the presence of the author, the writer. It is the author speaking, in reality. We must only listen and receive. Two positions: A and B. A solo can express a gigantic solitude. I think of Carmelo Bene's unbridled solos, as an example known to all. Carmelo Bene went beyond the concept of monologue with a homeopathic method. The actor took the place of the author [. . .]. A solo is unlikely to degrade into a moral lesson, because it shares or is born from the same solitude that the spectator feels.[19]

With the solo, the actor inhabits a different temporal space, an internal, emotional space where others cannot enter, because it is a personal space that concerns the experience of the speaker. In some solo performances, subject and object coincide, in the only simultaneous exhibition of the self and the personal reactions to the world that the subject has introjected. The solo in these cases connotes a mixture of thought and enunciation in a chain of reactions. An example is Beckett's *Krapp's Last Tape*, in which Krapp's present (as he listens to his recorded voice, reacting to it with physical actions such as closing his eyes, switching off the playback, cursing, wincing, etc.) dialogues with his past self, given witness in the voice of the tape recorder.

Another solo is the one performed by Sandro Lombardi in Heiner Müller's *Hamletmaschine* (1988): a mental dialogue consisting of lines directed at the principal characters (Ophelia, Polonius, the Ghost, Gertrude), in which the questions are amputated from the responses of the interlocutors, since that they are not present on stage, but only evoked by the actor playing Hamlet (who says "I was Hamlet"). The non-existent dialogue is interspersed with descriptions of the actions in each scene evoked.

In *La Camera Astratta* (by Barberio Corsetti-Studio Azzurro, 1987, FOCUS) as well, the mental is the action, a zone of human activity that psychoanalysis has made it possible to verbalize, through elements that overstep the bounds of the subject. The voice sets out on its own, as uncontrollable as thought, its movement facilitated by the music which seems to enwrap the nervous system of the spectacle, like a skin. There are no actions that have any relation to a world outside the psychic space, which is the true subject of the representation.[20] The actor possesses techniques that confer presence on stage to a phantasmagoria of figures with whom he has intense familiarity, calling out to them as vocal presences. This procedure functions such that the world exists as an *internal voice*, a mental landscape in which contemplation gives birth to visions. The past comes to life again in the present, thanks to technological memories that project invisible bodies onto the stage. As Helga Finter writes, "in the perception of the voice, it is the imaginary aroused by the hearable that determines the relation with the visible and creates a tie to it".[21]

In the dramaturgy of spectacles at the end of the millennium, the solo was developed through a wide range of compositional practices, giving form to a theater-world that redefined the difference between the tangible and the intangible.

8.4 Blocking the body and freeing the voice

Luca Ronconi (1933–2015) shared with New Theater the experimental method of the laboratory, a development process which devoted extended time to the construction of a spectacle, in collaboration with a stable group of actors, and a dramaturgy of the stage space that created new relations with the body-voice of the actor.[22] In his spectacles, the literary text (written or rewritten by Sanguineti, Wilcock, or others) was shattered, dispersed in space, offered up by actors whose bodies were blocked. In *Fedra* (1968), Seneca's text was rendered in the form of a reading, in declamatory style, with the actors immobile in illuminated niches positioned at different levels on a wall. From these isolated stations, each actor spoke his or her part, "a spectacle-oratorio, with all the actors always present, condemned to immobility, without any possibility of communicating or reaching one another, except through the word".[23] Imprisoned in neoclassical tunics throughout the spectacle, the actors charge the action with energy, shifting it from movement in space to words and waving arms, using a bombastic style of declamation. The actors concentrated on the study of metrics and rhythm, each character using a different cadence, "from the excited to the atonal, in a musical spectrum sustained by the *musique concrète* score by Vinko Globokar".[24]

Luca Ronconi's theater (we refer in particular here to his work before the Eighties) was woven with literary texts but did not place the actor at its center; rather, the performance style was labored, deformed, with a broken, geometric, sharp-edged gestuality, exaggerated like that of silent films. The actions, movements, costumes, and makeup turned the body into a plastic mass that suppressed individual human features. The leather costume worn by Vittorio Gassman in *Richard III*, for example, caged the actor and deprived him of free movement. Gassman in fact was dragged around the space by pulleys, or stood still in a niche from which he could not escape.

Using costume-traps that envelope the body (with rough cords that abraded the skin), the director forced the actors into positions that impeded movement and kept them from speaking in natural voices. "The meaning of the words is often sacrificed to the physical attitude of the actor, to sonorous monologues, to the physicalization of the relationship between two characters".[25] In the production of Giordano Bruno's *Il Candelaio*, "the exaggerated tonalities, booming sounds, the grafting of voice with often hopelessly bitter language, had the effect of rendering the vocal *impasto* of the spectacle incomprehensible".[26] This effect of obscurity was further increased by the text itself, which mixed Latin with pseudo-scientific and pseudo-Petrarchan language. *Richard III* unleashed an orchestration of sonic gestures such as sobs, screams, cackling, sharp and flat falsetto voices. About Ronconi's *Orestea* (1973), Angelo Maria Ripellino wrote,

> acoustic cubism marks the volumetric deconstruction, the rhythm is black, with an exaggerated breaking of phrases into their facets. This phonetic volumetric, this halting and fragmented scansion, is intended to express cold fury, ancestral dementia, the stuttering of myth. The phonic pattern does not coincide with the logical *ductus* of the spoken line, but is broken up into a sequence of fragments of varying timbre. The sing-song speech of Marisa Fabbri, tortured by assiduous, metronomic caesura, has been termed 'vocal spirit possession (*tarantolismo*)'.[27]

This privileging of the vocal and sonic register over movement can be found in other representative cases, such as Socìetas Raffaello Sanzio's *Voyage au bout de la nuit* (1999, based on Louis-Ferdinand Céline's 1932 novel; in English *Voyage to the End of the Night*), a spectacle in the form of a concert. While Hamlet had presented himself as an aphasic, autistic youth (capable only of emitting sonic gestures torn by the lacerating whistles of gunfire), here the actor-vocalists reduced Céline's novel to phonemes by inventing an acoustic universe that emphasized the peculiar traits of the author's writing, in which the syntactic structure of the sentence is exploded. This characteristic spurred the conception of a score in which listeners, "felt as though they were in the middle of a battle, where blows of sound landed as though in a fog, coming from all sides".[28]

Like an onstage deejay surrounded by digital processors, computers, sequencers, and samplers, Romeo Castellucci turned sounds into emulsions, or rather – suspended in the space of the vast, dark stage – made technologically-produced electronic sounds co-exist with the instantaneous sounds of the performers, whose bodies were paralyzed in plain sight. The firm voice of Claudia Castellucci and the modular flexibility of Chiara Guidi's voice coexisted with the sonic gestures of Silvia Pasello. The mix stratified diverse sources, both found and taped sounds, including musical selections processed to the point of unrecognizability, but ordered and woven into the score.[29] Employed like a blunt object, the percussion hit spectators in the guts, a weapon used against them. The sonic register of the spectacle produced a sensory and emotional impact through song modulated on breath, screams, onomatopoeic sound, and sonic clumps.

The stage was divided into two juxtaposed parts, vocal and visual. The vocal part engaged in a battle against being extinguished and overwhelmed by the other language codes of the spectacle, such as the plastic-visual dimension and the sonic plane produced by the deejay.

8.5 Word as event

For Mariangela Gualtieri and Cesare Ronconi of Teatro Valdoca, a spectacle must not consist of the execution of a project or a text, but must emerge from the choice of which abilities to put to use, whether voice, song, dance, acrobatics, or something else. These skills were brought forth and shaped during rehearsals with a band of young actors who inhabited the enclosed but infinite space of the theater. They established residence in the theater-place they found themselves in, recognizing it and living in it as a field of forces marked by innumerable footprints made while performing the initiatory rites that bound the little community together.[30] The point of departure was the people involved (who constituted the measure and form of the piece that would take shape) together with the poetic texts of Mariangela Gualtieri.[31] Gualtieri explained,

> I ask the actor to adopt techniques that will lead to the development of a mask that will push the actor toward a place to get lost in [. . .]. This state scares the actor [. . .]. It makes him lose track of time and take the time necessary to destroy everything.[32]

The objective was to discover "one's own center", "to enter into contact with a source within oneself", and receive a revelation. Doing theater is carrying out an initiatory ritual that integrates the actor into the tribe; the actor must be visibly marked, passing through a rite of membership in the group which is overseen by a master. Before every spectacle, in fact, the director painted the arms, necks, legs, and above all the mouths of the actors with red and black colors. Being marked was useful for the initiation into the game of cross-dressing, forming a new tribe in which men were not distinguished from women. In *Ossicine* (Little Bones, 1994), in fact, they all wore flowered clothing, and the faces of the young women and men (due to the gaudy makeup, together with the effect produced by the blazing light of the torches) looked like icons, their individuality transfigured. The *dramatic personae* of Teatro Valdoca's spectacles were prepared bodies, spots of color. In *Ossicine*, the fat, stupid queen who spat on the ground and grinned, emitting every so often a sound made of aspirated consonants, danced by herself, holding green reeds in her hand and wearing a giant hat, like something evaporated from a cruel dream of Lewis Carroll.

The Teatro Valdoca actor has a double valence: each one unique (with an unmistakable stamp) but simultaneously a part of a whole. "The uniqueness consists in that body with that voice, those muscles; only that person can speak those words to you".[33]

In this company's spectacles, the word was offered up in a particular way: the actor seemed driven by a need, or compelled by a duty, to carry out the task of pulling the words out of his or her mouth. In *Cantos* (1988), the voice of the actor emerged with pain, as though in the act of birth. In *Paesaggio con fratello rotto* (Landscape with Broken Brother, 2005, FOCUS), the figure of the oracle had a defective speaking apparatus that, again, made the emission of sound like a painful birth; the actress's voice was guttural, the oracle's body bent over, its life escaping, as though possessed by the god who inspired the words. She was held up by other actors (like a Greek chorus) in order to be able to yank out the words within. Speaking figures, in this spectacle, as a coming-into-light, the speaker's eyes closed. The chorus holds her arms and head, forcing the word to find the necessary narrow passage to fulfill its duty of being spoken. In this sense, the poetic word became sacralized through the impediment of the body. Just as speaking and being spoken was staged, so also was the action of listening to the word, which corresponded to the act of speaking as a dramatic stage action.

In *Paesaggio con fratello rotto*, the central space of the stage was set aside for the chorus, consisting of six women and one man, whose function was to observe the actions performed around them, illuminating them by pointing lamps, spotlights, and lighted poles. The chorus was both witness and actor: they observed and acted, danced, confused matters, struggled, slithered like animals, played rock-paper-scissors, ran around the animal, and poked it with red-painted sticks, in an cruel, infantile game. Single figures stepped out from the chorus, such as "the doll" carried in a cart who recalled one of the figures in *Las Meninas* by Velasquez. Another, touchingly, stepped away from the others and, on tiptoe, leaned toward the microphone, saying, "What does it take to cut a lamb's throat? But to make grain grow, that's something". Their young faces expressed amazement, ingenuousness, animal happiness, playfulness, aggressiveness, war, love: they represented humanity. The stage was a world with many people wandering in it; some were granted speech, which battled in a tragic struggle for integrity and fullness.

The actors existed on stage like parts of a single organism, each individual the energy of the other. In *Parsifal* (1999), an actor (Danio Manfredini) played a mythical character who took on the burden of embodying the non-hero, Parsifal ("old and lame", as described by Mariangela Gualtieri).[34] The spectator, however, perceived less an individual character than a chorality, in which each physiognomy assumed a sort of distinctive collective mark, which was the sensation of suffering that gave tonal unity to the spectacle. In this work, the distinctive trait came from the grain of the voice, from the way the words were given form (laments, prayers, litanies, doggerel), rather than from the speaker/characters, such as the mother, the hirsute Cundri, the Hermit.

8.6 Auto-fiction

The relationship between person and character shifted toward the side of the person in late-century theater. The actor was called upon to bring to stage his or her version of the world, along with a will (*pratton*) to change that world; that is, to weave a continuum between life and the artwork, while reducing the distance from the spectator.

A widespread practice of the anti-performative, anti-illusionistic New Theater actor was one that might be termed, in parallel with literature, *auto-fiction*.[35] The procedure consisted in mixing pre-existent materials in such a way as to confuse fiction with autobiography; to render reality directly, television-style, but also to adopt a confidential, intimate style, as though the writer were revealing herself to the reader/spectator. *Auto-fiction* short-circuits the separation between chronicle and invention *inside* a character, who says "I" in first person and uses her or his real name.

In the spectacles of Deflorian-Tagliarini, the self-reflexive conceptual mechanism of staging the construction of the spectacle itself can be considered a practice of *auto-fiction*, in which the character is the actor as she deals with the anguish, dilemmas, and doubts that invaded her during the development process of a play. In *Ce ne andiamo per non darvi troppe pre-occupazioni* (We'll leave to spare you bother, 2013, FOCUS), two dimensions intersect one another. The actor-character immediately offers herself up by saying, "I'm the one, Daria, who read the novel by the Greek writer Petros Markaris, *The Settlement*, and wants to stage the story of the women who commit suicide". At the same time, the first person is rendered as a compositional artifice for the spectator, to whom the actress, Daria Deflorian, is intent on demonstrating that she is performing herself, as she asks herself how to stage the story, taken from a novel, of four elderly women in Greece who killed themselves so as the relieve the state of having to look after them. Deflorian-Tagliarini's play was carefully constructed to represent the to-and-fro between giving body and presence to the four elderly women who prepare to commit suicide and the presence of the four actors (two women and two men) who perform themselves as they try to investigate the motivations (the effects of the Greek economic crisis) that drove the women to take their own lives. The characters in the novel are spoken of in the third person, described rather than performed, in a sort of literary epic form. The spectacle presents how the actors prepared the spectacle, adopting an explicit self-reflexive register ("How should we do it? We're not ready!"). The illusion that this mechanism produces in the spectator is that of witnessing the production process of the spectacle in real time. Rather than directly representing the suicide of the women, the spectators watch the rehearsals of the play that will present the deaths. This *auto-fiction* reinforces the mechanism of *as if*, the sense of "let's pretend that". To overcome the fictional aspect of theater, the fictional aspect is exaggerated by showing the existences of the actors intent on creating the work.

Auto-fiction is one of the ways theater in the new millennium has responded to the problem of the drama and the character. Instead of conceding "the impossibility of representation",[36] it highlights the ways in which theater represents. The pleasure of *auto-fiction* for the spectator, in this work by Deflorian-Tagliarini, resides in the sense of being admitted to the private realm of the actor, being comforted and seduced by the display of documentary data (as in a television or journalistic reportage) while also getting a peek inside the private space of the rehearsal room. *Auto-fiction* thus reinforces the actor's role as performer, just as the meta-theatrical aspect reinforces the theatrical.

8.7 Over-representing representation

Richard Schechner attributes to performative activity a concept he calls "restoration of behavior", by which he means an activity that recuperates, in the present, the oral and/or literary tradition of theater, including the "cultural patrimony of the performer, his or her personal experience". This means that performance always stands at a threshold: if it passes beyond the liminal dimension (on the part of the performer's experience), it obstructs the psychic distance of the spectator from the work, provoking discomfort.

This is the case of the version of Genet's *Les Nègres* produced by the Compagnia della Fortezza, entitled *I negri 1996*. Directed by Armando Punzo, the *dramatis personae* are two actor-prisoners in the theater company at the maximum-security prison in Volterra. They are body-books splayed open before the eyes of spectators, to whom each character details his personal story of violence and suffering, producing an effect that stings the spectator with a sense of authenticity beyond mere representation [FOCUS]. Rather than seeming to reveal meaning or offer an interpretation of Genet, the fragments extrapolated from the text, memorized by the performers, measure the distance between the present of the incarcerated performers and a spatio-temporal elsewhere, with which the prisoners have established a dynamic of appropriation and distancing. *Les Nègres* functions like a terrain where the social masks, behavioral schemas, and psycho-physical resistance typical of prisoners are shattered. Seeing spectacles by the Compagnia della Fortezza makes viewers understand the revolutionary value of having transferred the ability of the actor from the technical-professional plane to an ethical-existential one. As Jerzy Grotowski said,

> we feel that an actor reaches the essence of his vocation when he performs an act of sincerity, when he bares himself. Acting with sincerity

means being able to react totally, that is, to begin to exist. Because every day, we only react half way.[37]

When performing, the prisoner-actors do not interpret literary characters; neither do they work from Brecht's alienation effect. They neither perform characters nor tell about them, but take them into themselves, to the degree the characters can be contained within the inmates' own experience. The hymn of exaltation of negritude sung by the character named Bobò, given by the regal, tuxedoed figure of a prisoner-actor, is a conscious witness of a desperate condition, precisely because it is a prisoner who is singing it out. In interpreting Genet's character, the inmate-actor produces a non-coincidence between the role and himself, a (weak, in truth) ambiguity that pushes him into the space between "I am not Bobò" on one hand, and "I'm not myself, either" on the other. Instead, he is someone who – through the character of Bobò – is seeking to reveal something of himself. The liminal activity of the performer becomes a double pathway, an action that takes place before our ways but that enounces a *not here* and a *not now*.[38]

8.8 Actor-machine-sculpture-animal-cyborg

New Theater radically contested the centrality of the actor, as seen in the very first of Richard Schechner's *Six Axioms for an Environmental Theater* (1967): "Each element in the performance speaks its own language, and among the elements in the performance, the actor is not the most important one!" This means that the actor must establish a relation of interchangeability with the other elements of the staging. In place of a relation of inter-subjectivity among the characters, we find relations of body with objects, from which flows the actor's performance and the actor's ability to manifest bodily postures. These postures may include a body-sculpture, a body-machine, or a plastic composition in which the body blends with the objects it creates (Mario Ricci); or becomes architecture (Rem & Cap); or automatons, prosthetic cyborgs (Socìetas Raffaello Sanzio); a trace (Pathosformel); a detail (gruppo nanou); or a body composed of light. Franco Quadri observed about Luca Ronconi's 1968 version of *Richard III* that, "the performers become *props*, distinguished from the metal or wood accessories on stage only by their ability to speak. Actors as things, and the relations among them as forces, mechanisms, repulsion, annulment".[39]

In Mario Ricci's 1970 version of *King Lear*, the actors constructed and composed plastic forms and images on stage, using objects and various materials. Italo Moscati wrote,

> The stage no longer contains the characters and the events, but becomes the screen of a primordial projector that displays a series of spaces filled by something else. What is that something else? In the first place, the work of the actors with the objects. A shield can be made from the canopy of a children's merry-go-round, or may blend with other objects to become a

luminous wall behind which the unseen actors build a marionette theater. King Lear can play at having his portrait done, which the others then erase, or he can repeatedly compose his own image with blocks that silently slide on a structure that drops down from the darkness [. . .]. We should mention in this regard the battle scenes with wooden horses – with the actors' legs serving as those of the horses – that stand out in sharp relief over the projection of a color film of *King Lear*'s characters. The two overlapping dimensions create an anguishing double.[40]

The text of *Sacco* (by Rem & Cap, 1974, FOCUS) is composed of a series of drawings, like a storyboard. Spectators watch a figure emerge from a burlap sack, making sounds, singing little songs, making movements, finally achieving liberation from the container and the torturer who put him there. In the same company's *Richiamo* (1975), two workers in a body shop manipulate a mechanical device. "The real lead character is the car, which determines every aspect of the spectacle, generating the space, the time, the objects, the sound score, and even the text".[41] After *Richiamo* came other related devices: for *Rotòbolo* (1976), spectator-bypassers followed a complex procedure to enter one-by-one, and then exit from, an enormous sheet-metal cylinder constructed in a field outside Milan. In *Améba* (1986), two twin machines moved, then destroyed and reconstructed themselves [FOCUS]. The compositional means of Rem & Cap makes the spectacle consist of the construction of a stage mechanism: a sculpture in movement, an installation, a piece of architectural ephemera. Their theater-world presents a peculiar phenomenology of the actor that moves from presence to absence, toward the phantom, the shadow, achieving – through a sort of initiatory investiture – the status of *dramatis personae*. They then descend back into their ghostly condition, finally becoming mere heaps: a hat, a pair of shoes, a vest – the merest remains of a person.[42]

Up through the end of the Eighties, Giorgio Barberio Corsetti was both actor and author of his spectacles, presenting himself as a body-sculpture and as an architecture, a figure deformed by strange clothes that camouflaged the body in space, hiding in holes and small openings, disappearing and reappearing from cavities. The actor utilized aerial space, developing scenes in the air, flattening onto the walls, becoming shadow. At the same time, the body was disarticulated; dancing, it would lose pieces of itself. The character/figures of spectacles such as *Il ladro d'anime* (The Soul Thief), *Prologo a Diario Segreto contraffatto* (Prologue to a Counterfeit Secret Diary), *Descrizione di una Battaglia* (Description of a Battle, 1988) presented abstract monsters: icy, awkward, and cruel even as they would smile and behave in a way opposite to their claims. They were figures in a state of collapse who challenged equilibrium, without foreseeing, "the point of departure and arrival of a fall, a leap, as in a dance, which is mental risk above all. The fact of not knowing where they would land allowed them to play with imbalance and loss".[43] There was continuity between the body-objects and the architecture: chairs were anthropomorphized, reaching out to embrace the bodies who sat in them. Two-dimensional drawings became three-dimensional: Eyes and mouths opened and out came out actors who were body-bundles. The figures ironically and lyrically incarnated the division of the subject, the disintegration of the unity of the self, the impossibility of making action coincide with speech, and the neurosis produced by the disarticulation of language.

8.9 Spectral amplitude of the performer

The trends we have described as characterizing performance during the period under review should not be read as suggesting there was not an extremely wide range of activities underway, driven by many different drives and intentions.

In the United States, in the years between 1970 and 1976, performance actions by the first generation of performance artists such as Vito Acconci, Chris Burden, and Lisa Montano, among many others, employed both themselves and the spectator as subjects. Their works were both conceptual and concrete. Their ideas had to be presented in real locations, but within fixed time limits. Performances might last five days, seven hours, or an entire year. Actor and author coincided in a single body-action, both mental and corporeal at the same time.

Seeking a new status beyond that as an interpreter of texts – but similar to a conceptual art performance – the New Theater actor stood at a liminal point, neither person nor character. "I am myself on stage. I do not wish to live someone else's life". The actor furthermore tended to unify separate languages, such as theater and dance, and to take on the training traditions of diverse cultures, such as Nô Theater and Kabuki, Balinese and Indian dance. They included the production process within the spectacle, employing photography, cinema, video, graphic novels, etc. And they performed concrete actions.

Many New Theater spectacles made use of non-professional actors chosen for the singularity of their appearance: people with anorexia, obese people, people with handicaps, or a person who had recovered from a coma. In *Genesi* (Genesis) by Socìetas Raffaello Sanzio, the stage was populated by a repertory of singular non-actors, prodigious for their physical appearance: a person with phocomelia, a woman lacking a breast, a black bodybuilder, a contortionist. In *Inferno* (Romeo Castellucci, 2008), neither actors nor characters appear: the spectacle filled the stage with extras, enrolled like those in crowd scenes in films, who were required to perform simple actions. They were not *dramatis personae* in the Aristotelian sense of having action and character (*praxis* and *ethos*); instead, the main character was a crowd that was flagrantly extraneous to the traditional conception of the stage.

In *Untitled. I will be there when you die* (by Sciarroni, 2013, FOCUS), four professional jugglers would throw their juggling pins in the air, beating a rhythm in a different way at every catch, producing different sounds: dull, muffled, light, and so on. This action, reiterated throughout the spectacle, didn't evoke the circus, but worked strictly as movement and sound in the neutral stage space, a sort of choreography. The objects were extensions of their bodies, and their steady, repeated actions filled the present time of the performance, without evidencing any progressive tiring or collapse.

In *An Afternoon Love* (by Pathosformel, 2011), an African American professional basketball player stood alone on a stage empty except for a bottle of water, an old-style "ghetto blaster", a basketball, and a towel. The action was his solitary practice, from warmup to cooling down at the end.

CollettivO CineticO's 2012 spectacle *<age>* consisted of the nine adolescents who helped to compose the piece by answering a questionnaire about their behavior, a sort of self-portrait.

We can include all these different works within the ample spectrum of performance, as would Richard Schechner, seeing as how the historical figure of the performer covers all these multifarious figures, which function to deconstruct the statute of what an actor is.

The spectacles by Socìetas Raffaello Sanzio featured dysfunctional individuals (people with Down's Syndrome, autistics, anorexics) and manipulations of the body, such that the "spiritual" arose not in contrast to the "material"; rather, in these cases the material manifested and guaranteed the spiritual. The goal, unreachable by an actor, was to achieve the non-consciousness of an animal, something equivalent to "critical apnea", which is the ideal state for the spectator. *La Discesa di Inanna* (The Descent of Inanna, 1989) presented two baboons:

> The monkey is intended to substitute the human, to remind us of our intimate link to the animal, which on stage has a threatening effect [. . .]. The animal as carrier of the spirit is an hypostasis, the icon of the actor, his shadow, his hindrance, his dream, his desire, his tongue, his body, his pathos, ethos, his *rythmos* [. . .]. Because of this, I sought to knead together the movements of the actors with those of the animals, becoming a single magma.[44]

In this theater, the presence of the animal joined with the search for an inarticulate expressivity, bringing gesture, dance, and rhythm to the stage. In the company's *Orestea* (1995), the bodies of the actors were animated by machines (such as the mechanical arm worn by Orestes, a compressed-air device holding a dagger) that literally armed Orestes' vendetta, evidencing the *deus ex machina* of the tragedy, the violence that overcomes individual will. The automatic mechanisms fueled the inanimate objects with energy (Agamemnon's throne spun around on its own; plaster rabbits represented the chorus; a cadaver was animated electronically). The living beings were blocked by armatures, leather belts, prostheses, imprisoned in plexiglass chests, or boxed under glass. At the same time, the living bodies entrusted their vital functions (breathing) to mouthpieces and tubes, mechanisms that immobilized and impeded the flow of energy. In *Giulio Cesare* (1997), the character of Mark Anthony was played by a man who had had a tracheotomy. He inserted an endoscope into the hole, offering viewers a live video of his larynx and vocal chords, which was projected onto a large screen center stage, thus providing a literal vision of the flesh becoming word. Romeo Castellucci explained the action in this way:

> The machine, as opposed to the animal, is inhuman because it is pure function, pure operation purified of experience. The actor stands exactly between these two fields, between the animal and the machine, because he is both simultaneously, pure function and pure exposed body, pure being.[45]

In the episode of their nine-part *Tragedia Endogonidia* cycle entitled *M#10 Marseille* (2010), which was the company's final production as a collaborative, the stage was devoid of human presence. The lead characters of the spectacle were the visual and sound components. Castellucci observed,

> *M#10 Marseille* is the spectacle of the paradox of the invisible, the negative foundation of phenomena, but this absence of people and the immaterial presence of colors act here as the traces that penetrate the cutoff valve of history, leaving an impression on the film of memory.[46]

Presence was thus no longer an exclusive property of the actor, but could be transferred to chromatic, sonic, plastic, and visual materials.

From the repertoire of these actorial figures, analyzed in terms of a triangulation between *ethos*, *pratton*, and performance (the languages with which one expresses oneself), a constellation of figures emerge that interfere with the mediatic systems of image and sound, and with the visual arts (still life, ready-made, the plasticity of the body). These motifs contribute to the philosophical redefinition of the subject during the later twentieth century and beyond (figures of splitting, doubling, hetero-direction, and the vulnerability of diseased bodies). The repertory includes both choral entities and singles speaking solo, where gesture and word both coincide and split, with acousmatic presences and bodies composed of light. Grasping this private cosmogony without actors at the center entails recognizing that the world has lost its center.

8.10 Sonic body and actant

From the agglomerations of informal sounds – the phonetic collages of Dubuffet's Art Brut – to the use of the body as a musical instrument – as in the work of Charlemagne Palestine, Meredith Monk, and Laurie Anderson, and Carmelo Bene's voice-orchestra – the path has led the actor into a symbiotic fusion with technological devices.

Technologies of amplification enter both into the production of sound and its reception, involving the acoustic space of the listener. Carlo Serra has observed that,

> the work of dilating the sonic masses naturally encompasses the sense of spatiality of the listener, in terms of resonance: the acoustic space that surrounds the listener opens and contracts, oppressing the listener with the vivid power of the gigantic sonic object. Thus are created diverse typologies of spatialization of the experience of listening.[47]

The reproduction of the voice (the magnetophone came on the market in 1950; Beckett used a tape recorder on stage for the first time in *Krapp's Last Tape*, 1954) had effects as profound (and still unstudied) as the photographic reproduction of the body. The amplified, recorded voice causes a sort of sonic self-reflexivity, a distancing from and return to one's self, with a slight delay that shatters the continuum of the verbal text and the identity of the actor. It functions, in sum, like the reflection of a sonic mirror, where the subject no longer coincides with itself, because the enunciated sound stands outside the body.

In Beckett's plays, the stage is inhabited by bodiless voices that operate in the space as "actants" – entities endowed with agency – which give voice to thought, bestowing voice on something without voice, which had heretofore resided on the written page, but not in a theatrical setting. Some things may not be heard, and some words may overlap others. The experience of the voice as separate from the body becomes central to New Theater, which experimented with diverse modalities of relation with acoustic technologies. The most visible of these consist in separating words from the people who offer them up and put them into action; we no longer know who is speaking, or where the voice is coming from.

The contemporary sound scene has enormously amplified the vocal capacities of the actor through new technologies of playback, live amplified voices, stereo effects, surround sound, and others. The microphone is no longer only a prosthesis of the voice of the actor, enlarging and dilating it. Analogously, the recorder no longer serves only to capture the voice. Technology contributes to experimentation in new expressive dimensions, freeing the voice from its natural intonations, rendering it abstract and sensual at the same time. The voice now intercepts the signs coming from the world and the "interminable echo of the self . . . that manifests the presence and adherence of the subject to the concept".[48] Sometimes the voice is a medium which establishes contact with the beyond. It is an off-stage voice, as in Carmelo Bene's *Lorenzaccio* (1986) that designates what exists elsewhere, a mental image which may reside internally or externally.

Recorded sound is an "actant". Sandro Lombardi interacts with a sonic magma coming from a tape recorder in Act Two of *Ritratto dell'attore da giovane* (Portrait of the Actor as a Young Man, 1985): the magma consists of magnetic jolts and hissing that mediate the communication with another world, with voices from beyond the grave that the sound equipment has imprisoned. In this case, the recorded voice is not an extension of a corporal consciousness dilated in time, nor an external memory that can be manipulated back and forth, reified like a photographic image. Rather, it puts listeners in contact with another reality; it evokes spirits, becoming a true medium rather than a support to human perceptual faculties. In fact, the recorder is suspended as its captures subterranean frequencies. No longer a mirror of the actor's voice, it is a vehicle of communication with the other world.

Notes

1 Cfr. Chapter 3 in EAD, *Mondi, corpi, materie*, cit., dedicated to the actor. In particular, the section *Questions on the Death of the Humanist Subject* examines the concept of *corpus* elaborated by Horkheimer and Adorno in the *Dialectic of Enlightenment*, concerning the condition of the individual in capitalist society of the means of mass communication, and the effects that produce reification, cancellation of the past and of history, separation of body from spirit, isolation and flattening of individuality.

2 For a bibliography of vocality, see V. Valentini, ed., *Drammaturgie sonore*, Bulzoni, Rome, 2012; H. Finter, *Le corps de l'audible*, Peter Lang, Frankfurt am Main, 2014, at www.gruppoacusma.com/

3 C. Meldolesi, *Le forze in campo*, cit., 38.

4 A. Attisani, *Le forze in campo*, cit., 95.

5 F. Acca, "L'attore e il suo dopo", in *Culture Teatrali*, n. 13, 2005, Seminario sull'attore, 29–35.

6 For Aristotle, *dran* and *prattein* are the verbs of action, and drama is the imitation of people who carry out actions. The quality of the actions is defined on the basis of thought and character: ". . . characterization is what allows us to judge the nature of the agents, and 'thought' represents the parts in which by their speech they put forward their arguments or make statements". Character is "the element which revelas the nature of a moral choice", or in other words the moral disposition by which character is revealed in actions. *The* Poetics *of Artistotle*, trans. and commentary by Stephen Halliwell, UNC Press, Chapel Hill (NC), 1987, Chapter 6, pp. 37-38.

7 G. Celant, untitled text in *Arte povera*, Gabriele Mazzotta Editore, Milan, 1969, 225.

8 Cfr. J. Grotowski, *Per un teatro povero*, Bulzoni, Rome, 1970. Original edition, *Towards a Poor Theatre*, 1968.

9 G. Celant, *Arte povera*, cit., 227.

10 Ivi, 229.

11 J. Kounellis, "Del corpo, del comportamento, del 'natural', del 'vivo' come autenticità teatrale", in G. Barttolucci (ed.), *Mutations: l'esperienza del Teatro Immagine*, eds. M. Mussio, L. Ballerini, N. Cagnone, out of London press/la nuova foglio, Pollenza (MC) s.d., 54.

12 L. de Berardinis, *Per un teatro Jazz*: "I gave birth to spectacles out of the personalities of these individuals, which were not professional actors, but who claimed themselves to be actors on a cultural plane. That's how *Sudd* was born [. . .]. Sebastiano Devastato, who I'd met in Marigliano and took part in *Sudd*, was a writer who I tried to organized by making him aware of what he'd written, and ways to say it, putting together his methods, his style. It was no longer a relation

of contamination: a company had formed with its own identity, and the participants began to become aware of what theater is: and with the audience too, with institutions. Perla and I were the leaders". *Per un teatro jazz: Intervista con Leo de Berardinis, a cura di Oliviero Ponte di Pino*, in J. Gleber, *The Connections*, Ubulibri, Milan, 1983.

13 Giulio Carlo Argan, speaking of Gestalt psychology, defended and justified group theater research (Gruppo Uno in Rome, N in Padua, T in Milan, Zero in Dusseldorf) as deriving from a need for the artist to overcome the polarity between the individual and the mass, a polarity that produces alienation and resignation to the status quo. Cfr. G. C. Argan, "Au taut", in *Vitalità del negative*, CentroD, Florence, 1970.

14 AA.VV., "Elementi di discussione per un convegno sul Nuovo Teatro", in G. Bartolucci (ed.), *Testi Critici*, cit.,113–121.

15 C. Bene, *Il Monologo*, in *Opere*, Bompiani, Milan, 1995: "In my first decade on stage, without even a microphone cord, I produced myself as though endowed with futuristic phonic amplification, employing the same oral constants of an indispensable elementary research: the *verticality* (metrical and prosodic) of the *verse* (and free verse), the internal accents of the *prose poem*, the *canto fermo* (from Gregorian chant to lieder, as against *belcanto* vibrato), the *attention to defects* which have not been studied enough, the *amplitude* of the *timbric spectrum* and the *tonal variations*, the *staccato*, the emission (chest-mask-head-palate) of the voice, etc., but always constraining highs and peaks *within* the monotonic diagram of the harmonic band (to cloak the sound with a halo) and the *basso continuo*, never disengaged; the inspiration and the breath withheld, the vocalic flickering marked to a point of exaggeration to drive the drastic logos out of its wits (ever since the first version of *Pinocchio* as a syntactic accident): from which came that *pissing myself with performance*, magic that may not be lost on the most sensitive listeners". C. Bene, "Autografia d'un ritratto", in *Opere*, cit., XXXIII-XXXIV.

16 Ivi, 1015.

17 I have discussed this theme in "Lo sfinimento del dialogo", in V. Valentini (ed.), *Dopo il teatro modern*, Politi, Milan, 1989, 87–92. Cfr. L. S. Vygotkij, *Lo sviluppo psichico del bambino*, Editori Riuniti, Rome, 1973; *Problemy psichiceskogo razvitija rebenka*, 1934.

18 C. Bene, "Il Monologo", in *Opere*, cit., 1000–1002.

19 R. Castellucci, conversation with A. Pirillo in *Fenomenologie attoriali negli spettacoli di Pippo Delbono, Socìetas Raffaello Sanzio, Teatrino Clandestino, Teatro Valdoca*, masters thesis by A. Pirillo under Prof. V. Valentini, University of Rome. 2008–2009.

20 Cfr. V. Valentini, ed., *Studio azzurro, G. Barberio Corsetti, La camera astratta*, Ubulibri, Milan, 1988.

21 H. Finter, *Le corps de l'audibile*, Peter Lang, Frankfurt am Main, 2014, 198.

22 Luca Ronconi occupies a controversial position with regard to New Theater. His role in the international panorama is equal to that of Stein, Gruber, Mnouchkine, and Brook. He went beyond the avant-garde model of the Living Theater or Grotowski and the theater of critical directing, as well as beyond the trends typical of late-century theater, with discontinuous results. Between 1976 and 1978, in Prato, he founded and directed the Laboratorio di Progettazione Teatrale, together with Gae Aulenti, Dacia Maraini, Ettore Capriolo, Franco Quadri, and Umberto Eco.

23 F. Quadri, *Il rito perduto: Saggio su Luca Ronconi*, Einaudi, Turin, 1973, 76.

24 Ivi, 77.

25 Ivi, 159.

26 Ivi, 69.

27 A. M. Ripellino, *Siate buffi*, cit., 61.

28 C. Guidi, *Voyage au bout de la nuit*, Quaderno di lavoro di Chiara Guidi, 1999, 1.

29 R. Castellucci, "Alla deriva di un torrente sonoro", *Art'o*, n. 2, giugno 1999, 14–16.

30 C. Ronconi, "Un perfetto salto mortale: Conversazione con Cesare Ronconi di Emanuela Dallagiovanna", in E. Dallagiovanna (ed.), *Teatro Valdoca*, Rubbettino, Soveria Mannelli (CZ), 2003, 55.

31 Mariangela Gualtieri, poet, playwright, and actor. In 1983 she founded Teatro Valdoca in Cesena with director Cesare Ronconi. She has published numerous collections of verse, including *Antenata* (Crocetti, 1992), *Fuoco centrale* (Einaudi, 2003), *Senza polvere senza peso* (Einaudi, Turin, 2006) and *Caino* (Einaudi, Turin, 2011). *Sermone ai cuccioli della mia specie*, Teatro Valdoca, 2012. Cfr. www.teatrovaldoca.org

32 C. Ronconi, *Un perfetto salto mortale: Converazione con Cesare Ronconi di Emanuela Dallagiovanna*, cit., 27.

33 C. Ronconi,*Un perfetto salto mortale. Conversazione con Cesare Ronconi di Emanuela Dallagiovanna*, 2003, cit. p.55.

34 M. Gualtieri, *Parsifal*, Teatro Valdoca (ed.), Cesena, 2000.

35 The term "autofiction" was coined in 1977 by French writer and academic Serge Doubrovsky, who used it to describe his novel *Fils*. An emblematic Italian version of this type is Walter Siti's *Troppi Paradisi*, Einaudi, Turin, 2006; another is G. Genna, *Italia De Profundis*, minimum fax, Rome, 2008.

36 R. Palazzi, "Deflorian/Tagliarini, l'immedesimazione senza personaggio", in D. Deflorian and A. Tagliarini (eds.), *Trilogia dell'invisibile*, Titivillus, Corazzano, (PI) 2014, 121–141.

37 J. Grotowski, *Per un teatro povero*, Bulzoni, Rome, 1970, 143.

38 Cfr. V. Valentini, "La forma nasce dal bisogno di comunicare", in L. Bernazza and V. Valentini, *Compagnia della Fortezza*, Rubbettino, Soveria Mannelli (CZ), 1998, 9–22. Cfr. R. Schechner, "Sul recupero di comportamenti", in V. Valentini (ed.), *La Teoria delle Performance 1970–1983*, Bulzoni, Rome, 213–301.

39 F. Quadri, *Il rito perduto*, cit., 48.

40 I. Moscati, "Sette Giorni", *L'avanguardia gioca tutto sulla fantasia*, dicembre 6, 1970.

41 S. Galasso, *Il teatro di Remondi e Caporossi*, Bulzoni, Rome, 1998, 81.

42 In "Colpo su Colpo", *Art'ò*. In the sequence of seven paintings that compose the micro-narration of the installation by Riccardo Caporossi (*Sconosciuto*, 2010), we see a man in a black suit seated on a chair, his face concealed by a hat. From one painting to the next, he becomes smaller and smaller, losing his human features until he becomes mere trace: a pair of shoes and a hat on a chair. The figure then appears on another wall, as the shadow of a full figure in human scale.

43 G. Barberio Corsetti, "Description of a Battle", in R. Molinari (ed.), *L'attore mentale*, Ubulibri, Milan, 1992, 20.

44 C. Castellucci and R. Castellucci, *Il teatro della Socìetas Raffaello Sanzio: Dal teatro iconoclasta alla super-icona*, Ubulibri, Milan, 1992, 112.

45 R. Castellucci, "The Simplest Place Possible", Romeo Castellucci Interviewed by Valentina Valentini and Bonnie Marranca, in *PAJ, a Journal of Performance and Art*, n. 77, May 2004, 16–26. In *Worlds Bodies Matters*, I wrote, "The theater and contemporary art represent an animalized world, filthy, fractal, they represent actants with their minds separated from their bodies, with mutilated, constructed, mechanical, hybrid bodies, non-human behaviors, bio-genetic experiments. Is this a diseased condition?" But Nancy objects, "There is no

longer a *state* of health, nor a *stasis* of disease a back-and-forth, an irregular or continuous palpitation that goes from one edge to another of the skin, of the wounds, of the enzymes of synthesis, of the images of synthesis. There is no integral psyche closed in a fullness or emptiness". J. L. Nancy, *Corpus*, Cronopio, Naples, 1995, 86, 87. (*Corpus*, A. M. Métailié (ed.), Paris, 1992).

46 R. Castellucci, production program, Teatro Comunale di Bologna, September 16, 2006.

47 C. Serra, "Lobotomia' e altri equivoci", *Forum Italicum: A Journal of Italian Studies*, April 14, 2015, http://foi.sagepub.com/content/early/recent

48 M. Grande, "Lingua e phône", in *La riscossa di Lucifero*, Bulzoni, Rome, 1985, 187.

Index